MARY STOCKS

MARY STOCKS
1891–1975

An Uncommonplace Life

Barbara Hooper

THE ATHLONE PRESS
London & Atlantic Highlands, NJ

First published 1996 by
THE ATHLONE PRESS LTD
1 Park Drive, London NW11 7SG
and 165 First Avenue,
Atlantic Highlands, NJ 07716

British Library Cataloguing in Publication Data
*A catalogue record for this book is available
from the British Library*

ISBN 0 485 11507 7

Library of Congress Cataloging-in-Publication Data
Hooper, Barbara, 1929–
    Mary Stocks, 1891–1975 : an uncommonplace life /
Barbara Hooper.
       p.   cm.
    Includes bibliographical references and index.
    ISBN 0-485-11507-7
    1. Stocks, Mary Danvers Brinton, 1891-   --Biography.
2. Women authors, English--20th century--Biography.
3. Women political activists--Great Britain--Biography.
4. Women teachers--Great Britain--Biography.   I. Title.
PR6037.T6Z68   1996
914.2′03′82092--dc20
[B]   96-8818
                                                           CIP

Typeset by Bibloset in 10pt Plantin

Printed and bound in Great Britain by
Cambridge University Press

Contents

List of Illustrations		vii
Foreword by The Revd Lord Soper of Kingsway		ix
Acknowledgements		xi
Chapter 1	The London Years: 1891–1913	1
Chapter 2	The Oxford Years: 1913–1924	31
Chapter 3	The Manchester and Liverpool Years: 1924–1937	50
Chapter 4	The Westfield Years: 1939–1951	95
Chapter 5	The BBC Years: 1951–1965	131
Chapter 6	The House of Lords Years: 1966–1975	164
Epilogue	The Mary Stocks Legend and Legacy	189
Notes		190
Bibliography		195
Index		197

To the memory of my parents,
who were of Mary Stocks's generation

List of Illustrations

Plate 1: Mary Stocks (née Brinton), aged 22, on her honeymoon in Rome, 1913. (Photo Mrs Ann Patterson.)

Plate 2: Mary Stocks aged 33, on holiday with (left to right) John, Ann, Helen, 1924. (Photo Mrs Ann Patterson.)

Plate 3: At a reception to welcome her husband John as Liverpool University's new Vice-Chancellor, 1937.

Plate 4: In her study as Principal of Westfield College, with Candida, her white cat, 1945. (Copyright Keystone Press.)

Plate 5: With Sir Frederick Marquis (later Lord Woolton) at an honorary degree ceremony (D. Litt.) at Liverpool University, 1955. (Copyright *Guardian*.)

Plate 6: Mary Stocks interviewing Nancy, Viscountess Astor, for the tenth anniversary of *Woman's Hour*, 1956. (Copyright BBC.)

Plate 7: The *Any Questions* team at Combe Martin, Devon, in 1959. From left: Gerald Nabarro, MP, Patrick Gordon-Walker, MP, farmer Jack Houghton-Brown, Mary Stocks and Freddie Grisewood as chairman. (Copyright Powell's Photographers, Ilfracombe, Devon.)

Plate 8: Baroness Stocks of Kensington and Chelsea with Lord Goodman of Westminster and Lord Evans of Hungershall, when Lord Evans was taking his seat in the House of Lords, 1967. (Copyright Universal Pictorial Press.)

Foreword

by the Revd Lord Soper of Kingsway

(Lord Soper, formerly Dr Donald Soper, the distinguished Methodist preacher, was a contemporary of Mary Stocks on BBC programmes and in the House of Lords, and he gave the address at her memorial service.)

I count it a privilege to write a short Foreword to this book about Mary Stocks. I came to know her, and frequently to meet her, in the early days of the BBC *Any Questions* programme. Although there were many aspects of her life and work which were outside my personal involvement, I would say that my participation in *Any Questions* justifies the claim that I knew her well. We met regularly during the 1960s.

She was a wise woman. Her command of incisive language and her comprehensiveness, in every meaning of that word, were outstanding. At the same time she was a formidable exposer of anything that smacked of what she often described as 'bunkum', and she said so with kindly but withering perception.

We entered the House of Lords within a year of each other. I was made a Life Peer in 1965 and Baroness Stocks in 1966. We both sat on the Labour benches, but she voted against the Labour Party on several issues, and in the end she gave up the Labour Whip and moved to the cross-benches. I understood her reasons, but it was a great loss to the party.

I most admired her robust common sense. Time and again she perceived the nitty-gritty of a situation and went to the heart of the matter. Morality concerned her. She would put into one pithy sentence what some of us parsons would take five minutes to say. She did not groan under a sense of sin, but she was on the Lord's side.

The pages of this biography are a testimony to the truth of this acclamation, and reading of it is the record of an inspiring life. I would regard the word 'inspiring' as the key word in an invitation to read this book. It lifts the mind and heart at a time when such encouragement is so much needed.

Donald Soper

Acknowledgements

First and foremost my thanks must go to the Hon. Mrs Ann Patterson and the Hon. Helen Stocks, daughters of Baroness Stocks. Both of them were most generous with time, hospitality, photographs and information about their mother which I could not have had from any other source.

I also had much help from Queen Mary and Westfield College, London University. The Principal, Professor Graham Zellick, and his predecessor at Westfield, Professor J.E. Varey, both encouraged me to go ahead with the biography. I had enormous support from Professor Alan Deyermond, who checked through my typescript with great thoroughness, adding much from his own personal knowledge. Any inaccuracies that remain are mine and not his. Dr Janet Sondheimer, Westfield College Archivist and author of the college history, enabled me to read the Principal's Logbook for the years 1939 to 1951, and other papers relevant to Mary Stocks's time as Principal.

Mary Stocks asked her family to destroy her letters after her death, so in the absence of personal correspondence I have drawn quite heavily on the two volumes of her autobiography and on newspaper articles relating to her various careers. These are acknowledged in the bibliography.

I am grateful for the unlimited access I was given to documents in the BBC Written Archives, the Library of St Paul's School for Girls, the Nancy Astor Archive at Reading University, and the Record Office of the House of Lords. My research in these libraries was facilitated by Mrs Jacqueline Kavanagh, Mrs Sara Childs, Mr Michael Bott and the House of Lords Clerk of the Records.

Three people who knew Mary Stocks well have generously allowed me to interview them, and this added much to my understanding of her character. They are the Hon. David Astor, son of Nancy, Viscountess Astor; the Revd Lord Soper, a fellow BBC panellist and fellow Labour Peer with Baroness Stocks; and Mr Frank Gillard, former managing director of BBC Radio. I also had helpful correspondence with Mr B.L. Rathbone of Liverpool, a kinsman of Eleanor Rathbone.

I owe a particular debt of thanks to Mrs Cathy Chesterman, who efficiently retyped my confusing typescript at very short notice. All these people helped to make the compiling of the biography a pleasant and rewarding task.

Chapter 1

The London Years: 1891–1913

When she was nearly 80, Mary Stocks summed up her life in her own brisk way:

> My record of activity cannot be called a career. On looking up the word 'career' in *Chambers Twentieth Century Dictionary* I find it described as 'a progress through life, but esp. advancement in profession.' I have never advanced in any profession, merely marked time in one or two . . . opportunities have come my way, to which I have responded, and a disjointed mish-mash of activities has been the result.[1]

She did herself a major injustice. Most of us would regard as a pretty remarkable career a 'progress through life' which began with a Victorian childhood, embraced the women's suffrage movement, moved on to twenty years as a university lecturer and pioneer social reformer, took on board a decade as a college principal and a further decade in the House of Lords; and by way of sideline created a broadcasting track record spanning forty years.

Most of us would also wonder what fuelled such an energetic life and what influences shaped the young Mary Brinton, a London doctor's daughter, into the septuagenarian Life Peer, Baroness Stocks of Kensington and Chelsea.

In 1975 politicians, academics and radio or television personalities flocked to her memorial service at the church of St Martin in the Fields in London's Trafalgar Square. They sang conventional hymns and one less well known, the 'Hymn of the Workers in their Search for Education':

> The people, Lord, the people,
> Not crowns and thrones but men!

1

Flowers of thy heart, o God, are they;
Let them not pass like weeds away,
Their heritage a sunless day.[2]

It was a hymn sung at her husband's civic funeral in Liverpool Cathedral not quite forty years earlier. It was relevant to his life and hers. Almost all of her 84 years had been concerned with enterprise to improve the health and education of people less advantaged than she was, especially women, and most especially working women. Her frankness and radicalism sometimes landed her in trouble, and occasionally she was perceived as a tiresome eccentric. But throughout a long life, Mary Stocks hardly deviated from that one objective: to abolish the 'sunless day' for victims of poverty, ignorance and prejudice.

Her roots can be traced back to several eminent Victorians and empire-builders, but the Mary Stocks story effectively begins with her grandparents: on her mother's side a distinguished civil engineer who married the daughter of New Zealand's first Governor; on her father's side a medical consultant married to a Midland industrialist's daughter.

Her maternal grandfather, Alexander Rendel, was one of four sons of James Meadows Rendel, a leading engineer responsible for building Portland Harbour. Three of the sons followed their father's career and the fourth, Stuart, became a prosperous politician under Gladstone, eventually rewarded with a peerage as Baron Rendel. Alexander was professionally the most successful of the engineering Rendels. He belonged to that generation of impressive Victorians who built bridges, docks, dams and railways throughout Victoria's empire. As well as helping his father to complete Portland Harbour, he designed and built the Royal Albert Dock in London, the Leith Dock in Edinburgh, and in part the Hardinge Bridge over the Ganges. His other achievements included substantial sections of the Indian railway system. With all this to his credit, he was knighted in 1887.

At 24, Alexander Rendel had met and fallen in love with Eliza Hobson, who was then only 17. She had returned to England after the sudden death of her father, Captain William Hobson, RN, the first Governor of New Zealand. Alexander and Eliza married in 1853 and had eight children, of whom Mary Stocks's mother, Helen Constance, was the fourth.

William Hobson's name is forgotten now in Britain, but not in New Zealand. Some eighty years after his death, an Auckland newspaper reported on a ceremony at which schoolchildren laid wreaths on Captain Hobson's grave. The *New Zealand Herald* records a portrait of an unusual pioneer:

> Hobson was a captain in the Royal Navy, and it is said that in his younger days he had some exciting experiences while serving on the West Indies station, chasing slaves and pirates up mysterious creeks. Hobson arrived in New Zealand, at Orakei, in 1840, and set up the capital at Russell; but the following year removed the seat of government to Auckland as being more convenient.
>
> The most important event in his short term of office was the signing of the Treaty of Waitangi, by which the Maoris ceded the rights of sovereignty to Queen Victoria. Hobson then became the mediator between the two races . . . it was often a very difficult matter to reconcile the conflicting interests . . . his early death being undoubtedly hastened by the manner in which he was attacked by certain sections of the early settlers – men who wanted a freer hand in matters connected with the land.[3]

Among the family manuscripts a letter survives, written by William Hobson to an old friend in Plymouth, Miss Emma Hamilton Smith. It is dated 10 October 1840 (eight months after the first landing), from Russell in the Bay of Islands, and it gives Hobson's early impressions of the land and its people: a possibly unique account of the earlier settlement of what was to become New Zealand's capital.

> The country is not a second Garden of Eden, but like other extensive Countries it possesses a variety of Soil and a variety of Climate . . . Taken as it really is, if men will divest themselves of the wild speculative notions they may have imbibed from false representations, they will find in this Country as ample a return for enterprise as in any part of the World.
>
> The natives are not to be feared; indeed if I could restrain the low blackguard Whites from insulting them, I should never have the slightest trouble with them, but they will sometimes take the law into their own hands, and punish in their own way the Misdeeds of the Pakia Mauries. The term is applied to the most dissolute, in contradistinction to Rangatira, a Gentleman.

3

I have had much trouble to find a faultless position for a seat of government, and have but partially succeeded. I have fixed on the Waitemata in the Firth of Thames . . . at a distance by sea of 30 miles is an excessively rich valley containing two millions of acres, one half of which is now ready for the plough.

William Hobson died in 1843, aged 49, and was buried with full military honours. A Maori writer nearly a century later gave an account of the ceremony that had been handed down among his people by word of mouth.[4] Officers and men rowed ashore from HMS *Victoria*, moored in the bay, and a firing party from the 80th Regiment led the funeral procession along a muddy track. The Acting Governor and officials walked four abreast behind the flag-draped coffin, and hundreds of Maoris brought up the rear. The writer of the article, Kia Kaha, described the Maoris, 'in their flax mats and variegated blankets gazing in wonder at the burial of a white Chief'. After the funeral volley they too let off their weapons.

Legend has it that the Maori chiefs petitioned Queen Victoria to send as their second governor 'a good man like this governor who has just died'. In 1924 the City of Auckland raised a handsome memorial to Captain Hobson, and on the 90th anniversary of his death the Governor General, Lord Bledisloe, bought the Waitangi Treaty site for the nation.

Hobson was the maternal great-grandfather of Mary Brinton. Although he died half a century before she was born, his exploits were well remembered in the family. His daughter Eliza Rendel kept a scrapbook of cuttings sent to her by friends in New Zealand each year on the anniversary of her father's death. Eliza had a sister, Polly, the almost obligatory unmarried daughter who stayed at home with her widowed mother after their return to Plymouth. Mary Brinton later recalled with pleasure seaside holidays in Devonport and remembered her great-aunt with affection as an amateur photographer and assiduous patron of church bazaars.

On her father's side of the family the chosen profession tended to be medicine. They were travellers, too, and her father practised medicine nearly as far afield as William Hobson had sailed. The Brintons were carpet manufacturers from Kidderminster in Worcestershire, a traditional place for carpets in the heart of England.

4

Her paternal grandfather, James Brinton, became a consultant physician at St Thomas's Hospital in London, specialising in the physiology of the digestive system, and was made a Fellow of the Royal Society. He married Mary Danvers, one of a sisterly trio of society beauties, and they had four sons and three daughters. One son, Herbert, was a master at Eton. Mary Stocks's father, Roland, followed his father into the medical world.

James Brinton died young, aged 43, from kidney disease. An obituary writer mentioned Dr Brinton's talents as a linguist, lecturer, draughtsman and writer ('far above the average of writers on Medicine'). Another found him peculiarly successful as a clinical teacher, possessing 'a remarkable power of pictorial illustration and a command of terse and vigorous language'.[5] These last two characteristics were surely inherited by his granddaughter.

One of his brothers was from 1880 till 1886 Liberal Member of Parliament for Kidderminster, and the family produced several aldermen and magistrates. They were a close-knit but widespread clan, the Brintons, and in 1932 they held a family reunion attended by more than sixty Brintons from both sides of the Atlantic. Others who could not be there sent good wishes from Ontario and Johannesburg. The hosts were two aldermen and the Rector of Henley-on-Thames, all Brinton brothers. The *Kidderminster Shuttle* devoted a whole page to 'this unique and historic reunion'. The report makes it clear there was a strong tradition of public service right through the family: in the Church, teaching, local government and politics.[6] Here are clear pointers to several of Mary Brinton's future preoccupations.

Roland Brinton was born in 1858 and went to Cambridge, where he collected a double first in mathematics. He moved on to qualify in medicine, and worked first at St Bartholomew's Hospital in London. After this he set off for Australia, anxious to extend his medical experience by working in the outback, and to get to know the country.

On his return in 1889 he married Helen Constance, the elder daughter of Sir Alexander and Lady Rendel, thus bringing together a family network which on his side included the founder of the W.H. Smith newsagent empire, and on his wife's side a clan interrelated with the Wedgwoods, the Irvings and the Stracheys, all great Victorians in the world of arts.

After his marriage, Roland Brinton settled down into general practice at Queens Gate Terrace, Kensington. It was a solid and prosperous middle-class area of London, soon to be dominated by a new wave of prestige buildings: the Albert Hall, the Imperial Institute, the Science Museum, the Albert Memorial.

It is probably impossible to overestimate the influence of the Brinton network and what she called 'the Rendel Connection' on Mary's childhood. Life was very much a matter of weekly visits to grandparents, aunts and uncles and cousins in the two London domains where most of them lived; Bloomsbury and Kensington. They spent clannish weekends together at the Rendels' country place in Surrey. They were in and out of each others' homes and the children were often included in parental expeditions to schools, workhouses, women's clubs. Mary grew up among a generation of well-off relatives who regarded it as absolutely and unquestionably their duty to concern themselves with the less well-off.

Later in life she named her aunt Edith Rendel as the chief formative influence in her life. Edith had taken on the expected duties of an unmarried daughter and ran the three Rendel homes: 23 Russell Square, Bloomsbury, an Edwardian country house in Surrey (Rickettswood, scene of many extended family gatherings), and after 1900 a seaside home in Dorset. Where Edith differed from many comfortably brought up Victorian single women was in her activities as a St Pancras Poor Law Guardian, and in running the St Pancras Girls' Club for young women factory workers, as well as a crèche for their offspring. The club was in Woburn Walk, near St Pancras Station, and the girls had bank holiday outings to Rickettswood. In time the club outgrew Woburn Walk and moved to better premises in Burton Crescent, on the other side of the Euston Road.

Next to the new building, Edith's niece Leila Rendel, who had at first trained as a gymnastics teacher, started a nursery school called the Caldecott Community (named after the artist of the children's pictures used to decorate the walls). Later it became a boarding school for disturbed children of all ages, in Kent, and Mary Stocks's daughter Helen taught there.

From her Aunt Edith, Mary absorbed a lifelong interest in community welfare work. Edith might today be misinterpreted as a patron merely dispensing charity. In fact she was one of a rare breed of Victorian women who devoted their lives to pioneering social projects which fifty years later would come under the wing of the welfare state. Her older brother, Herbert, was treasurer of a factory girls' country holiday fund run by a vicar's daughter at Saffron Hill in Clerkenwell.

James Rendel was a successful city businessman who delighted his father by marrying Elinor Strachey, daughter of Sir Richard Strachey. Strachey, as an Indian administrator, and Rendel, as a railway-builder, were old friends. This marriage linked the Rendel family with possibly the best-known of the great Victorians: a family that included the feminist Philippa, the artist Dorothy, the writer Lytton, the Newnham Principal Pernel, and the political writer, Ray. Philippa and Ray were to be important contacts for Mary in her own political enterprises. Like his sister, Edith Rendel, James was a Poor Law Guardian and indeed chairman of the Kensington Board of Guardians till the Poor Law was abolished in 1930. He took Mary as a child to visit the Kensington workhouse, a place she at once disliked and associated with 'utter friendlessness and destitution'. Later, when she found some of her relatives had friends among the inmates, she saw it differently.

Arthur Rendel, a medical man, married a deeply religious Scots-woman, Elsie Blair, whose sayings entered into family mythology – for example 'My husband accuses me of flirting with the Holy Ghost' and 'If Our Lord had seen the use they made of His Cross in this cemetery, he'd have wished to have died on something else'. The Rendel connection was a powerful backdrop to Mary's adolescence, and all of its members in one way or another made an impression on her. Inevitably the two closest to her were her own mother, Constance, and her Aunt Kate, who married an architect, Halsey Ricardo.

The Brintons figure less prominently in her childhood recollections. There were fewer of them, the grandparents died before she was born, and they exerted less influence. But one or two are well worthy of mention.

One was Great-Aunt Emily, one of that bevy of good-looking Danvers sisters who married among the Brintons. She became the wife of W.H. Smith, founder of the newsagent empire, and celebrated by Gilbert and Sullivan in *H.M.S. Pinafore*. When he died she was given a title (Viscountess Hambleden) in her own right, and Mary Brinton recalled Aunt Emily living alone at the corner of Belgrave Square in an enormous house with a large staff of servants. It was as well, she reflected, that Emily did not venture into the House of Lords: her beauty was not matched by her brains.

The Brinton grandparents had three unmarried daughters, Maud (an amateur pianist), Marion (a qualified nurse and a councillor on Kensington Borough Council) and Edith (nicknamed Tiddy), an amateur artist whose pictures delighted her nephew and nieces. She passed on her artistic skill to Mary.

There was a military cousin, Jack, who fought at the Battle of Omdurman, as Winston Churchill famously did. This seems to have been the only variation from loyalty to the Navy in Mary Brinton's immediate family. Another cousin, Dolly Baird, was a minor actress who married Sir Henry Irving's son H.B. Irving, and made her name in the title role of Gerald du Maurier's *Trilby*. She was a friend of Edith Rendel and shared some of her community work in St Pancras.

Roland Brinton and Constance Rendel were married at St Mary Abbots Church, Kensington, in 1889. He was a popular family doctor, visiting his middle-class patients on foot or by hansom cab, holding consultations each morning at eleven. His daughter described the routine of the house as 'orderly, comfortable and secure'.[7] There were three living-in servants and the children, when they arrived, had a full-time nursemaid. Dr Brinton had some non-fee-paying patients, subsidised by the more wealthy, and for 46 years he acted as honorary medical officer to the head office of W.H. Smith. Frequent mentions of him in the house journal, *The Newsbasket*, reveal his popularity among the staff. Into this serene and leafy part of London, and this stable home and family, Mary Danvers Brinton was born on 25 July 1891.

Astrologers would no doubt make much of her birth date: born under the sign of Leo, a positive person, one who makes things happen. In other years 25 July had been the birthday of the theologian William Burkitt, and the statesman Arthur Balfour, whose relative Mary Brinton would march behind in a suffrage rally. Seven years later exactly would mark the birth of Amelia Earhart, the pioneer woman aviator.

Anniversaries on 24–25 July are not without significance in relation to Mary Brinton's future. In years to come they would mark the introduction of British life peerages, the first cross-Channel flight by Louis Blériot (on Mary's 18th birthday, as it happened) and the birth of the first test-tube baby in Oldham, Lancashire, the very district where Mary and others would campaign for better facilities for mothers.

The Balfour links are particularly interesting. Arthur James Balfour was Prime Minister for three years during Mary's childhood, and therefore a strong target for the suffragettes. During the First World War he was appointed First Lord of the Admiralty in Asquith's coalition government, overseeing that Navy in which several of Mary's relations served. And in 1917 he signed the Balfour Declaration which led eventually to the formation of the State of Israel in 1948; it was the human problems attendant on this development which preoccupied the woman MP Eleanor Rathbone, subject of Mary Stocks's best-known biography, and probably caused Eleanor's death. Most of these events, though, were years away, as unpredictable to the Brinton parents' generation as the future of their infant daughter.

Number 8 Queens Gate Terrace, London SW7, was essentially the centre of the Brinton family's world until the outbreak of the First World War. Today it retains its imposing character. The street is a double-width avenue, high, wide and handsome, separating two nearly identical cream-painted mid-Victorian terraces. The houses are five storeys high with balustrades, balconies and heavily ornamented basement railings.

Number 8 is pale buff with cream stucco and woodwork. On the door is fixed a small discreet brass plate: *Maison de l'Institut Francais* (nearby is a branch of the French Embassy). There are potted geraniums, and round the corner the now desirable cottages of Queens Gate Mews. No. 6 is a Middle Eastern Embassy, number 26 an outpost of Richmond College in the United States. There are a few discreet commercial enterprises: an estate agent, a travel agent and, at the western end of the terrace, the only real concession to our times – a pizza parlour. Number 8 bears no plaque, but a more enduring reminder of Mary Stocks is the street name plate which carries the legend 'The Royal Borough of Kensington and Chelsea', incorporated uniquely in the title she chose 75 years later.

In 1891 Queens Gate Terrace symbolised solid and respectable Victorian virtues, standing a stone's throw from the Albert Hall, the Victoria and Albert Museum and the Imperial Institute. All these were witness to the grand concepts of High Victorian architects and builders. South Kensington was the showcase of the arts and sciences, an embodiment of middle-class values and aspirations.

In 1891 Victoria's global empire on which the sun was expected never to set was at its zenith, and few questioned the morality of colonialism. (Seventy years later Mary Stocks would speak out publicly against colonial rule in Cyprus.) In the Far East the murderous Boxer Rebellion was about to be launched against foreigners and Chinese Christians; South Africa was experiencing uneasy peace between the two Boer Wars. In France, Van Gogh had recently died; in the literary world, Browning had been dead a year and Tennyson was in his last year of life. The first petrol-driven cars were chugging slowly along the roads of Germany; Alexander Graham Bell's telephone was still a rich man's toy; Picasso, aged 10, was already showing artistic genius. Hitler was 2, Stalin 12, Churchill 18; Gandhi was practising as a barrister in London, Lenin was in semi-exile in Siberia for spreading Marxist propaganda, Freud was in France studying hypnosis before writing *The Interpretation of Dreams*.

This was the world, teetering between the nineteenth and twentieth centuries, of Mary Brinton's childhood. She was brought up in middle-class comfort with nursemaids, governesses and domestic servants always at hand. There were holidays by the sea and at the Rendels' country house, a galaxy of loving and interesting relatives, and within a few years a younger brother and sister completed the Brinton family. (Ralph Brinton was born in 1895, Joanna in 1897).

Their home district of Kensington was a mecca for shoppers at the new and extremely popular department stores which had flourished since the Great Exhibition of 1851. This had opened people's eyes to the prospect of a consumer-led society. The wealthy shopped at Harrods in Knightsbridge, the slightly less wealthy at Barkers in Kensington High Street, the comfortably well-off at Whiteleys in Bayswater. Carriages or hansom cabs dropped them off and collected them. There was also the Underground Railway, newly constructed and regarded with some suspicion.

For privileged children in the 1890s there were pantomimes, circuses and the endless pleasures of Kensington Gardens, where at about this time J.M. Barrie was spinning yarns to the Llewellyn Davies boys which in 1904 surfaced in the story of *Peter Pan*. Mary Brinton knew Lewis Carroll's *Alice* books, written some twenty years earlier, and possibly Beatrix Potter's *Peter Rabbit* series, begun in 1900. Robert Louis Stevenson's *Treasure Island*, *Kidnapped* and

A Child's Garden of Verses all appeared during the decade before Mary Brinton's birth, and Kenneth Grahame's *The Wind in the Willows* was published when she was seven. This was a golden age for children's classics, and a reading age.

Mary Brinton's childhood had been remarkably serene, yet from an early age she emerged as a rebel. Not against home or family, but against the (to her) stuffy conventions still imposed on Victorian and Edwardian girls at the very time when their horizons were opening out.

The Brinton household was strictly run. 'The nurse lived with us children on the nursery floor. The other servants slept in the attic, and we could hear the cook and parlourmaid tramping up to bed. The rest of their time they spent in the area' – the basement.

> My father was not a carriage owner. He hired a hansom cab every morning at 8 which took him on his rounds to patients, and he was back at 11. A few patients came to see him, and for them he provided *The Morning Post, Punch* and the *Navy List* in his waiting room.[8]

Interviewed for a national newspaper in 1973, Mary Stocks recalled sitting on her father's shoulders to watch the opening of the Imperial Institute a few blocks from her home. Her father wore his medical man's outfit of frock coat and top hat, and they clearly saw Queen Victoria. Seventy years on she fiercely defended the Institute against modernisers who wished to pull it down to make more room for Imperial College.

For household provisions Mrs Brinton had an account at Barker's, in Kensington High Street: 'I can still hear her saying "Put it down to my account . . . B R I N T O N, Queens Gate Terrace."' A favourite family story tells of the opportunist in the shop who overheard her saying this, and ordered for himself a York ham and a Stilton cheese to be charged and delivered to Mrs Brinton. When the goods arrived at the area door of 8 Queens Gate Terrace, the conman was waiting and made off with them.

The household routine was unvarying. 'In the morning my mother used to go down to the basement to order the dinner and interview the cook and see what was in the larder. Then she wrote down the order for Barker's.'[9] To the end of her long life, Mary was virtually unable to cook. There was always someone around to do it for her.

Even doctors' children were not immune from childish epidemics, and the family treasures a watercolour painting and poem produced in 1897 by the doctor's sister Edith Brinton ('Tiddy', the artistic one). It shows a girl aged six or thereabouts in various stages of illness: in bed, rather poorly, then recovering. What distinguishes this painting is that Mary is clearly identified in a jingle written by the artist.

> Good gracious me!
> What's that I see,
> Over the fender stooping
> And giving out a curious shout?
> Oh, it was Mary . . . [whooping]
>
> But if she's good
> She shall have food
> In parcels sent to Mummy,
> Nice grapes and such.
> Mary likes much
> To put these in her . . . [tummy]
>
> Now who sends this
> With a loving kiss
> To a little whooping kiddy?
> I don't suppose my Mary knows?
> Why, who but her aunt . . . [Tiddy].

Her childhood was, as she told her interviewer in 1973, 'ordered, comfortable and supremely secure'. So what was there to rebel against? She objected strongly to long skirts, petticoats, frills and flounces. Inheriting some of Aunt Edith Brinton's talent, she sketched her notions of appropriate and inappropriate clothing for girls at the turn of the century: her mother *en grande tenue* with vast ostrich-feather hat, Mary as dressed by her mother in a governessy outfit, and 'what Mary would REALLY like' – a crop-headed female in cook's gear with a convict pattern on the dress. One has to suppose this symbolises her sense of being imprisoned in fancy dress.

And seventy years later she wrote:

My first consciousness of the disabilities suffered by women was concerned with dress . . . longer whalebones would be inserted into my Jaeger stays, which would some day have to be laced up from behind. And hair would, at 17 or 18, have to be 'put up' – not merely twisted into a bun at the back supported by hairpins which tended to fall out, but also fluffed up at the sides . . . Horror of horrors were the hats, which did not sit firmly on the head but had to be balanced on the hair . . . speared with hatpins.

She believed that if she had been able to dress as her grand-daughters did, in tunics and tights and bikinis, she would have come to terms with clothes and 'advanced into middle age as a well dressed woman'.[10] What actually happened was that by the time she was 20, Mary Brinton adopted a shingled hairdo, no-nonsense tweed suits with shortish skirts and (if a hat was essential) a pudding-basin hat, and this remained her style for the rest of her life.

Another antipathy was to the idea of 'coming out', the presentation at Court and launching into society of upper- and middle-class daughters in their late teens. It was a phase in her life she never afterwards mentioned.

Domesticity was a foreign concept to her. Brought up in a household where there were always servants, and later in life similarly placed, she never acquired the expected female arts of cooking, sewing or flower arranging. She was simply not interested in jewellery, make-up or personal adornment.

All of these frivolities – as she might have identified them – were for Mary Brinton on the fringe of much more serious impediments for women. Women were barred from many of the major professions. They had no vote. They were not legal guardians of their own children, nor entitled to draw allowances for them.

Her view of the world was not unique among middle-class women in the early years of the century. There was a consist-ency about it. Clothes, cooking and deb dances were for social butterflies. Serious thinkers and educated women, encouraged by enlightened families, found self-expression in political or academic careers or in socially caring voluntary activities. This was the way ahead for Mary Brinton and others like her when they left school.

Holidays were the highlight of the Brinton children's year. In old age Mary still vividly recalled places she was taken to as a small child. One of these was Penlee House at Devonport, the home of her great-aunt, Polly Hobson. Penlee House was a country house on the outskirts of Plymouth with a large garden, stables and a full-time staff of four. From here the Brintons had trips by governess cart or wagonette (a kind of horse-drawn charabanc) to Plymouth Hoe, across the river Tamar, or even to Dartmoor. They watched naval vessels in the harbour and explored the pier. Mary would have been surprised to know that one of her closest friends later in life (Nancy Astor) would be one of Plymouth's MPs, and a woman at that.

She admired her Great-Aunt Hobson, and later wrote of her:

> Had she lived a generation later her life might have been very different. Social service in local government or on the Bench would have directed her natural qualities of wit, energy and kindness into more satisfying channels than entertaining neighbours or cherishing curates.[11]

Another favoured holiday place was the Rendel grandparents' country house in Surrey, where anything up to twenty of the clan would gather in summer. Rickettswood had 350 acres of farmland, gardens, orchard and woods – a paradise for children. Sir Alexander was constantly having the house altered or improved. He owned several cars, but purely for pleasure – he always commuted to the city by train. The (by modern standards) huge domestic staff was recruited at least partly because they were deserving (orphans, teenagers with an alcoholic father, the homeless) rather than well qualified, and the jobs were theirs for life. The farm was managed by an Irish bailiff, Murphy, whose daughter ran the dairy. Mary Brinton recalled her grandfather strolling round the estate arm-in-arm with Murphy. Rendels were never snobs, they all had a soft spot for those in need, and they trusted their servants absolutely.

The older Mary Stocks regretted that her own descendants couldn't experience the daily life of a farm as she had known it: cows, cats with kittens, haystacks, a living-in bull and a donkey they called Neddy – 'as for my great-grandchild, she will never know the sounds and smells of a real farm. She will know only of silos, batteries and a test-tube bull.'

Near the farm was The Cottage, summer home of the house-keeper who looked after the main house in winter. During summer, she boarded deprived children brought out from London by the Rendels for a holiday, or lame ducks the Rendels had somehow met and taken under their wing. The housekeeper was one of five generations of Relfs who lived in the neighbourhood. Mary knew the oldest of them, Granny Relf, who kept a sweet-shop when she was over a hundred, selling drinks for a penny and boiled sweets or biscuits for twopence.

A third holiday home was at West Bay near Bridport in Dorset, today perhaps not much changed from its Edwardian character: a bustling small fishing port and holiday resort at the seaward end of Bridport, still only slightly overrun with fast-food stalls and neon-lit amusement kiosks.

In the 1880s an enterprising local architect designed and built for speculative sale a terrace of solid four-storey houses, end-on to one of West Bay's two parallel piers. Pier Terrace, as it was inevitably called, was made up of eleven identical houses which could have been mistaken for four – several have now merged as a hotel. The terrace dominated the pocket-sized harbour. Behind it a shingle beach shelved sharply upwards. To east and west steep cliffs with attractive twisting paths flanked the resort.

Roland and Constance Brinton bought No.5 Pier Terrace in 1900. It had the same respectable air as Queens Gate Terrace, and it was for their children an ideal family base for swimming, sailing, rowing, walking and beach games. They were hardy children at the turn of the century, not despising damp and chilly seaside holidays. Number 5 remained a holiday home for Rendels and Brintons through six generations, and Pier Terrace has changed remarkably little. Some doorways have been modernised, there are parking spaces for cars, one house is called Thisuldome.

Holidays at West Bay played so important a part in her life that Mary Stocks devotes a whole chapter to them in the second volume of her autobiography, *Still More Commonplace*. Other relatives bought seaside houses nearby, so she met and mixed with innumerable cousins, sketched (her artistic talent developed fast) and at West Bay was courted by her future husband.

During the Second World War the older Brintons retreated to West Bay to escape the London blitz, and Mary's own children spent memorable summers there. For each generation, No. 5 Pier Terrace has represented a type of holiday continuity peculiar to large middle-class family clans. For such families the tradition of shrimping, beach picnics, messing about with boats and windswept walks (often in Norfolk or the Isle of Wight) is almost sacred; they would not dream of taking their children to villas on the Aegean or the Algarve.

Rickettswood in Surrey was a holiday home to so many Rendels that they had no need of social life outside the family. They played croquet, or cards, or charades, or chess, or read, or painted, or went looking for flowers and birds' nests in the woods. They were self-sufficient and happy in that cloudless post-Edwardian era. Mary Stocks called it a golden age. It ended with her grandfather's death in 1918, and the sale of the big house. For a time it remained a private house, then it was converted to a country club, and later demolished to make way for a housing estate.

It is hard to find any real flaw in Mary Brinton's personal world until well after the turn of the century. In 1902, aged 11, she started school with Pestalozzi classes in Clareville Grove near her home. This was a progressive form of preparatory school, emphasising a child's natural development, pioneered by the eighteenth-century Swiss educationalist Johann Heinrich Pestalozzi. It suited Mary's independent nature well.

The Brinton parents had traditional views about the education of boys, but were more open-minded where the girls were concerned. Ralph was sent away to a private preparatory school when he was nine, but there was (to their great relief) no question of boarding school for Mary or Joanna. At 13 it was time for Mary to move on to secondary day school. Briefly she attended Kensington High School, but within a few months she transferred to the newly opened and prestigious St Paul's School for Girls, in Brook Green, Hammersmith.

John Colet, an English Humanist and Bible scholar, had been appointed Dean of St Paul's Cathedral in 1505 and soon after established a boys' school linked to the Cathedral. His mother, Dame Christian, was said to be an early advocate of equal educational opportunity (one of the leitmotifs of Mary Stocks's public life) and the Dean had intended to provide for co-education. For various reasons, the birth of the girls' branch was long delayed; in fact it was 400 years before a site was found in West London, near the boys' school which with expansion had moved out there from the City. Houses were pulled down and a handsome red brick edifice went up in Brook Green, round the corner from the boys' school and about five miles from Mary Brinton's home. Probably she arrived daily by horse omnibus.

For uniform, the Edwardian pupils wore Harrow-type straw boaters with a black band bearing the school crest, the monogram SPS, and generally a white flannel shirt over a long dark skirt, some adding a striped tie. At the formal opening of the school in April 1904 by the Prince and Princess of Wales (later George V and Queen Mary), the 54 girls who made up the original establishment paraded in white dresses and sang 'God Bless the Prince of Wales'. There were bouquets, patriotic songs and macaroons made for tea by the domestic economy class – much enjoyed by the Prince, according to the local paper.[12]

Mary Brinton was admitted in October, aged 13 plus, and a copy of her register entry shows she was the 84th pupil to join the school. New girls were given by the governors a red leather hymn and prayer book bearing the crest and their official number. Sixty years later, in a newspaper interview, Mary recalled her number, though not quite accurately.

School is reckoned to be the most powerful formative influence in many lives. Mary Brinton began as she continued, a rebel against convention. She respected the headmistress, Miss Frances Gray: 'To be sent for to her room for admonition, which happened to me twice, was an experience one would wish to forget without being able to do so'.[13]

Miss Gray had reached St Paul's by way of teaching posts at two lesser girls' schools, but she had begun her career in 1883 (after Cambridge) as the first classics lecturer at Westfield College in Hampstead, a women's college of London University. No one could have imagined that the non-conforming and not conspicuously academic Mary Brinton, thirty years younger than Miss Gray, would one day take over as Principal of Westfield. By her time it was a college with a strong tradition in classics.

There was, she said, no subject she wished to pursue in depth when she left St Paul's. Yet it had a catholic timetable, advanced for Edwardian education. Alongside the more obvious academic subjects at that time, the girls were taught botany, physics and chemistry, algebra, Latin (with some Greek) and Scripture. They also did drawing and needlework and held debates (but not till the sixth form) on such topics as 'suffragism versus non-suffragism'. There is no record of Mary taking part in these debates, yet within a few years the women's movement would absorb most of her energies, and half a century later she would be a leading debater in Parliament itself.

At St Paul's much store was set by sport: gymnastics, hockey, netball, tennis, cricket, swimming. (Until the school had its own pool in 1909, girls had a police escort when they walked to the public baths in Latimer Road.) Sport was anathema to Mary Brinton and one can guess at her reaction to compulsory needle-work. Quite possibly her summonses to Miss Gray's study were for non-attendance at games or, more probably, refusing to wear a boater.

However, despite her disclaimers, two subjects unquestionably appealed to her. One was art and the other English history. She went on, though not directly from St Paul's, to study history with distinction, and the school magazine records two Brinton successes in art. The magazine, *Paulina*, has appeared quarterly since the day the school opened its doors. The issue for July 1907 records that M. Brinton was 'commended in second class and third class of the Royal Drawing Society Exhibition' – in other words she passed external art examinations at levels two and three.

In one of her books she mentions winning a gardening prize, and makes little of it as gardening was 'an excuse for missing hockey'. However, gardening was no minor activity at St Paul's. Among the early pupils – their school careers briefly overlapped Mary Brinton's – were two sisters, Chrystabel and Joan Proctor. Joan went on to study zoology and became Curator of Reptiles at the London Zoo; Chrystabel was from 1916 till 1925 the school's highly regarded gardener and gardening mistress. This was significant in the First World War, when the playing fields were used for food production and became home to pigs, hens, rabbits and a horse and cart.

Two other aspects of school life may have played their part in determining her later interests; the emphasis on social work, and on religious instruction. St Paul's was moving towards setting up a social work centre in Stepney, in the area where Dean Colet had lived with his mother Dame Christian Colet. Dame Christian was revered as the inspirer of John Colet's co-educational ideals, and by 1912 the girls' school had developed in Stepney their own Dame Colet House. This was the base for a school care committee (volunteers concerned with a school's social welfare), a baby centre, Girl Guides, a clinic and a fund for country holidays.

These were exactly the kind of activities Mary Brinton admired among her own relatives, and after leaving school she plunged into voluntary work as a school committee secretary, based in Stepney. Whether consciously or not, the school's ethos must have affected her, likewise its attention to Bible reading and Bible study, its hymn-singing assemblies and the devoutness of some of the early staff members.

Sketching remained a favourite pursuit (she included sketches in her books, and recorded incidents of family history) but she does not seem to have had any professional artistic ambition.

Miss Frances Gray was not only a classicist but a committed churchwoman. She wrote a highly moralistic autobiography with a Chaucerian title, *Gladly Wolde He Lerne and Gladly Teche.* She was also a practical woman, believing in the virtues of housecraft and gardening, and she devotes nearly a page of her book to expounding on a lesson about leeks which she observed during a visit to Brussels. In her journal she recorded that St Paul's Girls' School opened 'on the Nineteenth of January in the Year of Our Lord Nineteen Hundred and Four', with 54 girls and 12 staff. She has some trenchant comments about women's careers:

> In the year 1903, a great many young women had found employment in offices and were, as it seemed to me, endangering their chance of turning into good makers of homes later on . . . I knew that women had been introduced into the General Post Office in order that they might have a livelihood, but I could not believe that all these young people in the Savings Bank (a few minutes' walk from the school) were there because they were obliged to earn a weekly wage . . . but they liked the economic independence it promised.[14]

In spite of her own professional status, Miss Gray made it clear she favoured 'Back to the Home!', as she put it, above the 'mechanical existence' of office work. Mary Brinton no doubt observed and rejected this philosophy.

Thirty years later, when Mary Stocks became Principal of Westfield, she stamped her personal style on chapel services and made a name for herself as a broadcaster popularising the Old Testament. In her schooldays there was no hint of Bible interest. As an adult, she professed to be no churchgoer, but admitted she had been confirmed. Her name does not appear among the lists of

St Paul's girls confirmed each year in their foundation cathedral, so her confirmation was presumably at a Kensington parish church. There are references in passing to 'my confirmation class vicar' and 'a disastrous confirmation class'. She made no attempt to persuade her own children to be confirmed; indeed she approved when her elder daughter opted out of school confirmation. Nevertheless, the St Paul's ethos, the Christian inheritance from Dean Colet and his mother, the commitment of women such as Frances Gray, must have left its imprint on her. There is no other visible church influence in her childhood, though she was to marry into a Church family.

In one more way Mary Brinton played down her school achievements. She seems almost to boast in her writings that she failed the Higher Certificate of the Oxford and Cambridge Joint Board, and was forced by her parents – after leaving school – to have coaching and re-sit the exam, thus qualifying for university entrance. In fact in the November 1908 issue of *Paulina*, her name appears second in the roll of those who passed, not the Certificate of the Joint Board, but the Oxford and Cambridge Joint Board Letter. Mary Brinton's success is recorded next to that of Elizabeth von Arnim, related to the writer (with the same name) famous for the novel *Elizabeth and her German Garden*.

So Mary Brinton left St Paul's in July 1908 by no means certificateless, and although she chose to belittle her four years there, the evidence suggests that school did more for her than she chose to admit.

The roll-call of famous Paulinas (old girls) is long and distinguished, and a hundred years after her birth the name of Baroness Stocks heads the list of those who made their name in public life. She had some noteworthy contemporaries, among them the musician Imogen Holst whose father Gustav was the school's first singing master and director of music. He composed *The Planets*, as well as a suite and a masque for the school, during his thirty years on the staff.

One of the same generation at St Paul's was Charis Barnett, later a midwife in France in the First World War, a magistrate, social reformer and childbirth campaigner whose path was to cross Mary Stocks's in Manchester in the 1930s. Other contemporaries or near-contemporaries were Kathleen Kenyon the Middle East archaeologist, Dame Evelyn Sharp – the first woman to reach the upper ranks of the Civil Service – and the novelist Dodie Smith. All of them are commemorated by their Alma Mater. As it nears its own centenary it continues to educate highly successful career women.

What explanation can there be for Mary Stocks's brushing aside of her four years at St Paul's? Academically she must have been one of its brightest pupils at the time, to judge by her later achievements. In her memoirs there is no mention of friends among girls or staff, or any of those semi-joking school reminiscences autobiographers usually work in. It is almost as if she wished to forget St Paul's.

The only explanation her family can offer is that she felt most of its activities to be irrelevant to her: sport, music, natural history, domestic arts, parading in school uniform, official assemblies. Yet it is hard to believe she would not with enthusiasm have joined in debates, art gallery expeditions or visits to the House of Commons. And in 1907 she took part in what was afterwards called the 'Mud March', a massive demonstration by women's organisations campaigning for votes for women. This was at the instigation of some of her older feminist cousins, Stracheys and Rendels. Mary gloried in the event, her first major feminist public event, and was delighted to find the exploit won nothing but approval from the school staff.

As the Women's Social and Political Union heightened its public image with newsworthy events and propaganda, so the older suffrage societies began to follow suit. In February 1907 the National Union of Women's Suffrage Societies organised the first public open-air demonstration held by the non-militants. The aim was a mass march from Hyde Park to the Exeter Hall, Westminster, timed to coincide with the opening of a new session of Parliament. The plan was launched at a meeting in November. Advertisement space was taken in the *Morning Post* and the *Tribune*. An organist, tickets and marshals were booked. The only unknown factor was how many women would turn up, for this was middle-class Edwardian London, where women's place was totally perceived as in the home, not parading about the streets.

Mary Brinton, aged 16, uninhibited, and beginning to be politically aware through the influence of her Rendel relations, must have rejoiced at the prospect. On the afternoon of 9 February, she assembled with an estimated 3,000 women at Hyde Park Corner.

It was wet and foggy, with slush under foot – hardly ideal for a public demonstration, even if the women had been seasoned campaigners.

Defying the weather, they set out with bands playing and the silk banners of the women's trade unions leading the way. Red and white were the colours of the day: rosettes, posies, programmes, ribbons attached to carriages, buttonholes. Out in front went the banner of the National Union of Women's Suffrage Societies, with its legend 'The Franchise is the Keystone of our Liberty'. Other banners proclaimed 'Failure is Impossible', 'For Hearth and Home', 'Representation our Goal'. The procession was led by the veteran Labour MP Keir Hardie, by the NUWSS President, Millicent Fawcett, by Lady Frances Balfour and Mary Brinton's aunt by marriage, Lady Strachey (her daughter Philippa was secretary of the NUWSS London branch). The *Times* newspaper reported soberly:

> Not one class of women alone was represented in this great procession of voteless citizens who had come to plead at the bar of public opinion for the right to representation in the counsels of State . . . there were high-born dames . . . literary and professional women by the hundred – the woman doctor, the high school mistress, the woman artist – and there were the women of the great industrial north . . . who had left their factories in far-away Lancashire to take part in the march.[15]

It came to be known as the Mud March because of the atrocious conditions, and many spectators acquired a new respect for women who could face public ridicule in such adverse conditions. For there was public ridicule, and more than one paper remarked on the insults flung at the marchers. The *Manchester Guardian*, with implicit snobbery, reported:

> It requires some courage for a woman to step out of her drawing room into the street to take her place in a mixed throng distasteful to many or most of her acquaintance, and to see herself pilloried in the newspapers next morning. That old ladies and delicate ones, and timid ones to boot, should have done this quite simply and bravely argues at least a good deal of quiet conviction.[16]

Pictures from the *Daily Mirror* and the *Graphic* show women of all age groups with their long skirts trailing in the mud, waving rolled papers and umbrellas, struggling to keep banners up against the wind, climbing park railings, debating with policemen, distributing badges. For Londoners it was an extraordinary spectacle, though one to be repeated from time to time in the next few years.

For Mary Brinton the Mud March was an exciting introduction to ten years of campaigning, though always by peaceful means, for votes for women. This was a cause she espoused wholeheartedly, something she could identify with intellectually and practically. Sixty years later in her autobiography she vividly recalled the Mud March:

> As we moved off through the arch of Hyde Park Corner, we met a barrage of ridicule from hostile male onlookers. 'Go home and do the washing', 'Go home and mind the baby' were the most frequent taunts flung at us . . . the balcony of the Ladies' Lyceum Club was crowded with members looking down from their safe vantage. Some of the marchers shouted 'Come down and join us'. I do not know if any of them did. It was a great adventure for a sixteen-year-old.[17]

Her later suffragist exploits included addressing a street-corner meeting in Hackney (much to her mother's displeasure) and chalking pavement notices about a meeting in Edinburgh. During the First World War she served on the executive committee of the NUWSS and was involved in the carefully orchestrated campaign which led to the partial granting of votes for women in 1917. By 1919 Millicent Fawcett had been succeeded as president of the organisation (renamed the National Union of Societies for Equal Citizenship) by the future MP Eleanor Rathbone, and thus two of Mary Stocks's most admired mentors held that office and helped to imprint on her a deep conviction that politics was a career for women as much as for men.

Public meetings greatly appealed to Mary as a teenager. They satisfied some burning desire to stand up and be counted, and for the rest of her life she was powerfully drawn to public platforms and the media as vehicles for shaping opinion. However, her approach was not fanatical: she persuaded others by prosaic common sense rather than rhetoric. In old age, Mary admitted to being perhaps motivated by enjoying the sound of her own voice as much as by reformist zeal. In the light of her subsequent careers, this may be a perceptive comment. Yet she undervalues her own total commitment to the causes she cared about. Alongside politics, her youthful enthusiasm was engaged by the social reform movements emerging before the First World War.

The early years of the century, Mary Stocks wrote, were great days for social workers – 'and it was one particular piece of pioneer reform which engulfed me as I emerged from St Paul's Girls' School on the eve of my seventeenth birthday'. A family friend, Margery Frere, a member of the London County Council education committee, had set up a network of voluntary care committees attached to every London elementary school. One such was at Saffron Hill, in the King's Cross area near Hatton Garden and the Farringdon Road. And Mary Brinton's first unpaid social work was as honorary secretary of the Saffron Hill School Care Committee. The committee members' task was to liaise with teachers, check on the homes of children who might need free school dinners, and recommend medical treatment based on the reports of school doctors. The 16-year-old Miss Brinton was thought too young for home-visiting, but she collated case studies and did the paperwork for committee meetings. For this her only preparation was one evening's instruction in how to draft agendas and minutes and the proper use of an LCC minute book.

In this, her first social responsibility, Mary clashed with the redoubtable social and housing pioneer Octavia Hill, who took the view that free medical treatment for schoolchildren undermined parental duties, and that public relief for the unemployed would weaken their resolve to find work. Despite the difference of opinion, the younger woman was much influenced by Octavia Hill's campaigning for slum tenants and her vision of freedom of access to the countryside for all, culminating in the formation of the National Trust. She admired Octavia's books, *The Homes of the London Poor* and *Our Common Land*. In fact Mary Brinton was a regular visitor to Miss Hill's Marylebone Road home, and she cherished a letter written to her about housing management and slum clearance schemes, in which Miss Hill wrote: 'Some day you may be able to hear, to see or to help in similar work'.[18] There seems little doubt that Octavia Hill fired Mary Brinton's enthusiasm for social reform.

Whether it was her contact with Octavia Hill, a meeting (also engineered by a relative) with the political activist Mrs Beatrice Webb, or the impact of the school care committee, one way or another, she became fascinated by the history and practice of London local government. And this in turn led to the discovery that she could study politics, social history and related subjects in far more depth as a university student, at the London School of Economics and Political Science, which had opened in 1895 in Houghton Street, off Aldwych.

She had retaken her failed Higher School Certificate, and now added chemistry as a further subject in order to matriculate; and in October 1910 she was admitted as an undergraduate to study for a Bachelor of Science (Economics) degree, aged just 19. It was the year of accession of George V and the year when Florence Nightingale died.

There is no evidence to show if Mary Stocks secretly longed to go to Cambridge like two of her Rendel cousins who became doctors. In so far as there was a university for Bloomsburyites, Cambridge was it. It nurtured Virginia Woolf's brother and husband, Lytton and Ray Strachey, George Rylands, Bertrand Russell and his wife Dora, John Maynard Keynes and others who might be regarded as fringe Bloomsburyites. Mary Stocks in her writing never mentions the Bloomsbury Group. Since she was related to several of its members, she cannot have been unaware of the Group's high profile. Probably she felt its almost exclusive emphasis on the arts irrelevant to her own interests.

The LSE she went to was 'a small institution in a tall Edwardian building'. The University of London had been officially founded as an examining body in 1836 and all its degree courses were opened to women in 1878 – just one generation ahead of Mary Brinton's.

Her three years at LSE were immensely full and happy – her triumphant progress towards finals and increasing political activism is charted in detail in the sixth chapter of her autobiography. She found a student body mixed in age, nationality and social background, but – as one would expect – predominantly male. However, in 1912 the balance was somewhat redressed by a social studies diploma course which attracted mainly women.

In her first year she was expected to pass in six subjects: economic theory, public administration, banking and foreign trade, economic geography, economic history and logic. This was good grounding for a future adult education lecturer and radio debater, let alone a member of a dozen government-appointed committees.

Mary Brinton's chief mentor at LSE was the brilliant Dr Lilian Knowles, her tutor and head of the Economic History Department – 'a stimulating lecturer and a magnificently flamboyant personality'. Lilian Knowles was a Cornishwoman who after Truro High School took two firsts at Cambridge, in history and law. At LSE she was successively lecturer, Reader and Professor in Modern Economic History from 1904 onwards, an amazing achievement for a woman on the staff of a mostly male college in the early years of the century. Eventually she became Dean of the Faculty of Economics for the whole of London University.

Four students chose in their second year to specialise in economic history honours, with Lilian Knowles as tutor. They were Mary Brinton, Vera Powell, who as Vera Anstey became an expert on Indian history and returned to lecture at LSE, Theo Gugenheim, who in 1914 changed his German name and eventually became Sir Theo Gregory of the British Economic Mission to Greece, and William Piercy, later a distinguished financier. They formed a Gang of Four, sharing tutorials, meals, student union activities and pub evenings. And all four gained first class degrees – Lilian Knowles had little to complain of in that year. What makes the achievement even more remarkable is that one of the four was a woman who had left school with few examination passes, and two were first-year evening class students who won London County Council scholarships to pay for their full-time studies.

William Piercy and Mary Brinton were elected joint secretaries of the Student Union (it was called Clare Market Parliament after a nearby street market) and plunged with relish into debates on adult suffrage (this was seven years before women gained the vote), Irish Home Rule and disarmament. Through the Union they met some of LSE's memorable postgraduate students, including Hugh Dalton (a future Chancellor of the Exchequer) and Eileen Power who went on to become a Fellow of Girton, a professor at LSE and writer of outstanding books on mediaeval history.

Arranging for visiting speakers to the Union brought Mary Brinton in touch with older women who were already powerful political activists, Millicent Fawcett and Beatrice Webb. She was by now a committed socialist and, but for her studies, would have been more deeply involved in suffragism. Her years at LSE, her friendship with like-minded fellow radicals, and the extent to which her own family's voluntary social work had rubbed off on her, were pushing her towards beliefs and values which stayed with her all her life. How astonished she and William Piercy would have been to be told that one day they would sit together on the Labour benches of the House of Lords. Friendship with Millicent Fawcett, with Beatrice Webb and Mary's own cousin by marriage, Ray Costelloe (who married Oliver Strachey in 1911) all made a strong impact on her politically.

Beatrice Webb, born Beatrice Potter, the daughter of a Gloucester railway magnate, was in her fifties when Mary met her. She had spent a few years in the business with her father, fell in love with Joseph Chamberlain, and gravitated to London where she worked as a rent collector and a charity visitor. Beatrice Potter's social conscience drew her into first-hand investigation of London dockland life and the sweated labour system in London's East End. Her first book, *Life and Labour of the People of London*, was published in 1887.

In 1892 Beatrice had married the leading theorist of the Fabian Society, Sidney Webb. They formed a unique partnership, together researching, writing and campaigning on urban living conditions, as well as on trade unionism and local government. Most importantly for Mary Brinton and her future, the Webbs were deeply involved in the foundation of the London School of Economics in 1895 and the Labour Party in 1906.

Beatrice Webb was one of several friends of Mary Brinton who served on the 1905 Poor Law Commission. She and three others (among them George Lansbury, a Labour MP and editor of the *Daily Herald*) drafted a minority report which partly paved the way for William Beveridge's proposed national insurance scheme in Lloyd George's Government. The whole concept of national insurance was something that Mary later wholeheartedly supported and often spoke about publicly.

Beatrice and Sidney Webb were active and pioneer members of the newly established Labour Party, and founders of the left-wing weekly journal, the *New Statesman*. Soon after Mary Brinton had graduated Beatrice wrote *Wages of Men and Women: Should they be Equal?*, a classic feminist treatise.

All of this was fascinating to a young economist busy discovering people and ideas increasingly opposed to urban and rural poverty. The Webbs' anti-Poor Law propaganda was largely disseminated from the basement in Clements Inn which Mary passed on her way to college. She joined them as a Saturday volunteer, addressing envelopes and sticking on stamps, until the Webbs turned their attention to other activities. In 1892, Sidney Webb was elected as an MP, serving later as a minister under Ramsay McDonald. The Webbs influenced Mary Brinton in several directions. During her time at LSE she joined the Labour Party, became an anti-Poor Law activist and began a lifelong commitment to adult education.

One of Mary's strongest memories of Beatrice Webb was of her views on religion, indicated in a 1913 Fabian lecture: 'The Bankruptcy of Science'. The Webb thesis was that science dealt with the process of life, answering the question: How? But as to the purpose of life, religion is needed to answer the question: Why? This deeply impressed Mary Brinton, then aged 22. Sixty years later she wrote: 'I found it comfortably satisfying in 1913 and have been content with it ever since'.

The other political arena which Mary Brinton entered whole-heartedly in her student days was the cause of women's rights, and for this Dame Millicent Fawcett must be held largely responsible. Millicent Garrett, the daughter of a Suffolk merchant and sister of England's first woman doctor (Elizabeth Garrett Anderson) was over 60 by the time Mary Brinton met her at LSE. She had been involved in the women's movement almost from childhood. She is generally regarded as the British leader of the constitutional suffrage movement, acquiring much of her political wisdom as secretary to her husband, Henry Fawcett. He was Professor of Economics at Cambridge and a mid-Victorian Radical MP for Brighton.

Millicent Garrett Fawcett served on the original suffrage committee, and thirty years later, in 1897, she became President of the National Union of Women's Suffrage Societies (NUWSS). This was in effect a rival body to the more militant Women's Social and Political Union, founded in 1903 by Emmeline Pankhurst and her daughters. Millicent Fawcett concentrated her efforts as a writer and public speaker in three directions – against Irish Home Rule, in favour of a Married Women's Property Act, and against the Boer War concentration camps.

Mary Brinton met Mrs Fawcett five years before the first vote for women was granted, when Millicent was at the height of her lobbying and propagandist careers. Although the NUWSS had existed since the time of John Stuart Mill (his polemic, *On the*

Subjection of Women, had appeared in 1869) it failed to gain a high profile until the Pankhursts set up their parallel organisation. Each stimulated the other. Whether it was militancy or the constitutional method that achieved more is a debate that may never be settled.

Mary could hardly be described as a militant. 'The nearest I ever got to breaking the law was chalking notices of a meeting on the pavements of Edinburgh, and running away before the police could tell me not to'.[19] Not only Philippa but the whole Strachey family, including their formidable mother, Lady Strachey, aligned themselves with the NUWSS. One summer at Rickettswood they and the younger Brintons held an open-air political meeting which rather shocked the local rural community. In a sense, wrote Mary later, the WSPU was parasitic on the NUWSS. In 1913 she and her brother Ralph watched the huge funeral procession for the suffragette Emily Davison, killed when she threw herself in front of the King's horse at the Derby. Despite their disapproval of militant methods the Brintons were much moved by the emotional atmosphere of the event. Mary believed that political leaders trusted Millicent Fawcett more than the firebrands of the WSPU because of her assets of temperament: her reasonableness, liberalism and sense of humour.

During the First World War Mary Stocks (as she was by then) served on the committee of the NUWSS, and she carried on the fight until equality of suffrage was fully realised in 1928. But, at the time of her schoolgirl and student involvement, Millicent Garrett Fawcett was for her a role model hard to better – the voice of reason, commitment and organisation.

Mrs Fawcett was invited to become the external figurehead President of the Student Union at LSE, and Mary Brinton as its joint secretary had many meetings with her. She recalled a hilarious inaugural lecture on the subject of gossip, and numerous tea parties to plan annual general meetings and dinners. The friendship between the two women, with nearly fifty years difference in age, was a mutually refreshing one. In her broadcasting years, the 1950s and 60s, Mary Stocks paid more than one radio tribute to both these mentors, Mrs Sidney Webb and Dame Millicent Fawcett. Beatrice Webb was recalled on Women's World Day of Prayer as having influenced 75 years of social reform. Millicent Fawcett had a *Woman's Hour* talk devoted to her on the anniversary of her birth.

Mary Brinton, with her first in economics, might well have

moved on to postgraduate research alongside Eileen Power, Hugh Dalton and Vera Anstey, but it seems that she had set her sights on some form of social work, though what form it might take had not yet crystallised in her mind. Another possibility was a more active political life. What was undoubtedly clear in 1913 was that a very bright future lay ahead of her.

But even before graduating she had met John Stocks. He was deputed to show Mary around Oxford when she spent a weekend at St John's College with Sidney and Mary Ball, friends of the Webbs. Mary Brinton was then 21, in her second year at LSE. John Stocks was 29, a Fellow and Tutor in Philosophy at St John's, and as radical as her in his views. In the summer of 1912, he visited the family holiday home in Dorset and proposed. The engagement lasted a year, mainly to give her time to graduate. Weekends were spent in Oxford and London, and they wrote to each other every day in between.

Chapter 2

The Oxford Years: 1913–1924

John Leofric Stocks was born at Market Harborough, Leicestershire, in 1882, one of six sons (there were also five daughters) of Canon John Edward Stocks and his wife Emily, the daughter of an Oxford solicitor.

John Edward Stocks had married Emily Jane Mallam at Oxford in 1871, after a four-year stint as chaplain at Christ Church. He then took charge of various Leicestershire parishes, spending thirteen years at Market Harborough where most of the family were born. Several of them were given Saxon second names – hence Leofric and Frideswide – which they rather disliked. John Stocks senior's career had followed a classic mid-Victorian clergy pattern: university, ordination, a country parsonage or two, a place in the Cathedral Close, and (as a matter of course) a large family. In time he was appointed an Honorary Canon and later a Residential Canon of Peterborough Cathedral, and here at their house in the Cathedral Close the children of John and Mary Stocks visited their grandparents. Helen Stocks remembered it as a rather cold and gloomy house, but 'always full of family'.

John Leofric Stocks was educated at Rugby, where his friends and contemporaries included William Temple, later Archbishop of Canterbury, and Reginald Harry Tawney, to become a leading economic historian. They all went on to read classics at Oxford. John's college was Corpus Christi and his passion was hockey. He captained the university eleven in 1904 and a year later played for England, as several of his five brothers did. It was said the eleven Stocks siblings were good enough to have formed a mixed England team, though mixed hockey would hardly have been thought proper by Edwardian society.

Resisting some pressure from family and friends to enter the

31

Church, John was appointed in 1906 Fellow and Tutor in Philosophy at St John's College. Some years later he was deputed to show Mary Brinton round the college while she was staying there with the Balls. The arrangement worked better than anyone could have expected. Within a few months he had proposed, and by the end of 1913 they were married.

Around the time of his marriage John was made Oxford University Junior Proctor, an ancient office carrying some prestige (it admitted the holder to various councils and committees) and some rather onerous policing duties. During his eighteen years at St John's he published a number of books, mainly on Aristotelian ethics, and worked on producing a classical Greek dictionary.

The partnership was an ideal one. John Stocks and Mary Brinton shared not only academic enthusiasm but many interests – radical politics, the theatre, travel, public speaking, political and social reform, a love of art, an attraction to the sea.

The wedding was at St Mary Abbots Church, Kensington, near the Brinton family home, on 16 December 1913. The groom was described as Bachelor, aged 31, son of John Edward Stocks, Clerk in Holy Orders. The bride appeared as Spinster, aged 22, daughter of Roland Danvers Brinton, Doctor of Medicine. The register was signed by Sir Alexander Rendel, Charles Donald (the best man), E.C. Petriburg and Lilian Knowles (Mary's tutor in economics at LSE). No photographs exist, for none were taken. Before the First World War, it was not common practice to photograph wedding ceremonies. The Pilgrims' Chorus from *Tannhäuser* was played while the register was signed, and the newly weds left the church to the Wedding March from *Lohengrin*.

After a reception given by the bride's parents, John and Mary Stocks spent the first night of their honeymoon at the long-vanished Grand Hotel in Trafalgar Square. On the wedding evening they went to the theatre to see an old family friend appearing as Catherine the Great, and after the show the leading lady entertained them to supper. Next day they set off for Italy. It was Mary's first night away from friends or family, her first night in a hotel, and her first trip abroad.

A very few honeymoon snapshots have survived. These are faint black-and-white views of the happy couple with some unidentified companions near the Forum in Rome and again in Florence. They did not visit Italy again, but the honeymoon was for Mary the start of a lifelong interest in European travel. The family photo album has scenes taken between the two world wars of the pair skating in Switzerland, walking in the Black Forest and visiting friends on a German farm.

The honeymoon had to be cut short because John's appointment as a University Proctor demanded his presence in Oxford at the start of the Lent term. Soon after Christmas married life began at 17 St Michael's Street, Oxford, a fairly quiet lane off the Cornmarket, five minutes from St John's College and in what is now a conservation area of historic interest.

Number 17 is a plain well proportioned late Georgian house on three floors, with a strip of garden and a handsome front door. In the 1990s it is cream painted and used as a quantity surveyor's office. Opposite are a pub and a guesthouse, and round the corner a cottage bearing a plaque to record that John Wesley stayed there on a preaching tour. Two doors along St Michael's Street stands the mid-Victorian pile of the Oxford Union, its library filled with faded murals of Arthurian scenes painted by Rossetti, Burne-Jones, Morris and other Pre-Raphaelites.

In Mary's time as a housewife, 17 St Michael's Street was sandwiched between a livery stable and a bookbinder's premises, with St Michael's Church and Infant School close by. It was a pleasant street in which to start married life, conveniently close to the heart of Oxford.

The Oxford of 1913 was almost unimaginably different from the Oxford of 1939, when by coincidence Mary Stocks again came to live in the city in the shadow of another world war. In 1913 single- and double-decker horse-drawn trams ran right across the city. They were notoriously unpunctual and liable to run off their tracks – a college porter called them 'the laughing stock of all Oxonians and certainly all visitors'.

However in that same year, 1913, another William Morris, later to become Viscount Nuffield, introduced a fleet of motor omnibuses in the face of much opposition. This man was the pioneer manufacturer of Britain's first small home-grown private car, and locally famous for starting out by making cycles in an Oxford backyard shed. Motor buses had an uphill fight to be accepted. At first it was declared illegal to pay fares on an omnibus. Books of tickets had to be bought at local shops.

At dusk a lamplighter went round the city centre with an oil lamp on a pole. Donkeys pulled barrow-loads of hot chestnuts for sale. Italian organ-grinders played popular tunes in the streets where John Stocks patrolled after dark to keep an eye on delinquent undergraduates. Delinquency ranged from being out after 9.15 p.m. (the curfew hour for all students in prewar Oxford) to drunkenness or being seen with a prostitute.

The Stockses could hardly have found anywhere more inspiring for a start to an academic marriage. The university had 28 colleges (four for women only) with a population of some 8,000 students. Despite its ancient appearance, St John's, founded in 1555, was in fact younger than 16 others. University College, the oldest foundation, predated St John's by 300 years. The first occupants on the St John's site in what is now broad tree-lined St Giles, Oxford's main approach from the north, were Cistercian monks. Their college had been founded by Archbishop Chichele in the fifteenth century and named after St Bernard. A weather-worn statue of the saint still presides over the main entrance, though the monastic building fell into disuse after the Dissolution of the Monasteries under Henry VIII.

Oddly enough St Bernard's was never formally suppressed, and in 1555 it was rescued and given a new lease of life by Sir Thomas White, a prosperous merchant tailor, twice Lord Mayor of London. The story goes that Sir Thomas was advised in a dream to build a college where three trunks of an elm tree grew from one root. Legend has it that the unorthodox tree flourished in St John's gardens for 150 years. Indeed from its earliest foundation, St John's was noted for its gardens, even in a university especially proud of its college gardens. And John Stocks too had a personal interest in one feature at St John's, the large-scale rockery built up from unusual geological specimens.

The remains of a fifteenth-century foundation even older than St Bernard's College survive in the crypt under St John's Buttery. Parts of Archbishop Chichele's college can still be seen in the first quadrangle, and the monks' kitchen was turned into the Hall. The monks' chapel remains, but much restored. Its chief glory is a five-lancet stained glass window which commemorates two archbishops, William Laud and William Juxon. St John's Chapel has a warm and well-used atmosphere; it is home to one of Oxford's best choirs. The Italianate second quadrangle dates from the time of Archbishop Laud, a little before the

English Civil War, around 1635. The Library has at various times housed a Chaucer printed by Caxton and a portrait of Charles I (who made Oxford his Civil War base), devised from lines of the Psalms.

Among so much history and romance, still one more story deserves to be told, of honest endeavour finding a just reward. The rooms above the kitchen were built by a college cook, Thomas Clark, at his own expense. In return the college allowed him to collect the rent from certain sets of student rooms until he had recouped himself. This story would have appealed greatly to the egalitarian Mary Stocks.[1]

She described her first year in Oxford as 'living a double life'. During the week she was continuing to lecture in economics at Kings College for Women, in London – she had started a year or so after graduating – commuting to London by train at a time when commuting was not the standard practice it has since become. In between she did a little economics tutoring to men and women Oxford students, by virtue of her first-class degree. She was pleased that a woman student she had tutored for a while at St Hilda's, Doris Odlum, went on to become an internationally known medical psychologist.

Another academic activity made possible by residence in Oxford was taking classes for the Workers' Educational Association. From this developed a lifelong association with the WEA, and forty years on Mary Stocks became its vice-president. Her first class was an afternoon one for farming wives at Ascott-under-Wychwood, about fifteen miles from Oxford. It was exciting to talk about economic history in a village hall where Joseph Arch, the pioneer trade unionist, had encouraged local people to fight for an agricultural union.

At weekends Mary Stocks became happily absorbed into Oxford's social life. Early acquaintances included Maria Montessori, who pioneered nursery education, and Annie Besant, the free-thinking social reformer. John and Mary Stocks loved the theatre and met Sybil Thorndike and Lewis Casson at the New Theatre. Another Oxford friend was the poet Robert Bridges, who made a lasting impression by keeping pigs, most appropriately, on Boars Hill. Boars Hill before the First World War was a village reached by walking across fields.

Other Boars Hill residents were Professor Gilbert Murray, the

great classical scholar, and his wife Mary. Despite their unconventional lifestyle – they were Quakers, teetotal and vegetarian
– the Murrays made the much younger Stockses very welcome
at their distinguished dinner parties, where the only drink was
lemonade.

The men shared a specialism in Greek classics and enjoyed
each other's intellectual company. Mary Stocks played her part
in furthering women's integration by chaperoning their daughter,
Agnes Murray, to teatime meetings of the (mostly male) Fabian
Society; this she was allowed to do as a married woman – a small
social breakthrough. Mary remained a close friend of Gilbert
Murray until his death in 1957, at the age of 91.

Other aspects of prewar Oxford life nostalgically recalled in Mary
Stocks's autobiography were bicycle rides to Otmoor, familiar to
her from agricultural history studies, but 'remote as a distant
foreign land'. She responded to Oxford's loveliness:

> There was Oxford, so beautiful, and in those far-off days so
> strangely withdrawn . . . As for architectural beauty, it was all
> within reach, all down the High Street to Magdalen Bridge, all
> up the Broad, and round the corner in St Giles where was St
> John's College, the most beautiful College of all.[2]

But she was also acutely conscious of inequalities she had not found
in London. The women's colleges, she commented, were there on
sufferance. Women students could sit the men's examinations but
not receive degrees; they played no part in governing the university;
they were not allowed in male common rooms. But John and Mary
Stocks were actively helping to change all that.

The idyllic life of a young don's wife lasted for barely eight
months. In August 1914 war was declared, and John Stocks almost
immediately enlisted as an Army second lieutenant. At Christmas
he was posted for officer cadet training, and his bride of exactly a
year returned to her parents' home for much of the war. At the end
of July 1915 John went to France as a captain in the King's Royal
Rifle Corps. A week later their first daughter, Ann, was born at her
grandparents' London house.

The absence of many male dons in the forces gave Mary Stocks
the opportunity to become first a part-time economics lecturer at
LSE, and later a full-time lecturer at King's College for Women,
which became Queen Elizabeth College of Domestic Science, in

London University. The College was in Campden Hill Road, not far from her Kensington base. This work continued even after the birth of her son John, the third-generation John Stocks, at 8 Queens Gate Terrace in 1918.

Later in life she often referred to her good fortune in having a nanny and domestic help whenever she needed them. Combining the roles of mother and career woman for her was never a problem, yet something rarely achieved by women of her generation.

Several of Mary's close family served in the forces through the war and, against the odds, survived. Dr Roland Brinton served in the Royal Army Medical Corps on the hospital ship *Asturias*, which was torpedoed in the English Channel on her way back from the Mediterranean, with the loss of sixty lives. Dr Brinton was rescued and, according to his daughter, the whole experience gave him great personal satisfaction; indeed he wrote articles about it for learned journals.

Her brother Ralph joined the Navy and came unscathed through the Battle of Jutland. In the 1930s, as a retired commander and documentary film-maker, he took part in filming Fleet manoeuvres for the Admiralty archives. The film, *Our Island Nation*, earned a place for itself in film history. The *Daily Telegraph* naval correspondent wrote: 'It offers a succession of thrills unsurpassed by any production from Hollywood'.[3]

John Stocks was less fortunate during the war. After 18 months commanding an infantry company in the trenches he was seriously wounded leading his men in November 1916 at Beaucourt-sur-Ancre, on the Somme. For this he won the Distinguished Service Order. After a long period in hospital he ended the war training cadets in the 19th Officer Cadet Battalion at Pirbright Camp, in Surrey. Here Mary and the children joined him for short spells in furnished houses.

Looking back much later on the First World War, Mary Stocks was struck by ways in which it differed from the second: in particular 'the indiscriminate rush of men into the Army', which led (in her view) to a disastrous waste of manpower without regard to men's special skills. She criticised strongly the incompetent method (at home) of setting up food rationing, which outraged her practical economist's mind.

One of the saddest material consequences of the war for the Brinton family was the sale of the grandparental home,

Rickettswood, the scene of so many Victorian and Edwardian family holidays. There would be no more shared sporting and intellectual contests, no more huge gatherings of the Rendel clan with Sir Alexander as paterfamilias. On the plus side, Mary rejoiced at wartime side-benefits such as the granting of votes for women in 1917 and the introduction of family allowances in 1918.

Her involvement in the fight for these social reforms led to a long and mutually stimulating friendship with Eleanor Rathbone, at first a Liverpool city councillor, later one of the first and most effective women Members of Parliament. During the war Mary Stocks had joined a committee of six, under Eleanor, drafting a scheme for child allowances to be paid directly to working mothers (rather than fathers). In 1918 their pilot scheme was published in a pamphlet, *Equal Pay and the Family*, yet the proposals were not implemented until the Labour Government of 1945.

Another campaign begun in the First World War was one to improve childbirth conditions for working women. This too was launched with a small but telling pamphlet, *Maternity*, composed of letters from mothers describing experience of childbirth without benefit of anaesthetics, midwives or hygienic conditions. The appointment of a woman chief maternity officer at the Ministry of Health advanced the cause, and so did the publication of *Married Love* by Marie Stopes. (The paths of Mary Stocks and Marie Stopes were to cross more than once in the 1920s.)

These and other forays into the minefield of women's health and women's rights, in the years during and after the war, led to positive and practical action by Mary Stocks and like-minded women a few years later. Gradually her activities began to focus on specific concerns; she followed eagerly in the steps of Beatrice Webb, Octavia Hill, Marie Stopes, Eleanor Rathbone and one other formidable pioneer whom Mary had not yet met. This was Nancy Astor, later elected to Parliament to succeed her husband when he unavoidably entered the Lords, and so almost by chance the first woman to take her seat in the House of Commons. All of these remarkable women exercised their influence on Mary Stocks. Her own contribution to improving the quality of life for women in twentieth-century Britain can be seen as a fusion of their ideas.

Armistice Day 1918 was not without trauma for the Stocks family. It was uncertain when John Stocks would be demobbed – indeed he was set the long-term task of devising educational programmes for Army returners. But for Mary, improvising in a rented house near Pirbright Camp, a much greater anxiety came when three-year-old Ann went down with an illness eventually diagnosed as typhoid, caused by contaminated milk.

When the demobilisation of all teachers was announced, and John was free to take up his Oxford Fellowship again, Mary, Ann and the baby John returned to Queens Gate Terrace for a while. In any case Mary was obliged to complete a year's lecturing at Queen Elizabeth, and it probably seemed wise to have Dr Brinton keeping an eye on his granddaughter's health.

Family life began again in earnest in October 1919, not in St Michael's Street but at St John's House, the house allotted to the Senior Tutor of St John's College. Here, Helen was born in the summer of 1920, and christened in the College chapel with R.H. Tawney and her aunt Joanna (later Mrs Baillieu) as godparents. (Ann and John had been christened at St Mary Abbots in Kensington.) Ann's godparents were William Temple and a Rendel aunt, also Ann. John's were Millicent Fawcett and an uncle. It is worth noting that in spite of her antipathy to confirmation and what she called organised religion, Mary was not averse to the ritual of baptism.

All three children remembered with affection their comfortable home within the precincts of St John's, with its own entrance in Museum Street, and its garden shaded by a mulberry tree. There were friendly college personalities to entertain them, archery contests on the college lawn, and the special privilege of watching Eights Week boat races from the St John's College boat.

When she was old enough Ann went to Oxford Girls' High School, whereas John was sent away to preparatory school and then to Rugby. In spite of their shared belief in equality of opportunity the Stockses were not quite radical enough to treat son and daughters alike. Ann enjoyed special status at school: 'I was enormously smug. To have two academic parents was very prestigious'.

There were family pets, a cat and a dog. John Stocks believed in bringing up children with animals. Unfortunately, the dog, a lively Jack Russell, did not get the attention he needed – so he went back to his home farm.

All this busy-ness – tutoring, family life, university activities – did not for a moment dampen Mary Stocks's enthusiasm for the cause of total women's suffrage. The 1917 Act had granted the vote and candidature rights only to women over 30. The suffragettes were not discouraged. The election of Constance Markiewicz as a Sinn Fein member for South Dublin in 1918 did not advance the cause, and she never took her seat – a principle still adhered to by successful Sinn Fein candidates 75 years on. Constance startled the reactionaries by having a 4,000 majority over a Nationalist who had held the seat for 26 years. In the same general election sixteen other women were unsuccessful candidates.

In the summer of 1919, Viscountess Astor took her seat in the Commons, to the outrage of Mary and her colleagues.

> Not for this had we laboured so long and hard . . . Here was an American millionairess, known to us only by reputation as a society hostess, stepping into a safe seat vacated by her husband on his elevation to the peerage: not by reason of her own qualification, but merely qua wife. We feared the worst.[4]

The fears of women's suffrage supporters proved unfounded. Nancy Astor emerged, in spite of her background, as an able fighter for women's rights who worked closely with some of the most radical women's suffrage campaigners. She and Mary Stocks became genuine friends. The two women had much in common, according to Nancy's son David, and their friendship deepened over the years.

However, Mary Stocks's main political involvement was still with the National Union of Women's Suffrage Societies, and her sympathies remained very much left of centre. This was strengthened by growing friendship with J.L. (Lawrence) and Barbara Hammond, the social historians. She also joined pressure groups demanding full Oxford University membership for women.

Full academic status, with conferment of degrees, finally came in 1920. One of the first women graduates to have her degree formally conferred was the novelist-to-be and theological writer Dorothy Sayers, a Somerville student. She was almost identical in age to Mary Stocks; their paths crossed in Oxford (where Dorothy for a time worked at Blackwell's) and in years to come Dorothy was invited as a speaker to meetings organised by Mary.

A generation of famous women passed through Somerville in the years after the First World War: Dame Janet Vaughan, later Principal of Somerville for 22 years and an internationally respected haematologist; the Oxford linguist Dr Enid Starkie; the writers Winifred Holtby and Vera Brittain. But for the work of the university pro-rights campaigners, none of them would have been allowed full academic status.

John and Mary Stocks came in contact with communism within a few years of the Russian Revolution. Sidney and Beatrice Webb at first embraced the ideology wholeheartedly. Other friends were more cautious. A Russian trade diplomat came to speak at the Oxford Labour Club and it fell to Mary to entertain his wife. Refreshments were on offer at one of the men's colleges, but women could not be admitted after a certain hour. So they made do with apricot jam at St John's House. Having no common language, they were unable to discuss 'the strange Oxford custom'.

The same Labour Club (John Stocks was its treasurer) clashed with the Vice-Chancellor over a proposed visit by Bertrand Russell. The undergraduate secretary (a woman) sought permission for a public meeting to be held. Mary Stocks, in her autobiography, quotes at length from the Vice-Chancellor's reply, intolerant even by 1921 standards. The Vice-Chancellor wrote that he objected to the Labour Club holding any kind of public meeting perceived by him as agit-prop and class divisive. He objected to the title chosen by the Club and even to the wording of the invitation ('quite apart from the question whether Mr Russell is a suitable person to address undergraduates on questions that involve social morality'). There was more in the same vein, and it provoked a deputation from the Union and representations by senior university members before the fracas died down.

This same Vice-Chancellor, Lewis Farnell, was the victim of a practical joke which delighted the press: he was sent a box of chocolates dusted with kitchen cleaning powder at a time when the papers were full of a poisoning-by-chocolates case. As it happened, the author of the 'gumpowder plot' was a St John's undergraduate. Altogether John Stocks's college must have been somewhat unpopular with the university establishment.

Mary Stocks was also indirectly involved in a row over the unexplained banning of another meeting, at which the distinguished theologian Maude Royden was to speak about women and the Church. A college head told Mary Stocks he supposed the Vice-Chancellor must have confused Dr Royden with a nude West End dancer of a similar name.

There was also the question of Irish independence. In 1921, shortly before the creation of the Irish Free State, public opinion in England had turned against the violence of the Black and Tans (a special force sent to quell the IRA of the day). A major meeting was organised in Oxford at the Corn Exchange. Mary found herself replacing posters of the meeting torn down by objectors. In the end, it all went off quietly ('Sunday School orderly', she called it).

Mary remained convinced that it was protest meetings like this, and others held almost daily in Oxford, that forced Lloyd George's Government into agreeing to the partition of Ireland. In her view this fundamental freedom to write, speak and hold public meetings could always affect government policy, if enough activists cared. This was a cardinal belief she held all her life, whether over great international issues or something as parochial as preserving an historic house. What made her unusual, if not unique, was that she practised what she preached for very nearly seventy years.

Amongst all this activity she found time to write an economic history textbook for evening class students. *The Industrial State, a Social and Economic History of England*, was published in 1920, the same year that Mary's younger daughter Helen was born. There was nothing tentative about this first publication, forerunner of twelve more. With self-assurance and a brisk style, she put together a social and economic history of England to appear in a textbook series of continuation manuals. These were intended for mature students anxious to continue their education beyond the compulsory elementary school stage ('young citizens earning their living, who want so to live and work as to preserve the gains of civilisation, and yet to help the world to a better future' as the general introduction has it).

Under its rather uninspiring title, *The Industrial State*, the small volume traces the growth of Britain's political economy from the Middle Ages to what the author called the New Age of Paternalism – the social benefits of the early twentieth century. The book is very much Mary Stocks the social commentator talking. Early in the first chapter she sets out her world view:

> We want, or imagine that we want, a whole host of things which our forefathers never dreamed of wanting; and we have means for satisfying those wants which our forefathers would have regarded as rank black magic. As a result the majority of us, in

this country at least, have become dependent on big industries and are obliged to live herded together in overcrowded smoky town areas which perhaps a hundred and fifty years ago were green open country.[5]

A little further on her socialist principles begin to colour the academic approach:

And now we must turn to a fourth feature of our Great Society – its lamentable imperfection. With all its accumulation of capital, with all its network of specialisation, communication and exchange, it has not really succeeded in making our own 46 million people reasonably comfortable. Masses of them are forced to live in houses which are a disgrace to civilisation. Masses are obliged to work too hard, or work under conditions which make life hardly worth the living . . . Either our Great Society is not producing enough wealth, or . . . distributing it so badly the majority of people are not getting enough.[6]

There is more than a touch of satire in that (often repeated) capitalising of Great Society. Mary Stocks, reading that passage aloud, would have invested it with a good deal of wry bitterness.

The tenth chapter is headed 'The Great Society Comes of Age', and it examines the dilemma of western industrialisation. Mary Stocks recognises the immense benefits of the industrial revolution in four main areas: metalworking and mining, textiles, transport and agriculture. Clearly, she argues, it should have brought the common man more wealth and more leisure. It should have freed him from grinding toil and 'the valley of the shadow of poverty'. And yet:

For some reason (which the reader may determine himself after hearing the facts) . . . somehow the words 'Industrial Revolution' have come to be associated in our minds not with human happiness, but with human suffering. We connect it with the growth of slums, with the overworking of women and children, and with the coming of something like a class war.[7]

The book demonstrates capably that this human suffering stemmed from the failure of housing provision, worker–employer relations and working conditions to match the enormous population explosion (from 9 million to 20 million in 60 years) of the nineteenth century. Factories sprouted in green fields. Men became slaves of machines, doing little more outside working hours than sleep. Family life deteriorated. Out of this was born the trade union movement, and pioneer social legislation to make daily life more tolerable. Mary Stocks is writing for a very specific reader – the ordinary working man or woman wishing to be better educated – and she has the skill to make economic history relevant to them.

This is by no means a dry little manual. Political economy is not a subject that lends itself easily to humour, yet there are flashes of humour. The Elizabethan traders laid the foundations of an empire 'in blunt-nosed little sailing ships with abominable quarters, scant storage room and an uncomfortable habit of driving to leeward in a strong wind'. Various historical or quasi-historical figures are referred to as 'our old friends' – Dick Whittington, the Three Musketeers, 'Turnip' Townsend. And 'as suddenly as it had begun, canal construction stopped dead in 1830. Why? The question is easily answered. In that year the Manchester and Liverpool railway was opened'.

Another way in which the author, perhaps unwittingly, revealed herself was by the use of highly subjective quotations to front each chapter, showing a preference for Victorian poets. She borrows, among others, from Ruskin, Hood, Crabbe, Masefield, Wordsworth, Shelley, Matthew Arnold, Shakespeare's *Richard II*, Lewis Carroll, Kipling and (less predictably) Goethe.

Lines by John Drinkwater preface the final chapter, which is headed 'Quo Vadis?' Crystal-gazing, Mary Stocks foresees that three major problems will bedevil the twentieth century: those of labour versus capital, international relations, and the relationship of the individual and the state – not unrealistic insights, given that she was writing just after the First World War and before many modern technological developments. Her conclusion also gains in immediacy in the light of recent history:

> We may be tempted to feel as though our ancestors had bequeathed us an enormously powerful ship to navigate with out compasses on an uncharted sea. Nervously we ask ourselves 'Quo Vadis?'

A newspaper reviewer wrote ambiguously: 'Mrs Stocks's work may be warmly commended to those who wish to take a bird's eye view of economic history. They will find her a most capable and entertaining pilot'.

For a year or two, family life, social observation and writing for a very specific public went hand in hand. After the economic textbook came two short pamphlets on economic topics, written at the behest of (and published by) the Labour Party: *The Meaning of Family Endowment*, costing one shilling, and *Equal Pay for Equal Work*, costing twopence. There must be a moral here in the price disparity.

In the earlier pamphlet, Mary proposed a halfway house between a state-prescribed £7 per week minimum wage (described at the time as 'sufficient to keep a family of five or six children at the period of their maximum needs') and the existing inequality between family size and income levels. Ahead of her time, she saw family endowment as a fundamental element in a comprehensive social system. This was Mary's own belief, her philosophy of social justice. An over-cautious reviewer found her arguments 'sober and persuasive, if not always convincing'.

In *Equal Pay for Equal Work* she dismissed the latest theory, proposing deductions for inferiority, and came out firmly in favour of the rate for the job. *The Manchester Guardian* found her pamphlet the best published argument so far for equal pay. But it echoed her warning: 'If, handicapped as they are by muscular inferiority and domestic obligations, women are to compete with men on equal terms . . . they must be allowed to make the best use they can of their capacities'. In other words, no sex barrier in the workplace – still the feminists' cry seventy years later.

The picture that emerges of Mary Stocks in her thirties is of a young married woman seizing every opportunity that lay before her – certainly not deterred by 'muscular inferiority or domestic obligations'. She opened many doors that others might have supposed shut: lecturing, tutoring, campaigning – especially on women's issues – but also enjoying family life in a way denied to earlier or later generations. She was a career woman, yet domestically privileged; an Edwardian, yet acutely conscious of the injustices of post-Edwardian society.

Family life in the years between the wars was full but without pressure for the three children and their parents. Many photographs show them on holiday, mainly in Dorset, with a car – still a rarity in the early 1920s. There was always a nanny, and domestic help was easy to come by. Later on Mary Stocks acknowledged on radio how much was made possible by the constant supply of nursemaids. Her younger daughter, Helen, said:

> We always had a nanny. I remember picnics and walks. Mother invented secret picnics and used her scarf as a flag to mark the place. Our parents were always busy, marking exam papers, checking a Greek lexicon, that sort of thing. I thought all parents were like that.[8]

Ann, being slightly older, recalled some of the famous people who came and went at St John's House, or whose homes she was taken to as a seven- or eight-year-old. The Murrays made an impression on her, and so did Margaret Bondfield, elected to Parliament in 1923.

There was much reading aloud to the children, with an emphasis on Robert Louis Stevenson on John's part and a preference by Mary for Beatrix Potter and Kipling. Inevitably, living in Oxford, they listened to the story of Alice, written by another Oxford don. They almost certainly picnicked on that same bank of the Cherwell where the child Alice Liddell inspired her elderly admirer, the Revd Charles Dodgson, the painfully shy mathematics tutor who created one of the best-known characters in all children's fiction.

What Ann remembered most vividly from the Oxford years was the acquisition of the family's first car, when she was six:

> My parents went to the first Motor Show and came back with an air-cooled Rover. Then of course they had to learn to drive. Very few dons had cars then, so we were very visible. On the basis that they wanted to go and we'd learn appreciation they took us everywhere – churches, museums – and we always travelled by car. My grandparents thought it was extremely reckless, but father kept accounts to prove the car was a saving.[9]

Soon cars were a common sight in Oxford, and the Stocks family moved on to a Citröen. It appears in quite a few family photos, mostly in connection with picnics near West Bay in Dorset. From Oxford to West Bay had become an easy journey, and the three children grew to love No. 5 Pier Terrace much as their parents and grandparents had. In the 1990s it remains in the family and is used as a holiday home by at least four generations of Rendel-Stockses.

When the Stocks sisters revisited Oxford in the 1980s they were shocked to find major rebuilding taking place at St John's College, their old home being demolished to make way for student accommodation. The distress was modified, however, when they saw their precious mulberry tree had been preserved in a polythene cocoon during the building work, miraculously surviving all the excavation.

The Oxford of the 1920s was not merely a world away from the Kensington where Mary Brinton had grown up, but one of the world's most desirable centres of learning. Only the *jeunesse dorée* studied then at Oxford, products very largely of the public schools, from blue-blooded families.

Mary Stocks, in her autobiography, says little of the undergraduate population, yet her husband's duties as a Proctor must have made her very much aware of the species. Indeed her own garden was a popular route for students climbing in and out of college at what she calls 'unauthorised hours'. She adds: 'Our house was never short of cushions, which could often be found on the ground because they were used by climbers to surmount the broken glass defences on the wall, and were not always retrieved'.

She noted the arrival of a new honours school – Modern Greats, nowadays familiarly known as PPE (philosophy, politics and economics). John Stocks was involved with the first two subjects and Mary Stocks tutored in economics. Why, she wondered, did the prescribed reading list include Marx's *Das Kapital*, but only its first nine chapters?

The Statute recognising women as full members of the University came into force in 1920. Mary rejoiced exceedingly over their new status, and also over the calibre of mature students who came up after the war. 'For women in particular' she wrote, 'the awakened Oxford did indeed present a brave new world'. The war had liberated women in terms of personal freedom, dress and public activities. Many Oxford women graduates went on to competitive careers in journalism, law, advertising and scientific research.

An outlet for the less inhibited postwar students was the Oxford University Drama Society (OUDS), and one of its brightest lights was a St John's student, Tyrone Guthrie. He went on to become a prominent theatre director in England, Canada and the United States. Mary knew him well and they renewed acquaintance some thirty years later. All her life she loved theatre, and a new interest was the opening of the Oxford Playhouse two minutes from her home, with a very young John Gielgud in its original company.

Among John Stocks's colleagues at St John's was an Austrian refugee with a passion for Masefield and Robert Browning (shared by the Stockses). Mary Stocks recalled taking him to meet Robert Bridges, who shocked the young man by giving it as his considered opinion that the greatest English prose writer was Jane Austen. ('In his view Bridges could not have been serious').

A small popular guide to Oxford in the 1920s gives a picture of it as a fledgling tourist centre. Not then the open-top tourist bus, the coachloads of Japanese photographers, the souvenir shops. Third-class return rail fare from London or Birmingham was sixteen shillings, but the smart way to approach from London was by river, taking two days with an overnight stop at Henley. Bed and breakfast at The Mitre cost twelve shillings, but only seven and sixpence at the Bridge House in Botley Road, or five shillings at Durham's in Beaumont Street. A ticket for a day's fishing could be had for a shilling, whereas a day's golf cost three and sixpence at the University Club, or sixpence less at the North Oxford Club. A horse-drawn cab cost one and fourpence a mile, or ten shillings by the hour. Oxford boasted some four or five cinemas and no fewer then ten men's clubs, six of them political.[10]

The guidebook mentioned disparagingly 'the frankly suburban aspects of Cowley and Headington',[11] but it told its readers that the High 'is considered by many the most beautiful street in the world'. St John's College was singled out for 'the pleasaunce formed by its gardens', which a century earlier had been 'the general rendezvous of gentlemen and ladies on every Sunday evening in Summer'.

The comment which might most have amused sensible and unromantic Mary Stocks was this: 'As a picture of bright young life, charmingly set, few can be prettier than St John's Gardens during Eights Week'. After detailing the architectural merits of the college buildings, the guidebook lists what it calls St John's notabilities, among them archbishops Juxon and Laud, the poets John Shirley and Thomas Campion, and the father of one of the Gunpowder Plot conspirators.

In this Arcadian setting the Stocks family spent the first five years after the First World War. It was the perfect environment for Mary to blossom in, surrounded by friends, involved in university social and political life, pursuing her own educational interests.

The happy and leisured pace of life, the car outings, the riverside picnics, the tea parties, came to an end in 1924 when John Stocks was offered a professorship in philosophy at Manchester University. They both welcomed the move, John for professional and family reasons, Mary because her curiosity in the industrial north had been roused while she was giving university extension lectures in Cheshire. She was more than ready for new challenges. Manchester beckoned to them both.

Chapter 3

The Manchester and Liverpool Years: 1924–1937

If Oxford had been a dream place, Manchester was a tonic. The entire Stocks family took to it as if they had simply been waiting in the wings for this experience. All that Manchester had to offer they grasped with both hands.

In the first place, the city in the 1920s and 1930s was an exciting place for adventurous lovers of the arts. John and Mary Stocks quickly fell under the spell of Gracie Fields, who more than any other entertainer embodied the spirit of prewar Lancashire. She was born in 1898, a mill girl who became an immensely popular singer and comedienne, exploiting the mass appeal of a homely North Country accent. Gracie starred in many comic sentimental films, the best known of them *Sally in our Alley* and *Sing as We Go*. Years later Mary Stocks chose a Gracie Fields song, 'The Little Pudding Basin that belonged to Auntie Flo', as a joyous reminder of her family life in Manchester, as a record to be taken to her 'desert island'.

They also discovered the appeal of Lancashire street and factory scenes, the classic mill cityscapes by L.S. Lowry, the Salford artist, long before he became world-famous. Mary bought two of his works, which are still in her family. Although Lowry was little known in the 1920s he was already perfecting his genre of city landscapes with matchstick figures and near-monochrome colouring.

Theatre had always been a central leisure activity for both the Stockses. In Manchester they encountered the plays of Walter Greenwood, another Salfordian, writing out of his own experience as milk delivery boy, signwriter, pawnbroker's clerk and so on.

He is best remembered for *Love on the Dole*, a 1933 comedy of urban deprivation. Mary Stocks described it as giving 'an accurate picture of Manchester, or rather Salford, poverty during the Great Depression', and she often referred to the realism of its characters.

Yet another 'spiritual centre' (so called by Mary) was a group of friends connected with the *Manchester Guardian*. Among them were the editors C.P. Scott, his successor Kingsley Martin and the correspondent Malcolm Muggeridge, later to become Editor of *Punch* and as prolific a broadcaster as Mary. All of these journalists were involved in amateur acting with John and Mary Stocks, and several of the families travelled to Russia sightseeing in 1932. The Stockses particularly valued the companionship of C.P. Scott, and it was largely through their manoeuvring that he met Jacob Epstein over high tea at their house, and agreed to have a bust made by the sculptor. This was presented to the City of Manchester on Scott's 80th birthday. Kingsley Martin and John Stocks acted together in a University Settlement production of Bernard Shaw's *St Joan*. Malcolm Muggeridge was based in Russia for the *Guardian* when the Manchester party travelled there; however, Muggeridge's love affair with communism rapidly turned to disillusion and he came home fairly soon.

So Manchester had a great deal to offer culturally, socially and in leisure activities, and there is no reason to suppose the Stockses regretted for even a moment their move from the dreaming spires of Oxford to the mill chimneys of Lancashire.

Quite early in their Manchester days the Stocks family discovered L.S. Lowry. Helen recalled:

There was a party at the University Settlement to encourage people to buy his drawings. He was rather unknown then. My father had seen his drawings in the *Manchester Guardian* and thought he was underrated. So my parents persuaded some of our relations to buy. L.S. Lowry did not make a great impact on me (I was about ten at the time) but I remember he had a beautiful white-haired girlfriend.[1]

The drawings which have been passed down in the family are *Going to the Match* and an untitled townscape. *Going to the Match* is initialled LSL, and dated 1925; it shows booted and cloth-capped figures (definitely not stick-men) plodding along a road against a familiar backdrop of factory chimneys and Rugby League goalposts. The untitled picture has been identified as a view of the railway carthorse sheds in Ancoats. This one is signed in full – L.S. Lowry 1930. Two other Lowry pictures in the family, believed to be copies, are a view of the Round House (scene of Stocks theatrical activities) and some children, signed and dated 1930, and an untitled drawing in pencil and pastel of Haworth High Street. Mary Stocks was a lover of the Brontës, and reputedly Lowry gave her this. A canal scene had also passed through her hands, but its present whereabouts is unknown. There can be very little doubt that John and Mary Stocks recognised the particular Lancashire genius of Lowry long before the art world lionised him.

The Stocks family arrived at 22 Wilbraham Road in the summer of 1924. John, the newly appointed professor, was then 42. Mary was 33, Ann 9, John 6 and Helen not quite 4. Mary saw their new home thus: 'One erupted from the aspidistra and lace curtain zone into an area of Victorian semi-detached houses, houses like our own . . . hideous but spacious'. The house was partly found for them by John's widowed youngest sister, Kitty Fletcher, who lived not far away at Leigh. She had married a colliery owner who died from pneumonia during the war, leaving Kitty to bring up three young children. In many ways her life mirrored Mary's: she was a magistrate, a county councillor, a pillar of the Labour Party and the WEA. The sisters-in-law were kindred spirits, and the six young cousins revelled in each other's company.

Mary Stocks described their Manchester life as revolving around the University, the *Manchester Guardian* and the University Settlement. John Stocks, as Professor of Philosophy, followed the flamboyant and highly respected Samuel Alexander OM. He was an Australian Jew, the grand old man of Manchester University, said to look like everyone's idea of Jehovah. Mary Stocks paid her own tribute to Samuel Alexander many years later in a BBC profile to mark his centenary. She said:

> When he presented Eileen Power for an honorary doctorate he said: 'My Lord Chancellor, I present to you a lady who by a strange dispensation of natural history combines the glamour of the butterfly with the industry of the bee'.[2]

Professor Alexander, a bachelor, had Wednesday 'At Homes' where he invited the great and the good of Manchester to view his giant aspidistra. Mary Stocks retold a perhaps legendary story of friends and neighbours gathering in his garden to photograph the old man in court dress (knee breeches and so on) after his investiture with the Order of Merit by King George V.

The Scott family, C.P. and his son Ted, together associated with the *Manchester Guardian* for half a century, also became friends. Both Stockses greatly admired the paper for its news sense and political judgement, and Mary was happy later to have her books and plays reviewed in it. There was in fact a network of *Guardian* journalists and readers in the 1930s who exercised no small influence on the Manchester social scene, among them Malcolm Muggeridge and his wife Kitty, and Kingsley Martin. Both men went on to become editors: Muggeridge of *Punch*, Martin of the *New Statesman*. C.P. Scott finally resigned as Editor of the *Guardian* when he was well into his eighties.

Two more city worthies were close personal friends of John and Mary Stocks. They were Ernest Simon (later Lord Simon of Wythenshawe) and his wife Sheena, leading activists in local government, education and social welfare. Thirty years later Mary Stocks was to write a biography of Ernest Simon, generally regarded as her best publication.

In this congenial social and cultural setting, Mary devoted a good deal of time to the WEA. She tutored, travelled across the Pennines to run economic history classes in remote villages, and tried in her own very positive way to find an answer to the question asked by so many of her intelligent working-class students in the twenties: 'Why is the Depression happening now, and why is it happening to us?'

She regarded it as her mission to teach her mature students not so much what to think as how to think. And her view of Manchester life between the wars, with its grinding poverty and unemployment, found an echo in the play *Love on the Dole*. It was the first and greatest achievement of Walter Greenwood, born in 1903 in working-class Salford (as was Lowry). *Love on the Dole* opened in 1933, in the depths of the Depression. It was a *succès fou*, repeatedly staged, filmed and broadcast with star casts. For Mary Stocks, Walter Greenwood's social message had more impact than any textbook.

Her own writing talent now shifted from textbook to theatre. In London and Oxford her world had centred on the academic scene. Manchester was radically different, and realism – as reflected in the pages of the *Manchester Guardian*, in Lowry's pictures, in Greenwood's play – took over.

In Manchester much of the Stockses' free time, and John's too, was devoted to the University Settlement. The title 'settlement' had perhaps a rather different connotation in the 1920s; a club or leisure centre run on charitable lines in a deprived inner-city area, usually funded by a church or college. Here at Ancoats, at No. 20 Every Street (and what address cold be more symbolic?), a disused chapel and a dilapidated builders' warehouse were used as a recreation centre for the University Settlement. Ancoats was an area of small houses built for nineteenth-century mill workers. It is mentioned in Friedrich Engels's classic social study, *The Condition of the Working Classes in England*, which had become bedside reading for the Stockses. It had been written in 1845, not long after his spell in a Manchester cotton mill, and in some ways Ancoats had not greatly changed.

John Stocks was co-opted to the Council of the Settlement immediately after arriving in Manchester, and soon became its chairman. Under his leadership and with a dynamic Warden, Hilda Cashmore, the old chapel took on a new lease of life as an amateur theatre, known locally as the Round House. The warehouse, previously written off as beyond salvage, flourished, and a legacy made the theatre conversion possible. The whole complex was 'rich in human ingenuity but poor in cash,' according to Mary. She recalled with special pleasure a Round House production of *St Joan* in which her husband played the ironic Inquisitor and their friend Kingsley Martin was the bumbling but well-meaning English priest, de Stogumber. Kingsley Martin had been a lecturer at LSE, for four years edited the *Manchester Guardian*, and for thirty was Editor of the *New Statesman*.

Later Mary was to write the history of the Settlement's first fifty years, but in the 1920s her main role was directing its plays – and herself writing plays for the Round House. In 1929 her first play was produced: *Everyman of Everystreet*, a nativity-morality drama in modern idiom with a strong infusion of contemporary Lancashire culture. The cast includes conventional figures from the Bethlehem story, but also Everyman, Everywoman and three Everychildren, plus an overworked landlady, the local descendants of the innkeeper and his guests. There is also a fat businessman called Dives ('Next year I'll have a depot out here. No more camel dumps for me') and three shepherds variously admiring wealth, conquest and priestcraft. Part of the play is in verse, and it ends with poetic kings and a declamatory archangel who speaks the words of Blake's 'Jerusalem'.

The play reveals its author at every turn. An introduction, 'Suggestions for Amateur Producers', offers extremely practical hints on cheap costumes, scenery and lighting. Round tins mounted on broomsticks and filled with spirit-soaked cottonwool will simulate torches. (Goodness knows what modern safety inspectors would make of this.) The Settlement's smaller angels wore blue-green robes, not the traditional white 'because of the extraordinary difficulty of keeping a company of excited angels clean . . . in the neighbourhood of Every Street. A dirty white angel is an abomination before the Lord'.

Dimmers, the playwright advises, can be constructed by anyone with a working knowledge of electrical engineering. (She rather avoids detail of this.) A problem area is the Centre back door, which must open and shut without suggesting an earthquake. Accent produces a very Stocksian comment: 'Under the auspices of the M.U.S. the Everyman family spoke with the accents of the industrial Lancashire. In a London Everystreet . . . Everywoman, instead of saying "The place was that dirty" would doubtless say "The place wasn't arf dirty".'[3]

Other Lancashire echoes crop up in the play. Everyman, a carpenter, referred to by his wife as Mr E., has landed a job in competition with the Woodworkers' Union. A sick neighbour had been taken to the Infirmary. Famine in the Ukraine evokes the response 'We got our own folk to look after.' Dives, the businessman, identifies the main current economic problem as one of storage, which may well have been inspired by a contemporary difficulty in the local cotton mills.

Everyman of Everystreet does not set out to be sophisticated. It is a parable written for an inner Manchester audience, cast and readers. It can be seen as a straightforward modern nativity, or one with strong references to Manchester's social problems. After five years in the city, Mary Stocks's ear for local dialect is not perfect, but it is not bad. The play is well crafted, integrating the Bible story convincingly into a twentieth-century Lancashire context, with interaction of song, music and humour. More than half a century after it was written it has not lost its freshness and relevance.

The attraction of the published version gains much from a series of bold Biblical woodcuts, the work of Winifred Gill, who designed the costumes for the first production. Winifred was a family friend and a member of the artistic Gill family, of whom Eric the sculptor and engraver was best known. Eric was at about this time doing his most famous work for Leeds University and Broadcasting House in London.

The play gained a good deal of critical acclaim. One reviewer wrote:

> The poetic quality of the play and ingenuity of the author's appeal to our emotions would make a performance thrilling even if the costumes came out of a child's dressing box.

A *Manchester Evening News* critic ('I.B.') said Mary Stocks's advice on improvising costumes reminded him of the old mediaeval mystery plays: a good buckram coat was needed for the Holy Ghost, a gilt beard for St Peter, and gloves for God. *Everyman of Everystreet*, he concluded, 'combines the serious playfulness of the old miracle play with the social criticism and urgency of the new'.[4]

Scene Two is in verse, simplistic but not without spirit. For example:

> That star led on most steadily,
> And when at length it came to rest
> They heard high Heaven's revelry.
> What should they care for Herod's furtive devilry!

The Wise Men encounter three secret service agents blinded by Herod because they had reported accurately to him. One of them addresses the Wise Men irritably: 'All babies play with their feet . . . the star which led you here was a star of your own crazy imagining.' The meeting of the Holy Family and the blind men is over-sentimental, but there is a rough charm about the chorus of children fleeing into Egypt:

> Desert skies are velvet black,
> Boundless is the desert track.
> We will make our beds tonight
> With the stars for candle light;
> We will make a baby's cot,

Light a fire and boil a pot,
We will picnic in the sand,
Journeying through Pharaoh's land . . .
Herod's men have clumsy feet,
They are marching up the street.[5]

The relevance of the blinded men, the fleeing children and the columns of marching soldiers, the whole concept of Biblical Palestine, is sharpened by our hindsight of what was to happen in Europe in less than ten years after the play was written.

A cleric writing about the play complained that most modern nativity plays had 'an affectation of simplicity . . . sheepish in language and ideas'. Not so with Mary Stocks's play: 'At the first word you know where you are, just here in this land of ours, on this very day and at this very hour of our fate.' He urged churchpeople, both young and old, to perform *Everyman of Everystreet*.

Mary followed this up with another modern nativity play published two years later: *King Herod*. It has a preface nearly half as long as the play itself, for the author was determined to leave nothing to chance. She mentions 'a judicious arrangement of coloured electric bulbs', and 'a white spotlight, borrowed presumably from some kindly-disposed institution.' She prescribes which editions of the *Oxford Book of Carols* or the *St Matthew Passion* shall be used, and suggests Woolworth's jewellery counter as a source for Herod's magnificence. (Woolworth's in the 1930s was popularly known as the sixpenny store – this was its top price.)

The character of Herod is spelt out somewhat unnecessarily, since this is both traditional and explicit in the play:

It is necessary to the drift of this play that Herod shall be a savage and rooted in savagery. Cruel, crude, stupid and suspicious, he personifies the bludgeon of material force in unending conflict with the spirit which eludes and baffles it.

It is worth remembering that Mary wrote this play two years before Hitler came to power as Chancellor. There may be a certain prescience in her delineation. Herod, described as 'one of Caesar's administrative blunders', interrogates the three Wise Men from the East, who are portrayed as middle-aged scholars. He is preoccupied with trumpets, standards and caravans as emblems of royalty. The palace scene ends with Herod's choice of music – 'a rhythmic drumming suggestive of the eternal tribal tom-tom, broken by the tuneless wail of a prehistoric saxophone'.[6]

These two nativity plays were much performed by schools and youth clubs, and copies are not impossible to come by sixty years later. It was a popular genre, making up in realism and directness what it lacked in subtlety. One is tempted to draw a parallel briefly with Dorothy Sayers, also a scholar, religious playwright and a writer in a range of modes. Her best-known play, *The Man Born to be King*, was written for radio, and first broadcast by the BBC in 1941. Here were two outstanding women born within two years of each other and with certain common interests: religion, radio, academic activities. Dorothy Sayers had been brought up in Oxford and graduated from Somerville in 1916, the middle period of Mary Stocks's residence as a don's wife at St John's.

A year later Mary Stocks published a third play, also written to be produced at the Round House, and even more local in context. This was *Dr Scholefield of Manchester*, researched from *Manchester Guardian* accounts of the Chartist movement in the 1840s. Chartism had centred on Ancoats, and it stood for a six-point People's Charter calling for (*inter alia*) universal suffrage, a secret ballot and payment for MP's. All of these aims would have been supported wholeheartedly by Mary Stocks, had she been alive in the mid-nineteenth century, and this is sympathetically reflected in her play.

The *Manchester Guardian* reviewer said:

> Ghosts of the Manchester of nearly a century ago came to life . . . at a time when democracy is threatened on all sides this play is not without significance . . . a prologue shows Friedrich Engels and a small be-shawled girl in conversation. One catches a glimpse of the spiritual darkness of those hungry forties.[7]

It is hard to judge the success or otherwise of this play; no other review of its stage production survives and it did not stay long in print.

A fourth play, published in 1933, was however much liked by the critics. It was given its première by a semi-amateur group, the Unnamed Society, formed in 1915 and based in the upper floor of a warehouse in Salford. *Hail Nero!* was itself hailed by a reviewer in the 1950s – after a world war and massive social upheaval – for its satirical invention and 'pretty wit'. This time

Mary Stocks turned her penchant for modern-idiom interpretation of the past to Roman history. *Hail Nero!*, published by Sidgwick and Jackson in 1933 (the year Hitler became Chancellor of the Third Reich), had a preface by John Stocks pointing out that Roman emperors were fair game for historical vilification. Nero was being rehabilitated by modern scholars, and the play took the process a stage further, almost deifying him – for even his detractors admitted he opposed gladiatorial combats, abolished cooked-meat shops in the interests of public health, and promoted imperial free trade and Greek home rule.

This is a three-act play with a much more substantial text than its predecessors. The dialogue is for the most part racy ('A wife can't be expected to entertain all the queer people her husband does business with, can she?') and the stage directions are once again excessively detailed ('His eye catches the wisp of waste paper he has just thrown down. Remembering the anti-litter league he rises and retrieves it, looks for a receptacle and, finding none, tucks it in his toga'.) The anti-litter league features largely in the dialogue. Nero arranges an all-day picnic at Antium for the Fire Brigade, and thus allows the great fire of Rome to burn unchecked as part of a massive slum clearance scheme. His friendship for Lucasta, the rat poisoner, is to be seen as a kindly act towards a misunderstood woman. He is Nero the hero.

The critics were enthusiastic. A national newspaper gossip writer said:

> We saw in this play a Caesar much maligned . . . whose fiddling was summed up as 'like a tea-time Palm Court orchestra'. He replied 'It was dreadful. But I had to keep those people quiet somehow, and you know the fiddle is not my instrument'.[8]

The *Manchester Guardian* reviewer referred to a play both ingenious and witty, and described the performance of Noel Tomlinson as Nero as 'a cross between a caricature of Sir Stafford Cripps and one of Lloyd George'. He (or she) did not justify this odd comment, so one can only conclude Mr Tomlinson deliberately evoked the two contemporary statesmen. Another character, Cleon, chairman of the property owners' association, is 'a Greek with all the vices with which Hitlerite Germany endows the Jews'.

There can be no doubt that audiences and critics enjoyed *Hail, Nero!* From time to time it was staged in London, and in the United

States. The notion of a misjudged emperor who had throughout history had a bad press had a degree of satirical relevance in the 1930s.

In 1938 *Hail, Nero!* was produced at the Playhouse Theatre in Oxford, possibly the first professional staging of a Stocks play. The review in *Isis* spoke of 'the wittiest, most hilarious evening you could desire'. The reviewer passionately defended Nero, an enlightened man before his time, 'even when he personally conducted mass observation tests to discover how many of his subjects slept in single beds'.

A *Daily Mail* reviewer summed the play up thus:

> Here was no tyrant, but the Town Planner of all time, who arranged for the slums of Rome to burn while the Fire Brigade was forcibly made part of a studio audience.

A *Manchester Guardian* report of Mary Stocks's election as a director of the Manchester Repertory Theatre referred to *Hail, Nero!* as one of Manchester's theatre successes of 1934. In April 1937 the *Washington Post* carried major headlines: 'Nero was first New Dealer, says University civic play' and 'Author sees fiddling Emperor as Misunderstood Emancipator of the Masses whose Humanitarian Motives were misinterpreted in history'. American playgoers saw the relevance of Nero's régime to dictator-dominated Europe. This year – 1937 – was also that of Orson Welles's highly successful Fascist jackboot production of *Julius Caesar*. Mary Stocks had hit a topical and controversial vein.

In a two-column review A. de Bernardi junior had much fun summarising the Nero situation in modern jargon – 'the only hitch was that when he sent out the praetorian guards . . . for this slum-clearance project he forgot to tell the boys when to stop'.[9] The fire guards 'were away at a well-timed picnic, thus establishing themselves as the first visiting firemen'. Nero was booed when he played highbrow music, but applauded when he switched to swingtime; and his intention was allegedly 'to bring the money barons to heel'. De Bernardi found *Hail, Nero!* 'a corking good play, loaded with laughable situations – the initial audience liked it immensely', and he predicted that seats at the University Civic Theatre, Denver, Colorado, would be at a premium. The programme mentioned another forthcoming production of the play by the Footlights Club of Boston.

Another critic approved of the play's conclusion and its high moral tone: 'Mrs Stocks is human enough to leave the last word with Caesar's secretary – "Of course I agree with Nero, but all the same if I were Caesar I would sometimes let the people have what they want".'

Mary Stocks's fifth and last play was a thriller, *Person or Persons Unknown*, performed by the Unnamed Society at Salford in 1931. Under the headline 'Professor's Wife's Melodrama', the *Daily Mail* reported:

> A Chancellor of the Exchequer who murdered six millionaires, and balanced his Budget with the resultant death duties, is the exciting theme around which Mrs J. L. Stocks, wife of the professor of philosophy at Manchester University, has written a stage thriller produced by the Unnamed Society last night at the Little Theatre, Salford.
>
> Mrs Stocks is a believer in fullblooded melodrama, and in this play crime, love and wit are served at high pressure.
>
> The love interest centres on the chancellor's infatuation with the woman Minister of Health. It was to satisfy her demands, as well as to save the Sinking Fund, that the six murders were committed.[10]

The author was interviewed by the *Mail* after the first night, and told the reporter that the idea for the play came to her during an economics lecture. 'I think I have found one way of balancing a Budget', she said, 'even though it means the introduction of gangster methods to politics. Of course the whole thing is pure melodrama . . . You hear about 100 per cent thrillers. I have been told that my play is 600 per cent murder'. She told another reporter there were no insinuations in the play against the private lives of known political figures, but parallels were inevitably drawn.

Although the play caused a stir at the time, there is no record of subsequent performances. With *Person or Persons Unknown* Mary Stocks ended her career as playwright. Of all her theatrical productions there is no doubt that *Hail, Nero!* attracted the most favourable public notice, but *Everyman of Everystreet* was the one most often staged. It was that irresistible form of drama, a modernised nativity play starring children and apparently identifying the Holy Family with contemporary local society. Everyman is Mr Manchester, with the idiom, the attitudes and worries of Lancashire society during the Depression years. It was a society with which the Stocks family strongly identified.

It was perhaps coincidence that shortly after the launch of *Person or Persons Unknown* Mary Stocks was appointed a member of the Committee on Habitual Offenders. She was one of two women appointed, described as members of the Labour Party. Oddly enough the secretary to the committee was a civil servant called E. E. Bridges, son of the Poet Laureate, Robert Bridges, who had often entertained the Stockses in Oxford.

Mary's period as a playwright was successful and brief. In the space of five years she wrote, saw produced and had published five short plays, of which one reached an international audience. All were greeted with enthusiasm by critics of some standing, but were soon forgotten.

Why this sudden burst of dramatic creativity, never repeated? There may be three reasons. In the first place John Stocks was deeply interested in theatre and in bringing it to underprivileged areas of Manchester. It was this kind of audience that Mary had in mind for her nativity plays, at least. She too had a passionate interest in live theatre, and here at the Ancoats Settlement and with the Unnamed Society there were ready-made stages and amateur companies to be grist to her mill. The North of England had a strong theatrical tradition in the 1930s. Mary admired Walter Greenwood; J. B. Priestley and *Hobson's Choice* by Harold Brighouse brought Lancashire and Yorkshire comedy to wider audiences. Realistic drama was competing, certainly, with radio, Hollywood and music hall, but Bible plays in a modern setting and plays with a social or political message were comparative novelties at the time.

Possibly she had exhausted her theatrical inspiration by 1935. What is much more likely is that the move to Liverpool in 1937, and her new duties as Vice-Chancellor's wife and public speaker took over. There is no record of her writing another play.

Another major preoccupation for Mary Stocks during the Manchester years was the growth of the birth control movement and the gradual public acceptance of a social need for contraception, for family planning. She threw much of her energy, powers of persuasion and reforming zeal into this cause and strongly admired the pioneering work of Dr Marie Stopes.

Among women intellectuals prominent in early twentieth-century Britain, Marie Stopes must compete to head the list. Strangely enough these two women, social and medical reformers, active for women's rights, public educators, were often confused because of the similarity of their names. Mary Stocks found this amusing. History does not record how Marie Stopes viewed the matter. Mary Stocks first met Dr Stopes in Oxford soon after the publication of *Married Love* in 1918 had (as she wrote) 'captured public attention, if not public approbation'. It was not, Mary Stocks argued, primarily a birth control manual, though that was how many readers saw it. It was about the technique of sex relations in marriage, and 'she wrote in simple terms . . . aimed at the heart of a personal relationship affecting millions of her fellow mortals'.[11] Seventy years later Marie Stopes's image is somewhat tarnished: she is seen as a preacher about the sacrament of love who herself lived through several deeply unsatisfactory relationships.

Mary Stocks knew something of the then less publicised aspects of Marie Stopes's private life, but for her they were less important than the light cast in dark places by such a public commitment to improving the quality of married life for the population as a whole.

Marie Carmichael Stopes was born in 1880, the daughter of an anthropologist. After a starry education, in which she accumulated prizes and degrees (a first and a gold medal in London, a PhD in Munich) she lectured in palaeobotany at University College, London, and Manchester. This led to fossil-hunting in Japan and elsewhere, and the translation of old Japanese plays, as well as the writing of novels and poetry.

But most of her many publications had to do with family life, sex and contraception, the most acclaimed being *Married Love*, *Wise Parenthood*, *Enduring Passions* and *Birth Control Today*. The first of these caused a massive sensation when it appeared, not least because its author claimed to be a virgin at the time, and it attracted long-running opposition from the Church, the medical profession and politicians. More than one writer denounced it as 'a handbook for prostitution'. In 1921, aged 41, Marie Stopes married as her second husband Humphrey Verdon Roe, son of the aircraft designer A.V. Roe, but she legally kept her own name. Recent biographies have revealed the existence of several lovers (with one much younger than herself she embarked on an affair when she was 60) and an amazingly repressive approach to bringing up her own son, born when she was 42. A reviewer of a biography published in 1993 described her memorably as 'the inventor of the how-to sex manual', one who had 'predictably difficult relations with her son', and 'deeply in love with the high drama of being her very exceptional self'. Another reviewer wrote 'A dottier or more hardened busybody it would be difficult to find', basing this on such eccentricities as sending a message to the Pope telling him where he had gone wrong with women, sending a copy of her poems to Hitler, and proposing herself for Churchill's War Cabinet.

Although she has been called 'the first agony aunt', Marie Stopes belied this epithet by cruelly exposing, in a preface to a later edition of *Married Love*, her husband's sexual inexperience and introducing young lovers at least in part to torment him. In short 'Marie Stopes could be as pitiless to those who loved her as she was compassionate to people she had never met'. These retrospective exposures of Marie Stopes's eccentricities and hypocrisy reverse a public acceptance, during her lifetime, of her suitability as the first prophet of sacred and controlled sex.

Mary Stocks had no such illusion about her. In the early 1920s Mary was acting as joint editor of a feminist publication, *The Woman's Leader*, and a series of articles on population problems caused Marie Stopes to call at the journal's London office, in Oxford Street. Afterwards she lunched in Soho with Mary Stocks and the other editor, Eva Hubback, who was then Parliamentary Secretary to the National Union of Societies for Equal Citizenship. During this lunch, Mary Stopes talked freely about her first (dissolved) marriage to Dr Reginald Gates, including this *bon mot* (since often quoted): 'After three years of married life I was still a virgin!'

Marie Stopes and her husband Humphrey Roe founded the world's first birth control clinic in London in 1921, and this prompted Mary Stocks and others to seek to enrol her on the National Birth Control Committee, later the Family Planning Association. But the co-operation did not last long. Mary Stocks wrote of this episode: 'I think that her desire to work in her own way on her own lines and without reference to anybody else was connected with a belief she had come to hold, that she was directly inspired by God'.[12]

But she always maintained she was glad to have known Marie Stopes, both socially and professionally. The two families spent summer holidays in Dorset, the Stockses at their West Bay seaside house; and the Roes in an abandoned lighthouse on Portland Bill, that strange tail of land that creeps out to sea beyond Chesil Beach, haunt of prisons and shipwrecks. Marie Stopes was attracted to the area for its fossil-hunting potential. Even on such informal occasions as bathing picnics Mary Stocks suspected that Marie was 'unconsciously or not, one did not know, projecting the image of her books'. The Stocks children were much entertained by the way she spoke to her husband and the fact that her 11-year-old son (Humphrey, nicknamed Buffkins) was compelled to wear kilts and skirts. She combined, in Mary's view, total personal vanity and total lack of sense of humour.

In these characteristics the two women were diametrically opposed. Mary's sense of humour, even over the earnest matter of birth control campaigning, is evidenced by two cartoon-type sketches in her autobiography. One shows Mary and Marie sitting on the rocks, swimsuited, discussing birth control. A fish is listening. The other shows fishermen some time later examining a haul of fish. In the net are two fish only.

In May 1926 the birth control pioneers held their first North Country public meeting, at Pendleton Town Hall. Eleanor Rathbone (prominent in public life, but not yet an MP) was in the chair, and the speakers were Lord Balfour of Burleigh, a doctor, a professor, and Mary Stocks. A supporter was philosophic about the success of the meeting: 'About 250 people came. There were only four votes against our resolution, and £4, mostly in coppers, was collected for the Clinic'. Within eight years the Clinic had advised 3,200 women, from as far away as Sheffield. As acceptance grew the clinic was allowed to move into Salford Health Offices. It could be said by 1934 that the theory and practice of birth control had arrived nationally.

June Rose's 1993 biography of Marie Stopes confirms a number of Mary Stocks's comments on her eccentricity. Harry Vernon Stopes Roe, her only child, born in 1924, was indeed dressed in kilts and 'loose knitted trousers' to protect his genitals until he went away to Charterhouse at 15; he was at all times largely shielded from society.

By this time (in the shadow of the Second World War) Marie Stopes's marriage had virtually ended and she had abandoned the birth control cause for a new obsession – writing poetry and novels. Muriel Spark, in her autobiography *Curriculum Vitae*, describes passionate scenes created at Poetry Society meetings and in letters by Dr Stopes, because her poems were not getting the recognition she felt they deserved. Her main collection was *Love Songs for Young Lovers*, which friends and enemies alike failed to enthuse over. She sent a copy to Hitler.

She let her Portland Bill lighthouse to a naval officer (as civilians could not go there during wartime) and had Cornish camping holidays with Harry. In the 1950s she carried on a flirtation, mostly by letter, with Lord Alfred Douglas, the former lover of Oscar Wilde. She sent him her poems, helped him out with money, and organised a petition for him to have a Civil List pension. In 1946, when Marie was 66, Harry was a postgraduate studying meteorological optics at Imperial College. Much against his mother's wishes, Harry became engaged to a fellow student, the daughter of Dr Barnes Wallis who invented the 'bouncing bomb'. Marie refused to attend their wedding in July 1948. For the rest of her life she saw little of the couple or her two grandsons.

She became fascinated by the occult, fancied herself in love with a young writer whom she met through H. G Wells (she was 72, he was 39), and still directed the Society for Constructive Birth Control. Mary Stocks remained a true friend until Marie Stopes's death from cancer in 1958. She was accorded a memorial service at St Martin in the Fields (as Mary Stocks would be later) and the deputy prime minister read the lesson. These two women had perhaps done more than any others of their generation to make life easier for working women.

In 1928 Mary Stocks had had the dubious privilege of proof-reading Marie Stopes's first novel, now long forgotten. The title was *Love's Creation*, and Mary viewed it tolerantly, though her family laughed at it. Marie Stopes wrote at length to thank her for her suggestions, some of which (to Mary's surprise) were followed. 'Even so it was never a good novel, and I doubt if she ever wrote another'.

Years later Mary visited Marie in an historic mansion near Dorking. She was proud of the house's past associations with the famous, proud of her son's scientific prowess, proud of her status as a hostess: 'But by this time her active absorption with birth control had grown tenuous. She had become a poet'.[13] Their final meeting was in 1958, shortly before Marie Stopes's death. The grand house and garden had become neglected, the marriage had ended, the son married against his mother's wishes, yet Marie Stopes still dressed with bravado and behaved as if she were half her age. She was 78 when she died, a lonely woman.

Mary Stocks's final judgement on Marie Stopes was essentially personal, kindly and tolerant:

> Where is Marie Stopes' pubic memorial? Nowhere, as far as I know, in stone or bronze. Surely one might say, in the fact that contraception is an accepted social need. And the story of that acceptance is made colourful by the vital chapter which Marie Stopes's militancy added to it. And it is certainly joy to know personally anybody who is in almost every respect almost wholly unlike anybody else.[14]

Charis Frankenburg in her autobiography, *Not Old, Madam, Vintage*, sheds more light on the origins of the Salford Birth Control Clinic. As Charis Barnett she had been a near-contemporary of Mary Brinton at St Paul's Girls' School. In 1925 she was doing a good deal of voluntary social work in Salford, having married a Manchester businessman, and was much concerned about the distress she saw among local working-class women:

> Having read the books of Dr Marie Stopes, D.Sc. (Palaeontology), and profited by her expertise – we had four children spaced exactly as intended – I wrote in the autumn of 1925 to ask her to tell me of someone near Manchester who might be interested in helping to set up a Birth Control Clinic. She suggested Mrs John Stocks. I recognised her as Mary Brinton whom I had known at St Paul's . . . On October 23rd, we collected a few friends and formed a committee.[15]

After visiting clinics in London and Wolverhampton, Mary Stocks and Charis Frankenburg recruited a woman doctor, Dr Olive Gimson, a nurse and a treasurer, and rented two rooms over a baker's shop in Greengate, Salford. The twice-weekly Mothers' Clinic for Birth Control opened in March 1926 with a capital of £190. At the first session there were nineteen clients. One shilling was the nominal charge, but some paid nothing. The whole project was an immensely bold step to take in the England of the 1920s, far more revolutionary than the introduction of the pill several decades later.

Repeated pregnancies, poor health and frequent miscarriages

were the rule, not the exception. Charis reported a number of harrowing cases: a woman who had had eighteen pregnancies, including four stillborn and three mentally handicapped babies; a mother who had gone through seven backstreet abortions; another with four living children, but seven who had died in infancy. Cases of abortion leading to septicaemia and haemorrhages accounted for many maternal deaths.

> The majority of the medical profession were at that time either ignorant concerning birth control, indifferent, or actively hostile . . . the subject was not included in medical training . . . the few medical students who wished to learn were regularly smuggled into a London clinic after dark.[16]

A young general practitioner practising in Oldham in the 1920s recalled: 'We did not have much information about what Dr Stopes was doing. We all distrusted her because she was not a medical doctor.' On the other hand a woman born in Leeds in 1926 said her mother swore by Dr Stopes's ideas, and read all the Stopes literature she could lay hands on, though she felt five years between children was an unrealistic gap. Charis Frankenburg, in her books, refers to a father of two whose health would be damaged, he was told, by sexual abstinence, and who had scruples about using contraceptives. His wife learned she might die having a third child. The couple took religious advice and decided to go ahead. The wife died in pregnancy.

Writers in the Catholic press attacked Charis Frankenburg not only for her reformist zeal but for her Jewish background.

> Mrs C. Frankenburg, who describes herself as the honorary secretary, has been appealing for funds . . . It is passing strange that this lady of the German-Jewish name should be exhibiting so much solicitude for the English working class. So far as can be ascertained she has never visited the slums.

There were newsworthy public protests. At St George's Road Congregational Schools in Bolton, where Mary Stocks was speaking at a meeting on the practical politics of birth control, the meeting broke up in disorder. The *Manchester Evening News* devoted three columns to its report, under the tabloid-style headlines 'Uproar at Meeting – Vociferous Objectors to Birth Control – Proud Boast of Father of Eleven'. The *News* report began:

A stormy meeting addressed by Mrs J. L Stocks, of Manchester
. . . finally broke up when Mrs Affleck, in proposing a vote of
thanks said 'Most of the speakers have been Irish'. Before she
could complete her sentence there were excited cries from all
over the hall of 'No' and 'Withdraw' and 'We shan't give her
the platform till she withdraws'. Mrs Stocks came to the front
of the platform in a good-humoured endeavour to discover the
objection to the statement, and the chairman, Dr Gray, said 'I
think Mrs Affleck was about to pay you a compliment. She is
Irish herself.' Finally Dr Gray smiled and said 'Well, I am going
home', and the meeting ended without a vote of thanks.[17]

Mary Stocks, the *News* reported, quoted the case of an unemployed
dock labourer's wife who came to the clinic for advice on abortion
'when it was too late for us to help her'. She went on to criticise
the churches for not giving desperate women better advice over
repeated pregnancies. At this point she was interrupted by an
excited woman who shouted 'It is murder, murder of the inno-
cents. Where should the people be who started this birth control
business?' There were cries of 'In Prison'. A doctor's wife from
Salford led the Catholic opposition, and a father of eleven said
he was proud to campaign against birth control – to which Mary
Stocks responded quickly 'But what about your wife?'
A letter printed in the *News* a few days later described Mary
Stocks as

> an admirable antagonist. From the moment when it became
> apparent that the majority of the meeting was hostile, Mrs Stocks
> only showed briefly any signs of nervous tension . . . She was
> collected, patient, ready with perfectly clear explanations of her
> attitude on every point at issue, and seldom even moved to a
> display of strong feeling. . . . After the meeting Mrs Stocks did
> not wait to be escorted from the platform, but hatless (as she
> always speaks) strode into the middle of the hall, eager to carry
> on the argument with all and sundry – and was soon surrounded
> by a large circle.

In spite of prolonged opposition from Roman Catholic communities in Lancashire, a cool reception from Anglican clergy
and sometimes less than sympathetic press coverage, the clinic
prospered. The women who came to it were for the most part

tired, middle-aged mothers of large families, often with health problems. Sometimes the woman, sometimes her husband, had heard of Maries Stopes or the local clinic. Hardly any were referred by doctors, who still regarded contraception with suspicion. Birth control, Mary Stocks wrote thirty years later, had been associated with irregular sex relations and many people believed it to cause infertility. The churches in general were reluctant to acknowledge the need for the Salford clinic. Charis and Mary were much amused to be described in a Roman Catholic journal as 'the kind of idle women who visit matinées and sit with cigarettes between their painted lips'. No amount of imaginative effort could produce a portrait less like Mary Stocks.

The success of the clinic meant much work for her: in helping to staff it, interviewing patients, keeping records and giving talks at women's meetings. At the same time she was campaigning for family allowances:

> I always regarded the two subjects as the positive and the negative of voluntary parenthood . . . We knew that we were right. Public opinion was on the move, and by the beginning of the thirties it has already moved a long way.

Her mentor on family allowances was Eleanor Rathbone, a stout defender of all moves designed to further women's liberty, and by now a prominent voice in the House of Commons.

With all her social work, writing, lecturing and broadcasting, with family and university obligations, it might be supposed that Mary Stocks's Manchester days were entirely filled. Yet the cause which claimed most of her time, energy and specialist knowledge was still the Workers' Educational Association. Whereas her WEA teaching in Oxford had been sandwiched in between various other commitments, in Manchester it became almost her main activity outside the home and university. She acknowledged 'I realised at the outset that in marrying John Stocks, I had married the W.E.A.', and increasingly it took hold of her.

Evening tutorial classes tended to be far from Manchester and hard to reach in bad weather. Fog and ice on the Pennines contributed to the problems, but the indefatigable Mary found night drives stimulating, her class contacts satisfying, and the existence of the WEA a godsend in the years of Depression:

golden years for adult education tutors . . . at any rate if their subjects touched on some aspect of economics . . . There was among thoughtful working class students a desperate urgency to answer the question: Why is this happening to us, and what should be done about it?

She welcomed also links with the trade unions. During the 1926 General Strike she was taking a class at the saltmining town of Northwich, and the class adapted itself to the crisis by studying in depth the report of the Coal Commission.

The WEA also brought for John Stocks renewed contact with two Old Rugbeians, and new family friends for Mary Stocks. William Temple, later the first President of the WEA as well as Archbishop of Canterbury, was Bishop of Manchester during the time of John Stocks's professorship; and R.H. Tawney, tutor to some of the very first WEA classes in Lancashire, a leading economist and professor at LSE, was a regular visitor. Tawney married the sister of Sir William (later Lord) Beveridge, and Temple's wife Frances was a particular friend of Mary Stocks and remained so into old age. The WEA remained an abiding interest for Mary Stocks throughout her long life. She was its Vice-President and wrote the official 50th anniversary history, published in 1953.

Meanwhile, her family was growing up. At first they all attended Lady Barn House junior school, run by a formidable Welsh lady, Miss Jenkin Jones. From here Ann won a scholarship to Withington Girls' High School (a member of the Girls' Public Day School Trust); John moved on to a preparatory school and then to Rugby, in his father's steps; and Helen (described by her mother as 'the most dedicated Mancunian of us all') started at Withington High School in 1932.

At about this time Mary Stocks's public life was really taking off. A family album of press cuttings kept by her mother, Constance Brinton, charts her progress. In 1931 the *Manchester Evening News* reported her appointment to a Home Office committee on the treatment of persistent offenders. The reporter indulged in some magazine-style prose about her:

> Slight, dark, with eyes that glow and flash with intensity, she says what she has to say without hindrance or hesitation . . . As a social reformer she has won many battles with her brilliant oratory . . . she will be the only woman member of the committee,

but this will not deter her from saying what she has to say, and saying it well.[18]

The family album includes a copy of the warrant of appointment authorised by the Home Secretary, J.R. Clynes.

In 1932 the *Manchester Guardian* reported on a stormy meeting called by the Women's Citizens' Association to discuss 'The Practical Policies of Birth Control', with Mary Stocks as chief speaker. When Dr Stopes's name was mentioned a heckler objected, on the grounds that she was not a medical doctor and should be referred to as 'Mrs Stopes'. Mary was quick to reply: 'It would give a wrong impression, for her married name is Mrs Humphrey Roe'. Supporters of the Salford Birth Control Clinic and its opponents wrote passionately to the press; for years the controversy simmered on.

A month later Mary Stocks was chosen as one of two women on the Lotteries, Betting and Gambling Commission. In 1934 she became a member of the Statutory Committee on Unemployment Insurance, and all this time was fully involved as a Manchester magistrate.

In 1932 the Stocks family broke new ground by going on a pioneering package holiday to Russia, organised by the Fabian Society and under the supervision of a fledgling Intourist Bureau. Socially John Stocks's standing as a university professor, as well as her own growing status as a public woman, had brought Mary into contact with a new circle of left-wing intellectuals among whom she felt very much at home. Malcolm and Kitty Muggeridge, *Manchester Guardian* friends, were spending a professional year in Russia. Before they left, Mary had been much impressed by Kitty Muggeridge's performance in Ibsen's *Lady from the Sea*. Eva Hubback, a feminist colleague from Mary's time in Oxford, arranged the trip to Russia and sent her son David on it.

To John the philosopher and Mary the economic historian the whole fabric of communist Russia was an absorbing study. 'All Fabians want to go to Russia', she said. And they felt it would be a useful experience for their older children. By now Ann was 17, John 15. Helen at 12 was considered too young; rather wistfully she saw the party sail from Hays Wharf.

To everyone's surprise the party included a Dorset squire, Sir Ralph Glyn, 'not at all the sort of person one would expect in a

Fabian group'. The idea was to follow in the steps of Sidney and Beatrice Webb, who had explored Russia after the Revolution, and were by now Lord and Lady Passfield. Ann Stocks recalled that her mother was astonished when the Muggeridges and others failed to observe the more obvious faults of the Soviet Union. (Within a year they did become disillusioned, and returned to England.) Ann said: 'My mother found a good deal wrong with the social experiment, especially in the area of food distribution'.

In order to make up a fixed-size group, as Intourist insisted, they recruited Robert and Brian Simon, sons of Ernest Simon (later Lord Simon of Wythenshawe) and members of the Rathbone family. In Leningrad (now again St Petersburg) they stayed in an Immigrants' Bazaar, and in Moscow in what passed for an hotel. The food was poor everywhere. The teenager Ann Stocks was shocked by what she saw:

> The factories were run so inefficiently, with workers sleeping on the floor. There was an exhibition of women doing totally unsuitable heavy work. And in a maternity hospital we saw little girls giving birth very publicly, and babies on trolleys kept away from their mothers.

Ann, a product of governess education and all-girl schools, noted an insensitivity to people's needs, and the visit turned her strongly against communism. 'Russia had a more powerful effect on the Muggeridges than it did on my parents,' she said. 'They were especially put off by the accommodation. We didn't say much while we were there for fear of the authorities, and of course we dared not take any photos.'

The group wished above all else to visit Tolstoy's home, but even twenty years after his death Intourist made it clear this was not on the approved itinerary. Eventually they did get there, and found it much as Countess Tolstoy had left it, with some of her old servants still at their posts. 'It was a museum but not yet a tourist place. We felt we were seeing the real Yasnaya Polyana'. Mary Stocks recalled Yasnaya Polyana in an article written for a WEA publication after her return. With her usual brisk commonsense view of the world she wrote:

> When I saw Russian villages I found it easier to account for the crowds of patient nomads who habitually camp around Russian

railway stations . . . and the influx of peasants into Moscow and Leningrad, with their devastating pressure on urban housing conditions. The point is, I think, that the peasant has so little to leave. His movable property goes into a few sacks.[19]

In Tolstoy's village the Stocks party met Leo's son, Serge. 'He is an old man now, and somewhat inarticulate with strangers, but he took us through the wood by moonlight to see his father's grave'. Fascinated by the atmosphere of the Tolstoy estate, Mary spent the night in his orchard (as she said, to keep company with ghosts) and found the experience charged with emotion. 'In spite of the cloud of propaganda which in the U.S.S.R. shadows your going out and your coming in, your sleeping and your waking, here you may forget the Revolution'.

Politically observant, she looked for signs of benefit from collective farming around Moscow and found none. But a rich peasant's house had been requisitioned as a day nursery:

And where had the Kulak gone? Our informants shrugged their shoulders. 'Perhaps to Siberia.' . . . Without Kolkhoz membership a peasant has no status in the village co-operative shop in regard to rationed commodities – and most essential commodities, including bread, are at present rationed in Russia. The inhabitants of Yasnaya were not afraid to speak their minds, and our official interpreter came in for some scolding as a government man. 'You officials drive in motors, while we peasants have to walk,' said the first and fiercest speaker.

In her conclusion Mary repeated the assumption that the Revolution could be forgotten in Yasnaya Polyana, and Tolstoy's God remembered. 'Even though one is conscious of no immediate need, except perhaps for a rubber groundsheet. And it is the business of the Five Year Plan to produce that'.

Other family visits in the mid-1930s were to Germany, where John and Mary Stocks met old friends for walking holidays in the Black Forest. It would be going too far to credit the Stockses with precise foresight about the future horrors of the Third Reich, but certainly they observed the socio-political scene there with some dismay. The predicted onset of a Second World War was, Mary said later, 'a terrifying menace, but one still hoped it was an avoidable menace'. In the early 1930s Manchester was already welcoming German refugees, and the Stockses played their part by giving a temporary home to a Jewish professor, Adolf Lowe.

Photographs of the German holidays survive, showing them in idyllic surroundings with university walking companions, in particular a professor of Greek from Strasbourg University. They also stayed with friends in Berlin and Hamburg, and observed inflation as it affected middle-class Germans: for example a retired music teacher living on a pension barely adequate to buy a pound of margarine.

Back in 1929, when Mary Stocks had attended the International Women's Suffrage conference in Berlin, she had felt Germany's post-1918 recovery was complete. Outwardly the country appeared prosperous and democratic, and she noted that women were prominent in the Bundestag. She regarded German society as in some ways more enlightened than English society because it was possible for women to walk in the streets without a hat. A few years later, in Manchester, her early broadcasts expressed a radically different view of Hitler's Germany.

Ann Stocks spent part of 1933 in Germany before going up to university. She was there when Hitler came to power. She studied German in Munich, and then lived with a family in Göttingen. 'I had to be very careful when I wrote home about what was happening. I went on an outing near Munich and there was Dachau. I knew Socialists and others were being kept there'.[20]

More of Ann's impressions were recorded in a letter home which was published anonymously – with a covering letter – in the *Manchester Guardian* of 29 March 1933. She wrote:

The windows of all the big Jewish shops were smashed in broad daylight by a troop of Nazis in uniform . . . all the one-price shops like Woolworth are forcibly closed . . . Many of the prominent burghers, especially the Jewish owners of some of the big shops, and former Social Democratic party officials, have hurriedly travelled to Switzerland. The Social Democratic Oberburgermeister was removed from his house by night in a police car under escort and imprisoned for his own protection; and three other prominent Jewish citizens were assaulted in the street and badly injured . . . The position of these people is perfectly dreadful – no one with Jewish blood can get any

position in Germany now or even feel safe . . . I suppose you
have noticed the new Ministry for Propaganda? The *Frankfurter
Zeitung* is now the only Liberal paper left, and why it has not
been suppressed is a mystery to everyone.[21]

The sender of the letter to the paper (almost certainly her mother)
added 'For obvious reasons her name and mine must not be
published'.

Many of her friends would have pointed to the postwar radio
decades as the golden years of Mary Stocks. In fact she was
broadcasting on and off from 1930 till the end of her life,
and she would undoubtedly have identified her golden years
(not a phrase she would have used, however) as the ones when
she was university-based. Broadcasting happily filled a vacuum
after her retirement as Principal of Westfield College, and before
grandchildren and the House of Lords increasingly claimed her
attention. As Mary Stocks herself said, she was in the right place
at the right time – with the right kind of voice – when panel games
and discussion forums became for a while the listening public's
darlings.

But she had established her popularity with the BBC long before
that. North Region talks producers discovered her in Manchester
in the early 1930s. They liked her unambiguous approach, backed
by her status as a magistrate, WEA lecturer and social economist.
As well as professional standing she had appeal through her
involvement with the Manchester University Settlement, Marie
Stopes's birth control movement and campaigns for maternity
and child welfare. What London and Bristol grew to love in the
1950s, Manchester had appreciated in the 1930s: a woman's voice,
astringent and humorous, commenting with authority on the world
as she saw it.

She was already collecting committees as other women at
that time might have collected sewing bees or women's guilds.
Between 1932 and 1934 she served on the Committee on Habitual
Offenders, the Royal Commission on Lotteries and Betting, and
the Statutory Committee on Unemployment. This was when she
attached to herself the much-quoted label 'a statutory woman'. She
was indeed the only woman on many committees all through her
public life, beginning as a solitary female Justice of the Peace on the
Manchester Bench as early as 1930, the year of her radio début.

Although her peak popularity was in the 1960s, she had made a considerable name for herself before the Second World War. The microfilmed scripts are there in the BBC sound archives to prove it, some handwritten, some typed, all much worked over. Sixty years on, they represent collectively a nugget of social history.

Her first encounter with radio was a weekly round-up of current events, decidedly personal and partisan. Apparently she had a free hand to choose her topics and express opinions. One is reminded of Alistair Cooke's *Letter from America,* and he too made his name in Manchester. ('The Mary Stocks Letter from Manchester' would have been a more appealing title than the impersonal 'Current Events'). Her comments have more than a flavour of prophecy. On 24 September 1930 she found the recent general election in Germany had 'some queer features about it'. She used a speech by the Labour Minister of Health, Arthur Greenwood, to berate the Government for its poor health insurance record. Her particular targets were maternal mortality in childbirth, and lack of provision for working mothers. She was displeased that insurance covered GPs' fees only, not those of consultants. As she was a doctor's daughter, anything to do with family doctors interested her all her life.

In the same slot on 8 October 1930 she said: 'One event overshadows all others – the loss of our giant airship and all that went with it – human bodies, human brains, human hopes'. The country had been deeply shocked by the wreck of the much-vaunted R101. Mary Stocks again was prophetic: 'The question for the experts is this: is there a future for the giant airship, in spite of its advantages over other aircraft?'

As she warmed to her role she became more outspoken. On 15 October: 'The trouble about this week's events – they are so party political I hardly dare mention them for fear of putting my foot in it!' One suspects some adverse reaction to a previous pronouncement. With hindsight the most far-sighted of these talks must have been the one delivered that day:

The meeting of the German Reichstag appears to have been something of a beargarden . . . the first day's business was only a general call, but it did give the National Socialists the opportunity to make derisive noises whenever a Jewish name was called.

Outside the building their friends went on the rampage, smashing the windows of Jewish shops, including Wertheim, the Central Berlin store which corresponds to our Harrods or Selfridges . . . As far as I can make out, the one fixed and definite point in the National Socialist programme is the persecution of the Jews . . .

Part of the fancy dress with which they entered the Reichstag was a symbol called a swastika, which in Germany is used as an anti-Semitic badge . . . The really odd part about it is that the leader of the National Socialist party, General Hitler, isn't a German citizen. He is an Austrian.[22]

Neither Mary Stocks not her contemporaries could then have foreseen how, eight years later, 'General Hitler' would start to devastate most of Europe.

On 25 March 1936 Mary Stocks, JP, was writing from Fallowfield Road, Manchester, to a talks producer about a proposed discussion on hire purchase. And on 17 January 1937 she was one of three speakers in a debate broadcast from Manchester on gambling, picked apparently because of her background as an economist. She spoke for eighteen minutes to a title of her own choosing: 'Gambling: what do we pay and what do we get?'. Not surprisingly, her conclusion was that gambling is a fool's game.

Two months later she was engaged in a rather less serious exercise, and one that set the pattern for many subsequent radio activities. This was an animated 15-minute discussion with the writer John Gloag entitled 'Men talking: women all over the place'. Later generations would have perceived it as yet another feminist versus chauvinist encounter, but in 1937 it was refreshingly novel. The producer afterwards referred to it as 'one of the best knock-about turns I have heard on the air'.

In July of that year Mary Stocks gave her first book talk, speaking by now as wife of the Vice-Chancellor of Liverpool University. After the war there were to be many of these book programmes, some scholarly and sophisticated. But the first was relatively lighthearted: a choice of summer holiday reading. A letter indicates that she chose biography and collections of letters, but there is no record of the authors or of her opinions. A safe guess might be Victorian poets, perhaps Browning or Coleridge, always favourites of hers.

Family life in Manchester was perfect. Both parents had prestigious and satisfying careers (even if Mary's was part-time), the children were happy at their various schools, home was still well supplied with domestic help, there were family holidays in Dorset and the Lakes and farther afield – Russia, France.

Helen Stocks recalled:

> Manchester was fine. I was three when we went there. We lived in an unadopted road, and the hay was taller than me – but by the time we left (when I was 16) the road had been made up and traffic had arrived.
>
> My parents were always busy, correcting exam papers or checking a Greek lexicon or planning W.E.A. classes. We had a nanny, and my mother read to us a lot: Robert Louis Stevenson, *Alice*, Grimm, *Brer Rabbit*, *Fritz of the Fiords*, and Robert Browning, her favourite poet. Father read us poems sometimes too.[23]

The children of an academic family in the 1930s might be expected to read constantly, but one is surprised to learn they made models and went in for sport quite a lot. Helen said:

> We were always making things – paper models, and toffee and soap which we sold to friends. We had ten shillings a month pocket money, and we did some gardening. With father we played tennis and cricket, and with mother we played backgammon and a game called 'Liar'.[24]

Helen's most revealing comment was made in answer to a question about family relationships: 'I don't remember any rules, or family disputes, except that we were a bit disunited over sport; not everyone was keen on cricket'.

As Public Orator, John Stocks was called on to entertain visiting dignitaries from time to time. 'Exquisite people came to the house because they were getting honorary degrees. I remember Epstein, Julian Huxley, one of the Toynbees'.

The arts still played an important part in the lives of the whole family. While John acted and directed plays, Mary wrote and produced. The children did not act in their parents' productions, but Helen was on one occasion Puck in *A Midsummer Night's Dream*. She recalled that her mother had played the Chorus, reciting Blake's 'Jerusalem', in her own *Everyman of Everystreet*.

Poetry reading was something that came naturally to them all and Mary Stocks's artistic taste is reflected in art objects she acquired during the Manchester years, for example a collection of tiles by the Pre-Raphaelite potter William de Morgan, who lived near the Brinton family home in London.

By 1935 Ann had started an economics course at LSE and John junior was about to embark on engineering at Liverpool University. There was, it seems, no great pressure on them to apply for Oxford or Cambridge, as family tradition might have dictated. (The Stocks family had favoured Oxford, the Brintons Cambridge.) Ann explained that her choice was determined by the fact that she had set her heart on reading economics, but Oxford offered only the mix of politics, philosophy and economics; while Cambridge, though home to the great J.M. Keynes, did not allow female students to attend his lectures. It pleases her that later, as a final-year LSE undergraduate, she was able to hear him on a study visit to Cambridge. In the case of John, Liverpool was felt to be right for someone with marine engineering in his blood, going back to three generations of Meadows Rendels.

1935 was something of an *annus mirabilis* for all the Stockses. Ann graduated, John entered Liverpool University, Mary was elected a director of the Manchester Repertory Theatre on the basis of her public work, and John stood for Parliament. This was the first of several attempts by the family to be elected to Westminster. Professor Stocks represented Labour in standing for Oxford University, one of several university seats which returned two members. Those entitled to vote were all graduates, wherever they might be living, and this meant there were nearly 23,000 voters with a dual vote for Oxford University and their home constituency.

The Conservative candidate was Lord Hugh Cecil, who had held the seat since 1922. The novelist A.P. Herbert stood as an Independent, and a second Conservative standing was C.R.M. Crutwell. The system of voting was by single transferable vote. What is surprising is not that this happened some twenty years after the proposal to introduce proportional representation had failed in the House of Commons (in 1917 the First World War caused the Bill to be dropped, and it was never resurrected), but that voting for Westminster by PR has ever taken place in mainland Britain.

The *Daily Telegraph* described the election campaign as 'leisurely and decorous'. The scattered nature of the electorate precluded any doorstep campaigning. However, Professor Stocks defied convention by sending out a letter signed by many of his well-known supporters (the paper called them 'the Old Guard of Socialist intellectuals'). Signatories included G.D.H. Cole, Julian Huxley, Harold Laski, Naomi Mitchison, J.L. and Barbara Hammond. Others were said to be 'pinkish Liberals'. The *Telegraph* offered an explanation for their new allegiance: 'This may mark the final retirement of Prof. Gilbert Murray, Liberalism's persevering champion, who carried his party's standard to the bottom of the poll in no fewer than four out of six previous elections'.[25] Another name to conjure with was Sir Stafford Cripps, chief speaker at the Stocks adoption meeting.

But the galaxy of intellectual support was not enough to win the seat. A.P. Herbert narrowly topped the poll on the second count with 5,206 votes; Lord Hugh Cecil (5,081) was also elected; C.R.M. Cruttwell came third with 3,697; and Professor Stocks, with a first vote of 2,683, did not qualify for the second round. The *Telegraph*'s final sentence was perhaps ironic: Cripps had said 'The Labour Party has to face the situation that it is a class party, a party of the workers'.

Among all this welter of activity Mary did not lose touch with her London suffragette colleagues. Eva Hubback was a frequent visitor to Manchester, and Mary kept up a lively correspondence with her cousin Ray Strachey, a pillar of the NUWSS.

There was also Nancy Astor. Mary Stocks devoted a whole chapter of her second autobiographical volume to Lady Astor, and letters survive in the Astor archive at Reading University which chart the long course of their friendship. They had met in 1920 after the – to the feminists – wholly unexpected election of Nancy Astor to Parliament in her husband's old seat of Plymouth. The leaders of the NUWSS, among them Mary Stocks, worked hand in hand with the new MP on women's matters once they realised that at heart she was one of them, however deceptive the image of American heiress turned British aristocrat.

During their Oxford days the Stockses were at times invited to Cliveden (the great Astor country house on the Thames), and feminist concerns caused Nancy Astor to consult Mary, who obviously inhabited a different world from the four-homes orbit of the second Viscountess Astor. (As well as Cliveden and a flat in Plymouth she presided over a London house and one by the sea at Sandwich, in Kent. Nancy's own family, the Langhornes of Virginia, gravitated between New York, London and the south of France.) In spite of the contrast in lifestyles, or perhaps because of it, Mary came to admire, one might almost say hero-worship, Nancy. In *My Commonplace Book* she enumerates Nancy's advantages: 'beauty, charm, physical vigour (which she owed to Christian Science) and enough money to secure expert help . . . her supreme initial advantage was that she was married to a saint-like and selfless husband': hardly a feminist ideal.

The earliest extant correspondence between the two women dates from December 1928. Mary wrote from Manchester on the printed notepaper of *The Woman's Leader and the Common Cause*, a self-explanatory journal. Its directors were listed as Miss Macadam, Mrs J.L. Stocks, Mrs Hubback and Mrs Blanco White. Half-jokingly addressing Nancy as 'Most honoured and gracious Lady', Mary was asking her to write an article on the American situation for a Christmas Peace number of the journal. The year was midway between the two world wars, the League of Nations still a respected international body. After issuing her invitation (she would not have consented to 'so tall an order' if she felt it was adding to Nancy's burdens) Mary's letter went on to refer to a Parliamentary debate on the financing of state maternity services:

> All the philanthropic, religious and feminist organisations in this dirty serious-minded city hang upon your speech of last Tuesday, and pray that you may be successful in delivering the Maternity Services from the block grants . . . I hunger for a sight of you . . . that is what comes of living in Manchester.

Presumably the article was forthcoming, probably with help from Hilda Matheson, Nancy's political secretary.

In September 1929 Mary was giving Nancy advice on setting up a social settlement in Plymouth, on the basis of her Manchester experience. As a compliment to Nancy it was called Virginia House. Mary wrote with some prescience from 22 Wilbraham Road:

> Some day Plymouth will be linked up with a University of the West and then it will be a thousand pities if there isn't a Settlement to work the practical side of a Social Studies department.

She would have been amused to learn that 64 years later there would be a Plymouth University. It seems Nancy was to speak at a Manchester meeting organised by Lord Stanford. Knowing this, Mary invited her to stay overnight at Wilbraham Road, inspect the Settlement and speak at a women's luncheon. Modestly she said that either John or Hilda Cashmore (the Warden) would be better equipped to explain the workings of the Settlement to Nancy. This letter was signed simply 'Yours, Mary Stocks'.

Nancy accepted for one night only, to discuss Virginia House. On 11 October Mary wrote:

> Dear Lady Astor, All Manchester is aware of your advent and is preparing to converge on you the moment you set foot in it – we greatly hope we shall be able to hold it at bay while you visit the Settlement for a secret conference with John and Miss Cashmore . . . We will meet you at the station, not in our little car Julia, but in her worthy successor.

She repeated her invitation to the women's luncheon: 'I myself shall probably be excommunicated and in disgrace because I am moving a birth control resolution for the N.U.S.G.C.'.

On 13 October, just before her visit, Nancy wrote setting out her very crowded programme for two days in Lancashire. First a conference, then a meeting at the Free Trade Hall, then 'a supper party afterwards at the Queen's Hotel to which I hope you will come with me', then on to Liverpool next morning for another speech. This was very much the pattern of Nancy Astor's public life. 'Now when am I going to see your Settlement? We must try to find a moment on Wednesday, somehow. I am so glad I am going to stay with you. Yours very sincerely, —'. Usually no record exists of how Nancy signed off, as her letters were always typed by a secretary who kept the unsigned carbon copy. Nor is it possible to deduce if the visit was a success. The Stocks children were much impressed to have such a famous name under their roof, and Ann said much later: 'I think she felt she was slumming'. It seems unlikely that circumstances again gave rise to such a visit; Nancy's normal milieu was a front-rank hotel.

There is then a long gap in the surviving correspondence between the two women until July 1936, when apparently the entire Stocks family was invited to a ball at Cliveden. Mary replied in characteristic vein, even to the insertion of a small sketch in the letter:

Dear Lady Astor, I have got into communication with Ann, in the middle of Dartmoor, and with my family in these northern mists. Alas – we cannot come to that dance. John and I live like those little figures in the Swiss weather guages [sic]: when one comes out, the other goes in. [Here she included a neat graphic of a mini-man and mini-woman emerging from a Swiss chalet.] If we are both out together our youngest daughter grows too independent. And on top of that Ann has a chance of remaining with her horses for another week . . . Not that she wouldn't have loved that dance. She would. Partly because she loves dances and human company, and partly because she loves making elegant clothes (in the intervals of heavy economics) and then finding occasions for wearing them. The multitude of the creature's activities leaves me tired! This month's B.Sc. exam results will show whether they conflict with one another.

Yours affectionately, Mary Stocks.

The salutations are becoming warmer. The doubts about Ann were quite unjustified; she sailed through with a first-class degree as her mother had.

Nancy's replies to these letters have not survived. They may have taken the form of brief notes sent by a secretary while Nancy was away from home. It seems possible that she wished to discourage too intimate a relationship; but the next correspondence between them – two years later – was to refer to a weekend Mary Stocks had spent at one of Nancy's glamorous homes.

Meanwhile major changes lay ahead in the public and private life of the Stocks family. 1936 and 1937 were for them all traumatic years. Early in 1936 it was announced that John Stocks had been elected Vice-Chancellor of Liverpool University. The *Manchester Guardian* pigeonholed him as a leading scholar in the fields of modern philosophy, ethics and politics and 'a not infrequent speaker on the political platform'. The newspaper paid major tribute to his involvement with the University Settlement at Ancoats. 'For ten years he and his wife have been the prime movers behind almost every activity there'. Among his achievements as Secretary and afterwards Chairman of the Settlement were the restoration of the Round House; and the setting up of community centres on the new housing estates at Wilbraham and Newton

Heath, forming a federation of centres, still maintaining close links with the University. 'The outside public . . . has from time to time enjoyed reading the humorous appreciations with which he presented honorary graduands'.

Another article praised both John and Mary Stocks for their 'scholarly, sympathetic and thorough teaching of the finest kind' on extra-mural courses, in university extension classes and through the WEA all over Lancashire and Cheshire. Mary Stocks was commended as Vice-Chairman of the WEA's north-western area and then its national Vice-Chairman. Its success, said the *Guardian*, was in no small measure due to her guidance. At the University Settlement and the Repertory Theatre she had done much to promote drama and literature. Together the Stockses ran fourteen classes in ten different areas, and lifted such places 'out of the rut of suburban mediocrity'.

Another local paper declared that Mary Stocks held a special place among voluntary women workers in Manchester. It mentioned her courage, wit, intelligence and lack of personal bias. 'Many will miss her vivid personality when she goes from Manchester'. The National Council of Women gave a dinner in her honour at the Grand Hotel. Tributes were paid to her work as a magistrate and member of government committees. But the most interesting comments came from Mary's old friend Sheena Simon (later Lady Simon of Wythenshawe) who talked about her articles and reviews for the *Guardian*, the time when she stood unsuccessfully as Labour candidate for the city council in Rusholme Ward, and her passion for the cinema. Lady Simon was most grateful that Mary Stocks had introduced her to Gracie Fields – 'we both adore her'.

At a farewell dinner given by the WEA north-western area, Professor Stocks said he had always felt the heart of the WEA was in the north. Harry Tawney had launched it in Rochdale, and the kernel of the whole movement was in Lancashire.

While these ceremonies were taking place in Manchester, an interesting and in some ways parallel ceremony in Auckland, New Zealand, commemorated the 94th anniversary of the death of Mary Stocks's great-grandfather, Captain William Hobson, the first Governor. A naval guard of honour, the Mayor of Auckland, the Minister of Education and 300 members of the public saw wreaths laid at Captain Hobson's tomb. Speeches were made referring to him as a national hero for his part in the Treaty of Waitangi, the founding of Auckland and his commitment to the integration of Maoris and settlers.

As an entertaining guest speaker at the speech day of Wirral County Girls' High School, Mary Stocks was extensively reported in the *Liverpool Post*:

> If girls went into the Civil Service with hardly any education they became what was known as writing assistants and they typed things they did not understand and would never understand, and they ran about the passages of Government departments carrying cups of tea. They would probably get married at an early stage out of sheer boredom (laughter).
>
> If, on the other hand, they had a secondary education . . . they became members of the executive grade. There they wrote letters which they understood, and (she imagined) other people ran about with the cups of tea (laughter).
>
> If they passed to the Civil Service from University with a really good degree, they entered the administrative grade . . . and they wrote the speeches of Cabinet ministers (laughter). If they wanted to get married they could choose their man, because they did not need to get married in a hurry.

She went on to advocate a sense of proportion in reading newspapers, equating headline size inversely with the significance of world affairs.

Possibly the headmistress disapproved of Mary Stocks's philosophy. In her report she doubted if office work was the best training for 'future mothers of the nation, and it did not seem to be improving the race'. One can guess what Mary Stocks's reaction to this might have been. Within days the anger of several correspondents spilled over in the local press. Some women signing themselves 'Three Ex-Writing Assistants' complained that she had her facts wrong. The writing assistant class of the Civil Service had ceased to exist the previous year. 'One would have at least have thought that the wife of the Vice-Chancellor of that mighty seat of learning, the Liverpool University, would have been sure of her facts'. They pointed out that writing assistants had been replaced by Clerical Assistant, Grade 1, and that 95 per cent of those holding this post in Liverpool had matriculated. They demanded an apology and finished their letter with a flourish which must have impressed Mary Stocks:

> While we appreciate that a speech is a difficult ordeal for some of us, we do hope that such a difficulty will not be used for the purpose of inflicting an injustice on a worthy class.

Mary Stocks replied at once, with characteristic vigour:

> I am very sorry indeed that my remarks should seem to depreciate the educational attainments of responsible public servants who have clearly made far better use of their secondary education than I did myself, seeing that my own final exploit at the secondary school was to fail in higher certificate . . . in reading your resumé of my ill-considered and offensive utterances it is borne in upon me that I must owe a whole host of apologies. I have it seems accused Cabinet Ministers of not writing their own speeches. I have accused members of your profession, Mr Editor, of a defective sense of proportion . . . I can only add that, though Cabinet Ministers may write their own speeches, it is all too clear that I ought to employ some responsible and well-informed person to write mine.

Another correspondent ('Government Typist') set out in 87 lines a comprehensive and very civil-servantish account of the structure, pay and duties of women in the Civil Service ('it is regrettable that so excellent an exponent of the benefits of education should fall short of accuracy in her statements'). And a writer signing himself T. Oupie suggested that women might well feel they could foresee and prevent murders next door (picking up another point in Mary Stocks's speech), but they could do little about the death of 10,000 in China. No doubt after this she chose her words with more care at speech days.

John's installation as Vice-Chancellor was an exciting time for the whole family. He and Mary were pulled by students though the city streets in a open carriage as part of the university's rag day. A *Daily Telegraph* photograph shows their evident enjoyment of this unorthodox welcome. For once in her life Mary was obliged to wear a despised long dress under academic robes for the ceremony. There were welcoming parties, distinguished lectures and a memorable introduction to the academic life of Liverpool.

At this time her reputation both enhanced and was enhanced

by her husband's. She found herself reviewing books and was much in demand for luncheons of women's organisations and school events. She was appointed to yet another statutory body, on unemployment insurance. And her plays were being performed not only in Manchester but in London and America. At about this time, speaking to a gathering of Liverpool Soroptimists, she argued the case for drama to be subsidised to bring it within the reach of everyone. She attributed its lack of appeal among non-professional people to the expense of theatre-going and the rival attraction of the cinema. During 1937 her *Hail, Nero!* was performed by the Footlights Club of Boston, Massachusetts, and the Civic Theatre of Denver, Colorado.

Soon after their arrival in Liverpool, the Stockses were guests of the Liverpool Chamber of Commerce at a reception for Walter Nash, the New Zealand Minister of Finance. This gave the *Liverpool Post* the chance to trace Mary Stocks's notable ancestry. It was an interesting coincidence, said the reporter, that Mrs Stocks happened to be the great-granddaughter of the first Governor of New Zealand. Moreover, she was also a great-granddaughter of James Meadows Rendel who had designed the first docks at Birkenhead, and the Birkenhead, Lancashire and Cheshire Junction Railway.

Despite a few infelicitous public utterances, Mary Stocks's personal reputation seemed set to grow in Liverpool as it had in Manchester. Her WEA work continued, she was writing, broadcasting and lecturing, her plays were in demand and her children were carving out their futures.

Shortly after graduating with a first at LSE, as her mother had, Ann sat the notoriously tough competitive examination for Civil Service administrators and was one of five women to pass, coming 12th out of 42 places. This was only the third year in which women had entered, 44 of them in 1938. Ann Stocks and one other candidate gained full marks on the personality test, and her chosen subjects were general economics, trade and industry, banking, money, public finance, social economics and economic history. This was only one of many ways in which Ann Stocks resembled her mother; their attitudes and interests often converged; a battle inspired them. The *Daily Mail* commented:

> Women are on trial in this competition as in no other in the Civil Service or outside it. Failure would mean a setback to all their

claims in every field, and a reflection on their mental capacity as compared with men.

Much the same could be said fifty years later.

Helen found it a little more difficult to adjust to the move to Liverpool after settling in happily at Withington Girls' High School. Because of this it was decided that she should go as a boarder to Talbot Heath School in Bournemouth, where the head-mistress was John Stocks's sister Frieda (Elfrieda). She finished her schooling here and moved on to Kings College for Women (Household and Social Science), (as it then was), in Kensington, to qualify in social work, which equipped her to follow in the steps of Edith and Leila Rendel at the Caldecott Community.

All seemed set fair for the expanding careers of the whole Stocks family. Then came the blow which shattered their glittering world. On 13 June 1937, towards the end of his first year as Vice-Chancellor, John Stocks was visiting University College, Swansea, to lecture to extra-mural students there, and staying as a guest of the Principal. A newspaper report mentioned that Professor Stocks arrived in Swansea by train and was driven straight to the University College. The weather was oppressive and onlookers thought he looked unwell, but he made no reference to this.

After delivering his address to the extra-mural students, John Stocks joined them for tea on the college lawn, then spent the evening at the home of the Principal, Dr C.A. Edwards, who early next morning found him very ill. He died soon afterwards, from a massive heart attack, aged 54. The news was brought to Mary Stocks in Liverpool by the police. She said later: 'rather a sudden knockout blow than a slow drip of terrible news.'

Glowing obituaries appeared in many newspapers, national and local. The *Liverpool Daily Post* praised John Stocks as philosopher, soldier, teacher, administrator and prolific author. He had notably fulfilled a pledge given on his first day as Vice-Chancellor to strengthen the bonds between town and gown. As a public speaker he had scholarly wit and charm; in civic life he would be much missed. 'His death is a loss to the city – to the University it is a calamity'.

The *Post* also paid tribute to Mary Stocks: 'a woman of out-standing ability and charm . . . who has made her mark on Merseyside. She is an ardent feminist and a keen and alert student of contemporary affairs. She has broadcast on modern social problems'. The paper went on to outline her earlier public work in Manchester. She had unstintingly supported her husband, and he had often spoken of this.

Published tributes to John Stocks came from his old friend William Temple, now Archbishop of York, from the Vice-Chancellors of Oxford and Manchester, from Samuel Alexander OM (John Stocks's predecessor as Professor of Philosophy at Manchester), and from the WEA: 'the death of J.L. Stocks greatly impoverishes university life in England'.

The funeral, in Liverpool Cathedral on 17 June, must have been an unspeakable ordeal for Mary. It was a grand civic occasion. The body was brought by train from Swansea to Lime Street Station, then in the early hours by road to the Chapel of the Holy Spirit in the Cathedral. In the afternoon, it was transferred to the choir and placed on a catafalque draped in red and gold. For an hour the public filed into seats. Then it was the turn of the family. Ann Stocks was on her way home from Mills College, California, and could not arrive in time. Mary was supported by John and Helen and seventeen members of the Stocks family as well as Mary's sister Joanna (Mrs Ian Baillieu).

Liverpool University was represented by almost the entire teaching staff, with Pro-Chancellors and senior officers (among them Sir Frederick Marquis, later Lord Woolton and a promiment wartime member of the Government). The Lord Mayor of Liverpool processed with nine aldermen and councillors. Fifteen universities sent representatives. The congregation included judges, headmasters and leading industrialists.

John's school contemporary R.H. Tawney was in the congregation, and so were members of the Rathbone shipping family. The Archbishop of York and the Bishop of Liverpool led the service, and the Bishop spoke this prayer:

> Let us pray in silence for the sons and daughters of the City and the University . . . and in the silence let us give thanks for our brother and for his service to God's truth, which sets men free.

One of the hymns was described as 'A Hymn of the Workers in their Search for Education', and this same hymn was sung (as we have already seen) at the memorial service for John Stocks's widow not quite forty years later:

Shall crime bring crime for ever,
Strength aiding still the strong?
Is it Thy will, O Father,
That man shall toil for wrong? . . .
From vice, oppression and despair,
God save the people!

It is hard to imagine how Mary Stocks and her son and daughter reacted to the pomp of a civic funeral (such a spectacle as Liverpool had rarely witnessed, said the daily paper). Almost certainly they would have preferred an intimate family service. But John Stocks remained a public figure, in death as in life. Archbishop Temple preached movingly, saying: 'Just now the sorrow of his death, and the shock of it, blots out all other feeling. But as the days pass this will give place to thankfulness for the varied and rich achievement of his life'. It was an appropriate funeral, perhaps, for the son of a canon and brother of three clergymen. Only the immediate family attended the burial at Allerton Cemetery, conducted by William Temple. Mary's hand can be seen in the filling of the grave with lilies and irises.

At the age of 46 she was now a widow and homeless. The Vice-Chancellor's house went with the job, and Mary had no wish to occupy a place no longer rightfully hers. She had no regular income, and John (aged 19) and Helen (now 17) were as yet not earning. All this had to be faced on top of sudden and totally unforeseen bereavement. A less resilient woman would surely have wilted.

Barely three weeks after the death of John Stocks, Mary's uncle James Rendel (the oldest son of Sir Alexander) died at the age of 83. His influence on her early years had been great, in view of his experience as a Poor Law expert and chairman of the Kensington Board of Guardians.

The widowed Mary dealt briskly with her practical problems. Within five months she had found a home and a job, both in London. She seldom mentioned the psychological effect of John's death, but the closing sentence of her autobiography gives a clue to her sense of loss: 'The finest opportunity that came my way was the opportunity to marry John Stocks . . . thank God I did not hesitate long'.

So she embarked on her first professional non-academic career,

91

as an embryo scriptwriter. Her introduction to schools broadcasting was through an old friend, Rhoda Power, author and sister of the historian Eileen Power. Rhoda was a BBC producer and she made her first approach to Mary Stocks, inviting her to write and narrate a radio documentary to be called *Coal, Iron, Cotton*. This was very much Mary Stocks's field as a social economist, and her experience as a playwright for the Manchester University Settlement came in handy too. In a nutshell, educational radio was tailor-made to bring together her various skills.

The gap was great between the Manchester magistrate invited to join in prestigious sociological debates, and the vice-chancellor's widow needing to earn her living. In the interval between *Book Talk* and *Coal, Iron, Cotton* John Stocks had died. For his widow, briefly homeless and jobless, the offer of BBC work must at first have seemed a godsend. She wrote from 37 Argyll Road, Kensington (having returned to her old home area) with enthusiasm, not at all intimidated by a stream of sometimes trivial BBC demands for alterations.

Another indignity which Mary Stocks bore with good grace was George Dixon's insistence on a voice audition, although he was well aware she had broadcast already for Manchester. Fortunately he approved of what he heard: 'Clear, deep voice. Grand broadcaster, able to go at our speed. Yes'. The 20-minute programme eventually went out on 5 May 1938, and favourable memos circulated among the BBC hierarchy.

By this time Mary Stocks had accepted the offered post of General Secretary for the London Council of Social Service. This fitted well with her pre-university welfare work in London as a young woman. Through most of 1938 she combined this with a good deal of radio work, mostly for Schools Broadcasting. Broadcasting House was conveniently located midway between Kensington and the LCSS offices at Bedford Square. Her diary was always full, but she enjoyed her radio commissions and fitted them in somehow.

On 10 June 1938 she joined a team of five to discuss football pools (Mary Stocks disliked them). This was a half-hour programme for which she submitted in advance an 850-word script. It now seems odd that apparently unscripted discussions should be based on approved scripts supplied by each team member, without reference to each other. In fact this was at the time perceived as a method of ensuring 'a balance of opinions'. Mary Stocks revelled in these semi-scripted programmes, and they groomed her for later roles in totally unscripted shows.

Surprisingly, she accepted without question the BBC's right to chop and change her scripts. With the football pools draft she sent this note: 'It will need a good deal of altering, I suspect, to bring it into hitting distance of what others will say'. Some drafts were altered repeatedly, and there is much evidence of her anxiety in the schools documentaries to work out an effective mix of dialogue, narration and sound effects. Dialogue she took particular pains with. Letters show that then and later she both valued and acted on professional advice.

In October 1938 Rhoda Power asked Mary Stocks for a dramatised account of the Tolpuddle Martyrs or the Great Reform Bill, together with an explanatory pamphlet for school use. She had scarcely started on this – to the accompaniment of the usual flurry of bureaucratic letters – when her circumstances changed dramatically, and her career took another momentous turn.

In November she was offered the vacant post of Principal of Westfield College, London University, to be taken up in a year's time. Partly this was the result of William Temple's influence as a former chairman of the Westfield Council, partly because the Council was looking for someone who would broaden the horizons of an all-women's residential college. For a time it looked as though this prestigious new job would put paid to BBC work, but Mary Stocks had no intention of relinquishing a sideline she enjoyed and knew she had a talent for.

In February 1939, interviewed on her new appointment, she described herself as 'not a very interesting person really. You see I never made a million pounds in a sweepstake'. She went on to say that possession of a university degree might tell one much about a girl's intellectual attainments, but little about her character. Challenged to confirm that degrees were of little use in most women's careers, she defended every girl's right to the opportunity of university education regardless of income. 'Speaking generally, I think it is becoming more and more a matter of routine for parents to send their daughters as well as their sons to university'.

N.G. Laker, a BBC administrator, wrote in December: 'Congratulations on your new appointment. I hope it does not mean you will be too busy to broadcast'. (In fact she managed little radio work in the next twelve years.) Mary Stocks replied, writing from her temporary home at 10 Holland Park Court: 'Many thanks for your mention of my appointment. It is a piece of great good fortune for me – but rather intimidating'.

Then came a cataclysmic event which was to affect the BBC profoundly, and to shatter the routine even of a relatively cloistered women's college. War against Germany was declared on 3 September 1939, barely a month before the start of Mary Stocks's first term at Westfield. Writing to the BBC from the college, in Kidderpore Avenue, Hampstead, North London, eleven days after the outbreak of war, she wondered if she should totally rewrite the nearly completed British history series: 'As it is, it is distinctly prewar'.

The BBC's reply came not from Portland Place but from a Post Office box number at Evesham, in Worcestershire, where various departments were evacuated almost as soon as the first air-raid siren sounded its eerie wailing note. The reply was brief, telling Mary Stocks to trust her own judgement in the matter of changing the British history series. This uncharacteristic vagueness was not the only signal of BBC agitation. The usual formal salutations were replaced by an abrupt signing-off: 'We are very busy, like you'.

Evidently, the Great Reform Bill went into cold storage for a few weeks, while Westfield moved into temporary (and very cramped) wartime quarters at St Peter's Hall, Oxford. Here Mary Stocks and her family, now in their early twenties, were on familiar ground. After her experience of commuting between London and Oxford in the early years of her marriage she was quite happy to divide her time between Oxford, 10 Holland Park Court, and the seaside home in Dorset which was still an escape for many of the Rendel-Brinton clan.

Chapter 4

The Westfield Years: 1939–1951

Mary Stocks had not sought the post of Principal of Westfield College in Hampstead, and she probably did not know it was vacant. Some twenty applicants had been nominated by vice-chancellors and college principals from other universities, and considered by Westfield Council, before her name appeared in the lists. Most of the other contenders already held academic posts of some standing elsewhere.

It is doubtful if she would have entered the lists of her own accord. The initiative in putting forward her name came from Archbishop William Temple, a former chairman of Westfield Council. As Archbishop of York he had preached the eulogy at John Stocks's funeral and was only three years away from becoming Archbishop of Canterbury. He knew Mary's potential as well as anyone outside her immediate family.

Temple's formal proposal was endorsed by Professor Eileen Power of Girton College, Cambridge, known to Mary since her student days at LSE. Recently (at the age of 48) Eileen had married Professor Michael Postan and together they were working on a massive history of English trade. Others who wrote supporting Mary included Sir Hector Hetherington of the University of Glasgow, Sir Walter Moberley of LSE and a Westfield staff representative on the college Council.

Months elapsed before a decision was made, and many candidates were interviewed. The recommendations of Temple and Power carried great weight, and a final postal ballot of Council members swung decisively in Mary's favour by 26 votes to two.

So, from the beginning of August 1939, with preparations for war in Europe already far advanced, Mary Stocks, née Brinton, social worker, suffragette, birth control campaigner, found herself in command of an all-women's residential college of some 150 students. (Her previous experience was perhaps not irrelevant.) The college had been founded with a constitutional bias towards missionary careers. Her face did not at once seem to fit. She wrote of 'an unlooked-for honour' and one that rather staggered her. Here was an irregular church attender, a non-academic since the early 1920s, family woman and mother of three (all previous Westfield principals had been single women), with teaching experience gained mainly among working-class adults. She was plunged at the deep end into a cloistered, even pious community of women aged 18 to 21, some of them contemplating Church careers, and this at the very outbreak of the Second World War.

As it happens, there existed from 1921 onwards a Principal's Logbook which tells the day-to-day story of Westfield through the eyes of successive principals, thereby revealing much of their characters. Mary Stocks's contribution to the logbook, written throughout the war and an equally testing postwar period, is a unique and highly entertaining journal. The style is brisk, laconic and often satirical. The first entry in her handwriting runs: 'Summer Vacation: August 24th. International Crisis develops, Bursars to Oxford'. The ensuing rapid upheaval was the start of a six-year evacuation from bomb-threatened London to the relative safety of Oxford. St Peter's Hall, a men's college in New Inn Hall Street, was made available to Westfield for the duration. All London colleges were evacuated – University College to Aberystwyth, LSE to Cambridge.

St Peter's Hall, near Oxford Gaol, must have startled Westfieldians: a former private hall of residence, upgraded as a college in 1928, with rather austere redbrick Georgian buildings framing the Victorian church of St Peter-le-Bailey. This was so called because of its nearness to Oxford's Norman castle mound, and when the hall was metamorphosed the church became in effect the college chapel. There was also a handsome pillared lodge of golden Bath stone, once the rectory; and an imposing Master's House which had been the offices of the Oxford Canal Company, built in 1827.

St Peter's was too small, far from cosy, and cold. But once the initial shock had worn off, the London exiles began to see some advantages. It was near the heart of academic Oxford and (more importantly in wartime conditions) a five-minute walk from the main railway station. For their new Principal, New Inn Hall

Street was familiar territory, running as it did at right angles to St Michael's Street, where her first married home had been at the start of an earlier world war. But this was not the time for sentiment or nostalgia (and when did Mary Stocks ever indulge in either?). It was a time for action and improvising.

War was declared at 11 a.m. on Sunday 3 September. By 8 September the logbook entry records: 'General H.Q. established at St Peter's'. Fairly quickly it became obvious that a quart had to be fitted into a pint pot. St Peter's held 90 students and staff, whereas Westfield expected 137 for its Michaelmas term. On 22 September Mary Stocks wrote gloomily 'All hope of extra accommodation at St Edmunds and Lady Margaret Hall now extinguished'. Term was postponed for a week. Study space, lecturers' rooms and book shelving all had to be squeezed into what had been simply male students' living quarters. Lecture areas were contrived in corridors, many books stayed in their packing cases. History classes were held in St Peter-le-Bailey Church. As the logbook records: 'Position not easily definable and wholly unprecedented'.

The new students arrived on 10 October, the second and third years on 11 October. It was difficult to say which intrigued them more – their new quarters or their new Principal. Old hands were at first very suspicious. Everything was compared unfavourably with their pleasant uncrowded campus at Hampstead, and among all the upheaval they missed the calm and comforting presence of Miss Dorothy Chapman, a classicist who had guided Westfield unremarkably through the 1930s.

The first drama happened on the first day of term. 'Evilly disposed person entered college between 6 p.m. and 7 p.m., posed as college doctor and medically examined four first year students – C.I.D. sergeant arrived and took description of man . . . More stringent regulations as to locking gates.'

November of the first term in Oxford was marked by some eminent visiting speakers, a custom which Mary Stocks kept up right through her 12-year tenure of office. Eileen Power gave the annual inaugural lecture in the afternoon and stayed talking to history students till 10.15 p.m. Later another old friend, Gilbert Murray, spoke to the modern politics club on the international situation, and Margaret Bondfield (who had been Westminster's first woman Cabinet Minister under Ramsay MacDonald in the early 1930s) gave an open lecture under the title 'I Remember'.

Apart from accommodation problems the first Oxford term went more smoothly than might have been expected, given that the Londoners assumed their stay would be very temporary. Christmas was celebrated with early morning carols on the last day and a college dance: 'Principal warned of possible insobriety of guests. Forewarned. Behaviour of guests above reproach. 4 male gatecrashers (one drunk) ejected by Principal'. And the last logbook entry of 1939:

> Discipline . . . Signs that the comparative freedom of Oxford and the presence of the male sex were mounting like wine to the heads of certain students . . . Problem remains to be solved.

For Mary Stocks it was a time of pain and pleasure, a season of picking up old threads, renewing friendships from her time at St John's, rediscovering the delights of Oxford. It must have seemed to her ironic that she came now as widow, once more to Oxford during a world war, and now part of John Knox's 'monstrous regiment of women'.

In January 1940 she started on a radio script on women's emancipation. 'We feel you are exactly the right person to do this', said the BBC mentors. The History series surfaced again in December 1940 under the title 'Movements and Men, 1800–1875'. The four components emerged as children in industry, Robert Owen, the Reform Bill and the Tolpuddle Martyrs. All of them had figured strongly in her 1920s textbook, *The Industrial State*. This was very much her field. Mary Stocks finished her drafting within a month and the programme went out in February.

Then there was comparative radio silence from 1940 till 1951. The BBC was concentrating its efforts as Britain's chief propaganda and home morale weapon. Mary Stocks was concentrating hers on guiding Westfield through five difficult years in inadequate accommodation in Oxford, and an equally difficult period of adjustment when the college finally returned to Hampstead in October 1945. She was also planning several books.

However, the radio silence was by no means total. In February 1941, she was working on a portrait of Octavia Hill, and followed this with 'Woman Doctor', a profile of Elizabeth Garrett Anderson. In April 1941 a producer wrote to let her know that her Dr Anderson piece was to be used, but so drastically revised that they proposed introducing it as 'from material supplied by Mary Stocks': rather a slap in the face for an experienced script writer, as she by now certainly was.

There were one or two overseas talks arising from her status as a university principal. The first went out in the *Calling West Africa* service in December 1943, on the highly relevant subject of women's education. She introduced herself as representing Westfield College, home of 160 women working for degrees, and an exiled component of London University. At the time of the broadcast several colleges had been bombed, notably King's and University, and Westfield in London was damaged by fire bombs.

Mary Stocks's central argument was that a nation aiming at cultural or political advance must carry its women along with it, educated to their maximum potential. After a long struggle Britain had achieved equal opportunity in university education. Nonetheless she believed there was still parental prejudice, and few women had been appointed professors. In a sentence, she summed up her own career: 'I do not remember ever feeling it was a disadvantage to be a woman'. Later she gave a radio talk to the West Indies on similar lines. Her message was clear and positive: higher education must be open to all who can possibly benefit from it. Her personal crusade was to widen the net, to extend the boundaries. Among the Westfield ranks a year or so later were blind and disabled students, mature students and ex-Servicewomen and two West Africans. Mary Stocks was presiding over possibly the first generation of women students for whom there was no barrier if they had academic ability.

Some years later Mary Stocks was to say of prewar Westfield: 'relatively small numbers, physical isolation from other London colleges and deeply embedded traditions had made it a peculiarly self-contained community'. No wonder Oxford went to the students' heads somewhat.

Mary Stocks was responsible for discipline, academic arrangements, the welfare of the undergraduates. The bread-and-butter running of the college devolved on its Secretary, an administrator appointed by the Council. Mary Stocks regarded herself as lucky to be working with Evelyn Gedge, whose remit included negotiating terms with Oxford University, overseeing all college finances and liaising with the Westfield Council. She had, according to Mary Stocks, 'the ideals of St Francis and the skills of Macchiavelli'.[1]

The Vice-Principal, Bursar, Assistant Bursar and a Registrar who doubled as Principal's Secretary made up the college's senior management team. It was their task to make as easy as possible the immigration of Westfield into Oxford. This inevitably included some pastoral care of young women, mostly from all-girls' schools, plunged suddenly into a mixed society, while enabling them to enjoy the benefits of a new world.

Early in the Lent term, the drama club had the advantage of a speaker from the Oxford Playhouse, Mary Stocks's former connections proving useful once again. Then came a college highlight: a talk by Dorothy Sayers on religious drama. The paths of these two, Stocks and Sayers, almost identical in age, had first crossed when Mary was a young don's wife and Dorothy a graduate of Somerville. In the intervening two decades their lives had diverged greatly but also had interesting parallels. After college, Dorothy worked briefly for the Oxford publisher Basil Blackwell, then at an advertising agency. At about the time Mary Stocks moved to Manchester in 1924, Dorothy Sayers had her first Lord Peter Wimsey book accepted (and had given birth to an illegitimate son). By 1939 she had completed the Wimsey series and written her first religious stage play, *The Zeal of Thy House* (performed in Canterbury Cathedral) and a children's nativity play for radio, *He That Should Come*. So the two women had a good deal in common, not least in the field of writing modern dramatisations from the New Testament. Their major works (Mary's biographies, Dorothy's *The Man Born to be King* and her translation of Dante) were yet to come. They had much to say to each other: 'Talk continued in the Principal's study till 4 a.m.'.

During this term, Mary Stocks began the practice of occasional High Tables with visiting speakers, stage-managed by various departments in turn. She herself spent considerable time and energy lecturing to non-college bodies. In the spring of 1940 she gave talks on unemployment insurance, on drama, social conditions in wartime Britain, and the novelist, Stella Benson.

So far the war had not impinged greatly on college life. Dunkirk and the Battle of Britain were yet to come, women's call-up a distant notion and the number of air raids negligible. In June came Oxford's first air-raid warning, and a scatter of small bombs at Weston-on-the-Green airfield a few miles away. Mary Stocks noted 'War tension continues unabated. Students seem . . . strangely unruffled. For members of the S.C.R. life seems strung out on B.B.C. news bulletins'.

However, the main theme of the summer entries in the logbook is to do with dress rather than danger from the sky. A resident staff meeting was devoted to debate on whether wearing stockings should be compulsory. 'Opinion unanimously against lax view of Principal that they are superfluous garments in warm weather. Result – stockings to be worn with academic dress'. By now she was beginning to earn a reputation as an eccentric dresser. A wartime college photo shows her with very short hair, jersey and check tweed jacket. The legs are not visible, but she had already adopted the almost uniform gear of flat children's-type sandals over woollen stockings. At the end-of-term staff entertainment to the finalists she excelled herself. 'Will the Principal's dignity survive her appearance in trousers and a beard, as Jonah emerging from the whale?'

The summer vacation of 1940 was marked by the temporary lodging of evacuees at St Peter's Hall, among them a hundred children of the Caldecott Community (which Mary's aunt had founded) bombed out of their Maidstone premises.

In October some incendiary bombs fell on Westfield's Hampstead buildings. Only one caused serious damage, but the fires attracted more German bombers to the area. In spite of this added anxiety for Westfield's staff (most of whom still regarded Hampstead as their home) the Michaelmas term was a lively one, with the hockey team beaten 5–6 by the Oxford and Bucks Light Infantry at Cowley Barracks, and an inaugural lecture on the Royal Prerogative by the college Council chairman, Lord Caldecote, soon to become Lord Chancellor.

Soon after this Mary Stocks appeared dramatically at Oxford Magistrates' Court on a double charge (there may be a touch of pride in her report) of blackout offences. (Because of increasing raids there was extra vigilance everywhere over the effectiveness of blacking out.) The college was fined 60s. and 40s., the actual culprit not named.

In November 1940 the college play was the Principal's own *Hail, Nero!*, though she did not name the author in her account of the production. The play had been often performed since its première at Salford seven years before, and several American universities had staged it. Modern dialogue or costume for a classical plot was rather in vogue in the early 1940s; Orson Welles scored highly with the Italian Fascist references in his version of *Julius Caesar*. Westfield's *Hail, Nero!* was staged in the neighbouring Wesley Hall, and the author noted: 'Locasta the poisoner a superb impersonation of an academic female two generations ago'. One wonders whom she had in mind.

For the autumn term 174 new students registered instead of the normal 50. The college's increased popularity was attributed to the extra appeal of academic Oxford. 'It seems to offer the best of both worlds', wrote the Principal, 'Oxford life at London fees'. The inaugural lecture was a novelty – a review of Hitler's speeches by an historian.

During the earlier part of 1941 the staff were much preoccupied with the implications (to them personally and to college organisation) of call-up, compulsory warwork and firefighting. Arrangements were made for students of an age liable to conscription to take their degrees in two years, instead of three, and after much debate certain forms of part-time work were judged suitable. The logbook does not specify what these were, but factory work and farming were among the options.

Meanwhile, Mary Stocks was serving on a government commission appointed to investigate conditions in the women's forces. The original composition of this body gave rise to a minor explosion in the press. The *Evening News* in its *Talk of the Day* commented that setting up an all-male committee for the purpose was 'doomed from the start'. Thelma Cazalet, MP for Islington East, asked witheringly in the House of Commons: 'Would it not be a good thing to set up an all-women's committee to inquire into amenities in the male Services?'[2]

Realising it had blundered, trumpeted the *Evening News*, the Government decided on a clean sweep and announced new names: Thelma Cazalet for the Conservatives, Edith Summerskill, a Labour MP, Violet Markham of the Unemployment Assistance Board, Mrs Walter Elliot, wife of a former Minister of Health, and 'Mrs J.L. Stocks, who knows especially well the minds of girls who go forth to make their way in the world at the end of their university careers,' as the *News* observed. There were also three men on the revised commission. Three of the five women, Elliot, Summerskill and Stocks, went on to become Life Peers.

The *News* columnist was very positive about the need for such a commission. 'Let us hope that the people now called upon will search out every allegation of unfairness, or that lack of the human touch that might mar a young girl's life in the Forces'. And so they did. In her memoirs Mary Stocks recalls visits to women's naval, army and air force units around the country, and the recommendations of the commission as to how they might be made more congenial for young women away from home for the first time. An added bonus for her was the start of a lifelong friendship with the commission chairman, Violet Markham.

From then onwards she was frequently quoted in the press on the status of women in the armed forces, commending their suitability to be officers, medical officers and chaplains – this last a rather revolutionary proposal, since women during the war could progress no farther than assistant chaplains.

At about this time Mary Stocks was reported as saying, in a speech at a school prizegiving:

> It is really no good to be nothing but a home-maker. You are fussy about details, and when you grow up you are a dreadful nuisance because you cannot occupy yourself. Your children ask 'What are we going to do with mother?' But if you are nothing but a professional woman, either you let all your emotions slip back into your work and you become a nuisance to your colleagues . . . Choose the right profession, a really responsible one; don't become a shorthand typist, a slave to other people's letters; don't be in too much of a hurry to marry; and give up the later middle years of your life to public service.[3]

She added that the three careers combined (marriage, job, public service) might be 'pretty burdensome' but 'each will do the others good'. This was fairly radical advice to give girls whose mothers had grown up in the early years of the century. Mary Stocks was beginning to earn a reputation for public outspokenness verging sometimes on the outrageous, but she was only preaching what she herself practised.

As the war dragged on into 1942 shortages and restrictions began to bite deeply into civilian life. In January 1942 Ann Stocks was married in the bombed shell of St James's Church, Piccadilly, to a fellow civil servant from Belfast, Arthur Patterson. It was a wartime wedding marked by austerity, but the officiating priest was the Archbishop of Canterbury.

Towards the end of the academic year Mary Stocks had one of her moments of puritanism which occasionally irritated the students. She gave a student what she called 'a scolding' over bread wasted at breakfast. Next day the logbook reported: 'Complete disappearance of all crusts – but how long will this virtue last?' Toasts to retiring members of staff were drunk in ginger wine, in pursuance of the new frugalism (or the shortage of old wine?)

In June a supper party was held in the garden of the Master's House at St Peter's, for students who were going down from Westfield that year. It was customary on these occasions for the dons to put on an improvised entertainment, but in 1942 they apparently failed to do so. The logbook comments: 'The S.C.R. having refused to contribute its quota, the Principal, Vice Principal and Miss White put on an impromptu triologue, in response to pressure from students. The result may or may not have been funny, but it was certainly vulgar.' The other actors were G.K. Stanley and Beatrice White. The following year the staff toed the line with *Hamlet Act Six*.

Throughout 1942 Mary Stocks continued to attract press attention. She was becoming what she afterwards called herself; a statutory woman on public bodies, a familiar enough name for newspapers to seek her comment on what might loosely be termed women's issues. The *Daily Telegraph* excelled itself with a cumbersome headline: 'Has Done As Much As Three Average Women But Doesn't Think Herself Interesting'. The headline was prompted by a typically sharp (and not new) Stocksian pronouncement: 'I am not a very interesting person really. You see I have never made a million pounds in a sweepstake and I have never been divorced'. The report described her as 'tall, dark-haired, with a fascinating smile', and quoted her as saying she believed in co-education at university level: 'After all when they leave university young men and women have to work together, and it is as well they should begin early'.[4]

Even with wartime newsprint restrictions there was still space to report surprisingly fully her major public lectures. One was at Manchester University on the Victorians, and in particular Victorian women – of whom she claimed to be one. A review of her talk referred to 'rapier wit' and 'rare refreshment'.

At Bridport Town Hall she spoke on Russia. The five-year plan was an attempt to do for Russia in five years what the Industrial

Revolution had done for Britain in 70 years. Lenin had an instinctive flair for mass psychology, and he stepped into the muddle of disillusionment of post-Tsarist Russia at exactly the right moment for his purpose. And the position of women in Russia? In 1932 she had found they had amazing freedom to become plumbers, engineers, wireless operators – or mothers of very large families.

Increasingly the impact of war was felt nationwide. Air raids intensified on the major cities; Oxford was spared direct attacks but suffered by being in the path of enemy bombers making for Coventry or Birmingham; food shortages grew more acute as more Atlantic convoys were sunk; the blackout, limited public transport and diversion of essential workers and resources into armaments all affected people's daily lives. Even sheltered women's colleges were not immune. In the autumn, as fuel controls tightened, term began with a régime of no central heating and no fires in rooms. Mary Stocks reportedly worked wrapped in an eiderdown, which must have inspired some cartoons for the college journal *Hermes*. Her uninhibited logbook entries continued with a 'clearly n.b.g.' observation on a competition essay she was judging, and a highly subjective review of the Easter Term college play, the *Electra of Sophocles*: 'Good performance of – to my mind – uninteresting play'.

In September 1943 the tradition began of an annual reunion for old students. This was held in Hampstead, at the invitation of the Women's Royal Naval Service who now occupied almost all the Westfield buildings. At Oxford even the grim turn the war had now taken did not deter a string of distinguished speakers from coming to dinner, among them Violet Markham, Gilbert Murray, Emil Cammaerts and Dame Katharine Jones, head of the Army nursing service. In a great coup Mary Stocks prevailed on Gilbert Murray to give the first public reading of his latest translation from the Greek, Menander's *The Arbiters*.

Outside the college walls she was still writing, broadcasting and giving lectures. A notable article on careers for women appeared in the *Sunday Times* in September 1943, and an even more controversial one in the *Manchester Guardian* in April. This was a review of a report, *Our Towns*, making public hitherto hidden facts about the care of Britain's wartime evacuees. Her argument was that the analysis of evacuation problems shed necessary light on the grim scene of 'urban destitution and degradation'. This was a subject she knew a good deal about, in view of her experience at the London Council of Social Service and in inner city Manchester. The article refers to nine social evils:

> Wrong spending, bad sleeping habits, bad eating habits, juvenile delinquency, dirty and inadequate clothing, lice, skin diseases, insanitary habits and bodily dirtiness. We are left with the uncomfortable impression that no scheme of social security will suffice by itself to lighten the darkness of this squalid scene . . . a mighty effort of education is needed.[5]

She goes on to reiterate the authors' pinpointing of 'the blood-sucking operations of certain diseducative influences . . . hire purchase agreements, moneylenders, commercialised gambling interests, pawnbrokers, clothing clubs, door-to-door commission salesmen, commercial burial insurance'.

The authors called for nursery schools, and serious study to be undertaken of urban deprivation. It is true this was a pre-welfare state book review, written in 1943, but one would have expected a more constructive and imaginative appraisal of urban poverty and its remedies from Mary Stocks and the *Guardian*.

The spring term of 1944 was chiefly memorable for an emotionally charged college domestic dispute. By now, for various reasons, students had taken on some of the domestic chores. At a college meeting 'certain grievances re domestic duties and meals were aired . . . students were alleged to be organising a petition to Bursar . . . Bursar in flames . . . return of Principal [from London] to find storm brewing'. Four days later the Bursar resigned.

In February, Mary Stocks left hurriedly for London 'to deal with bombed family mansion – return of Principal dusty and discouraged'. This was 8 Queens Gate Terrace, from which her parents had already been evacuated to Dorset. A few months later her infant grandson Mark and his nanny arrived at St Peter's Hall as 'refugees from robot plane operations'. His parents stayed at their desks in Whitehall, Ann rising to be assistant private secretary to Ernest Bevin when he was Minister of Labour. After her marriage, Ann was obliged to work different hours at the Ministry, with responsibility for women's call-up, foreign labour and eventually the resettlement of Poles in Britain.

In October Mary had a duty to perform which was personally a sad one for her: to organise a memorial service in the college chapel for the late Archbishop of Canterbury, her old family friend William Temple. He had died prematurely – many said from overwork – only a few years after his move from York to Canterbury. He and his wife Frances had offered Mary much comfort after the death of John Stocks; he had married Ann Stocks to Arthur Patterson, and christened their son Mark; and but for him it is unlikely Mary Stocks would have been Principal of Westfield.

In other ways the war affected Mary's family. Her son John followed his Uncle Ralph into the Royal Navy, serving for most of the war as an engineer officer. Helen gave up a course in social science at London University to work for a while in the Women's Land Army. She found this unsatisfying, and left agriculture to care for maladjusted children in the Caldecott Community founded by her great-aunt, following its wartime moves from Kent to Dorset and finally back to Kent. When Ann's second son Simon was born it was judged unwise for them to remain in London, so the boys were sent briefly to the school where John Stocks's brother Charles was headmaster.

Both daughters spent occasional weekends with their mother at St Peter's, and there were visits whenever possible to see Dr and Mrs Brinton, now in their eighties, by the sea in Dorset. 'Sometimes she talked to us about administrative problems', said Ann.

> The older members of staff found it difficult to adjust to wartime conditions. Sometimes she was irritated with the college Council, but this was an administrative challenge where her experience at the London Council of Social Service came in useful. To escape from the modern world she would retreat to Trollope and Jane Austen.[6]

The hopeful progress of the war after D-Day lightened the public mood in late 1944 and early 1945. The Principal reported on a college dance: 'All serene, no interruptions from outside. Only contretemps concerned mismanagement of three barrels of cider'.

Mary Stocks and Violet Markham found themselves together again investigating women's service units, this time in Europe. They visited France, Holland and Germany, passed files of German prisoners marching across the German border ('I must confess to finding it a pleasant sight', wrote Mary), flew in a light aircraft over the devastated Ruhr Valley, and signed the register at a Brussels hotel as Brigadier Markham and Colonel Stocks.

Mary enjoyed Violet's company; she was, among other points of interest, a racehorse owner, a bon viveur and author of a book on architecture.

By the Easter vacation of 1945 it was clear Westfield would be able to return to Hampstead by the end of the academic year. The long blackout was at last lifted in April, and Victory-in-Europe Day was celebrated with street parties, bonfires and fireworks. Westfield held a service of thanksgiving in St Peter's Chapel – 'the rest of the day was chaotic'.

The return to London was far from smooth. Weeks passed before the Admiralty announced the WRNS was leaving Hampstead, and staff were on tenterhooks in case the necessary plans could not be finalised for the Michaelmas term. On 4 July, American Independence Day, the Bursar made a decision to go ahead with plans for an August move.

In the middle of all this excitement and uncertainty, Mary Stocks added her quota of both by standing for Parliament, as her husband had done twenty years before. She stood as Independent Progressive candidate for London University against Sir Ernest Graham-Little, National Independent, who had held the seat since 1924. (An earlier candidate – for Labour – had been H.G. Wells.)

This was the dramatic postwar election which produced a Labour landslide victory, totally unexpected by Churchill's followers. There was strong Labour support among Service voters. The university seats (where the electors were British graduates of the university concerned, no matter where they lived) were a special case. In the absence of a Labour candidate there was a straight fight between Graham-Little, representing the broad right, and Mary Stocks, for the broad left.

Mary lost by 149 votes, capturing 49.5 per cent of the total vote. Sixty-three per cent of an electorate of just under 24,000 voted. Phlegmatically she recorded in the college logbook: 'University Election. Sir E. Graham-Little defeats M.D. Stocks by 149 votes on a recount'. She had indicated she was prepared to resign as Principal if she was elected. It is difficult to see how the two roles could have been combined, but Mary Stocks, if anyone, had the temperament to do it. We do not know how distressed she was at losing when the tide was running so strongly for Labour, where her true sympathies lay. We can only guess how vigorous a Member of Parliament she would have made.

In the same election J.B. Priestley stood, also as an Independent Progressive for Cambridge University. He came third. A.P. Herbert did rather better, standing as an Independent for Oxford University, and he was elected. For Combined English Universities – with an electorate of over 40,000 and two seats to be contested – Mary's old friend and feminist colleague from Manchester and Liverpool days, Eleanor Rathbone, stood as an Independent and topped the poll. She had held the seat since 1929 and was expected to hold it indefinitely. The last days of the wartime Parliament had seen Eleanor's great triumph. After a long battle (in which Mary had always supported her) the law was changed to allow family allowances to be paid to mothers instead of to fathers. When this was passed, the whole House of Commons cheered Eleanor.

So the second Oxford era came to an end with perhaps something of an anticlimax for Mary Stocks. The move from Oxford to Hampstead held no particular charm for her, except nearness to her family and the convenience of extra college space. She would be starting again, as it were, in new surroundings and with increased responsibilities. The close election defeat must have been a blow, though she scarcely mentions it in her various writings. She had flourished, essentially, on the challenges of wartime Oxford, and her acute sense of humour never deserted her. Hampstead might well be expected to lack Oxford's drama and tensions; it might even seem tame.

In the third week of August 1945 the remaining Westfield staff girded their loins for a return to home base after an absence of exactly six years. It took two years or more for what they called the Oxford myth to die away, until the last Oxford intake student had finished her degree. Even then there were a few postgraduates who felt nostalgic about Oxford, and some ex-Servicewomen returning to complete degrees begun years earlier. Rapport was good between the women from the forces and the new school leavers, but something like a generation gap yawned between them. The staff also fell into two camps, pre- and post-Oxford. All these groups Mary Stocks did her best to weld together into a homogeneous community, but the old Hampstead cloistered self-sufficiency had gone for ever.

Postwar women students (whether ex-Service or not) wore trousers most of the time, smoked, drank cheap sherry, had regular male visitors and haunted the West End theatre queues for cheap seats. Boyfriends included officers, a clergyman or two, an Oxbridge rowing blue, a junior diplomat, plenty of overseas students and the future general secretary of a major trade union. Cars and motor-cycles were still a rarity in postwar Britain, but around London these were scarcely needed. Coffee replaced tea as the universal stimulant, and nearly every student had a radio in her room. Coffee, toast and prototype pop music whiled away the after-dark hours.

Apart from the WRNS occupation, parts of the college had been taken over by the Tavistock Clinic, and briefly, during heavy raids, by the YMCA; so the buildings that staff and students came back to were by no means derelict. The gardens had been cared for, the resident Secretary Miss E.C. Gedge (that same formidable woman described in the logbook as combining the skills of Macchiavelli and St Francis) had kept a watchful eye on all the premises.

Mary spoke later of Westfield's 'definite and civilised ethos'. For her it was a shade too genteel and Victorian in 1939, but by 1945 the combined influence of the war, Oxford and Mrs Stocks had decisively liberated Westfield.

Back in London, Mary Stocks served on ever more government committees. As she confessed, with the back-up of a competent administrative staff she found it hard to resist invitations, and all her advisory work undoubtedly raised the college profile. The traffic was two-way, for many of her contacts in public life came to Westfield as guest speakers, something that would have been difficult to put in place without that network of public faces.

After some minor contretemps over burst pipes and what was described as 'occupational débris' left by the WRNS, Westfield reopened after its long migration on 12 October 1945. Mary Stocks wrote: 'Great hurly-burly. Everyone new to everything'. On the second day she observed 'Queuing system at breakfast didn't seem to work well' and a student called Pankhurst was elected as fire captain, which seemed symbolic. On the first Sunday of term Holy Communion was celebrated jointly by an Anglican bishop and a Church Army prebendary, in keeping with Westfield's broad church principles.

Three weeks after the start of term came a notable day for the Principal. Untraditionally, she herself gave the Inaugural Lecture, and her subject was London. Who better to speak to this title? A Londoner by birth, upbringing and education, Mary Stocks reserved for her birthplace a special respect not dimmed by years of relative exile in Oxford and Lancashire. The Mayor of Hampstead took the chair, and a crowd of eminent guests stayed for tea.

On Guy Fawkes Day (the first which could be wholeheartedly celebrated since the lifting of blackout) the logbook records student activities in its usual droll style.

> Bonfire on suitably chosen site in new strip of garden (i.e. with a view to burning garden debris and providing wood-ash for soil as well as entertainment for students) . . . Reason to believe that an effigy of a Wren was burned at an earlier stage – but this had better not be known.

It was during this term that a pleasant ceremony took place to mark five years of peaceful co-operation between Westfield and St Peter's Hall, where Westfield could so easily have been a cuckoo in the nest. Two members of staff and two students went to Oxford to plant a magnolia tree in St Peter's quad 'and to present a silver loving cup – really a very lovely one – in memory of our sojourn . . . it was received by the Master. Followed by sherry in the loving-cup'.

A postwar problem involving ex-Servicewomen unable to sit the entrance examination was resolved by deciding to admit them as non-residents (one detects here the Principal's commonsense approach to problem-solving). As always there was no shortage of distinguished speakers and overnight guests: Gilbert Murray; Miss M.E. Popham, the Principal of Cheltenham Ladies' College; Veronica Wedgwood (eminent historian and a kinswoman of Mary Stocks); E.V. Rieu (translator and editor of Penguin classics); and Lord Caldecote, the Lord Chancellor, who was presented with a portrait and a silver plate on his retirement as chairman of the college Council.

A very Stocksian comment was entered in the logbook while scholarship examination papers were being marked during the Christmas vacation – 'an unusually poor lot – astonishingly immature' – yet only days later at interview they were found to be 'unusually charming and mature. Do personal charm and academic capacity vary inversely? God forbid!'

In the fashion-conscious forties Mary Stocks's eccentricity of dress became more noticeable as many young women around her adopted the New Look, Christian Dior and elegant shoes. She stuck firmly to her baggy wool suits, thick stockings and childish brown sandals. The outfit was neither bizarre nor bluestocking, but somewhere between the two. It suited her no-nonsense personality and remained unchanged, more or less, for thirty years.

Other habits which might have seemed faintly annoying in others endeared her to her staff and students. One was a practice mentioned by several former students when they were asked what they chiefly remembered of her. The answer ran like this: 'She always sat in the front row for visiting lectures and appeared to be sound asleep. Yet when the lecturer stopped speaking she was always ready with the first question, and right on the ball'.

Mary Stocks had some pet dislikes. Hats, for one. Her family can only recall her wearing a hat for some government committees, the magistracy and her installation in the House of Lords. Make-up she abhorred and never used. Sport, except for sailing, scarcely entered her life (though some early married photos do show her as a reluctant performer on skates in Switzerland). Television she saw as an enemy of radio, and fought long and hard to delay the coming of commercial television.

As a college principal she was especially noted for her inability to remember names (admitted more than once in her writings). In dealing with students she overcame this problem by simply addressing everyone as 'Miss'. My own favourite memory is of one occasion when I was 'on the carpet' in her study for staying out after hours. Locking-up time was at the (to liberated women) now ridiculous hour of 10 o'clock. Later than that, the porter had to be roused and one's name and arrival time recorded in a special book. There were of course alternative modes of entry, but these depended on the connivance of friends who were quite likely to be out themselves. The dialogue next morning in the Principal's study went like this:

> *Principal*: Well, Miss – er – so you came in at half past eleven last night?
> *Student*: Yes.
> *Principal*: You do know the regulations, Miss – er –?
> *Student*: Yes.
> *Principal*: Well, that'll be two and sixpence and I hope it was worth it.

Her study door was virtually always open for student gatherings (with cakes and the now obligatory coffee). She encouraged a vast range of student societies, and often attended their meetings. She revived the college divinity lectures and made a special point of always taking the chair.

In January, as the Lent term of 1946 began, the Principal told the staff she was again standing for Parliament, 'with an offer of resignation if elected'. This was an altogether more realistic objective than her 1945 candidacy. She had been chosen to stand at a by-election caused by the sudden death of her former political ally, friend and mentor, Eleanor Rathbone. Miss Rathbone had been returned to Parliament as an Independent Member for Combined English Universities with – yet again – a handsome majority in the Labour landslide election of August 1945. Although she was 68 and had held the seat since 1929, she was at the height of her powers and passionately active over the question of refugees and Palestine. Her death happened without warning on New Year's Day 1946.

There were four candidates for one seat: H.G. Strauss (Conservative), Mary Stocks (Independent but supported by the Rathbonites), Sir Ernest Simon (Independent; an ex-Liberal moving towards Labour), and Sidney Wormald (Independent Labour). With Labour riding high in the polls it seemed there might be a close result.

Only 42 per cent of a total electorate of 43,438 bothered to vote. The tradition of not campaigning actively for university seats was maintained. If there had been vigorous campaigning it seems possible Mary Stocks would have won. In the event the final result was:

H.G. Strauss	5,483
Mrs M.D. Stocks	5,124
Sir E.D. Simon	4,028
S. Wormald	3,414

So the principalship remained unshaken, and a footnote was added by a debate in March between a team from Westfield and a Canadian Forces team from Watford, referred to as the Khaki University. The matter debated was 'Woman's place is in the home', and, to the mortification of the home side, the proposition was carried.

During the spring of 1946, food shortages intensified, so the main cooked meal of the day at college was transferred to midday, and only a light supper provided in the evening. This expedient carried on for nearly two years. All through the academic year dispute rumbled on about the possible abolition of the Botany Department, and considerable diplomacy was needed by Mrs Stocks to sustain morale in the threatened department. There was no lack of excellence in the department, but it was endangered by a process of rationalising the structure of a college which offered no other science subjects. However, the logbook for 17 May offered light relief. Various members of staff had kept up a vigil in darkness for a night or two hoping to catch a suspected intruder. 'On May 16th four students were caught engaged in illicit entry . . . And on May 17th the Bursar and Sister Adams caught one another'.

The spring term of 1947 opened with the presentation of a drawing of Mary Stocks done by Percy Smith, given to the college by the students in memory of Oxford. These were the last finalists who had begun their college careers at St Peter's Hall, still nostalgically recalled.

A secret ballot of the college Council voted by 16 to 6 to close the doomed Botany Department, on the advice of the university and the University Grants Committee. Westfield was to become mainly an arts degree school within London University. The situation was not an easy one for the Principal, but the records indicate no criticism of her handling of the Council or the botanists.

This was the time when student elections produced a Senior Student and a Secretary of the Student Union who were both ex-Servicewomen. Shortly afterwards the Principal's logbook recorded an incident which seems so far removed from today's world as to have legendary quality. A missing student was 'believed to have gone off in the company of a young man . . . It later transpired the young man appears unconnected with university activities – Allah be praised'. (The reference is probably to intercollegiate drama rehearsals.)

Almost the final entry for the 1946–47 academic year refers to a visit from a former student working for UNRRA (the United Nations Rehabilitation and Relief Association) in Germany. 'Miss Harvey fresh from Berlin and full of gruesome and discouraging tales'.

In April 1947 Mary Stocks found herself yet again on a government committee for which she had special qualifications – as chairman (this was before the days when the feminist left campaigned for the non-discriminatory title 'chair' or 'chairperson') of a working party set up by the Minister of Health, Aneurin Bevan, to inquire into the recruitment and training of midwives. There was a current shortage of practising midwives, and Mary's involvement with early birth control clinics, as well as district nursing, gave her a particular interest in the whole problem.

The opening of the Michaelmas term in 1947 again exercised her powers of diplomacy. A member of staff who had been on extended sick leave appeared in college unexpectedly, and made 'a very unseemly oration to first year students' which led to 'police intervention'. The Principal's logbook does not specify the nature of the offence.

A highlight of the new term was the arrival of two third-year students from Barnard College, in the USA, and of Tejumade Aderemi from Nigeria. Teju became one of the most popular students of her year, and her engaging personality livened up Westfield. The first logbook reference to her reads: 'All up. Newcomers include the coal-black daughter of an African chief.' At that time there was of course, no Race Relations legislation to curb such an uninhibited allusion if it had been made in public.

A duty the Principal carried out with regularity and dignity was to take morning prayers in the college chapel. In her books she stresses how important this was to her personally, and how it developed her talent as a Bible reader and commentator, later of value to the BBC. She was proud of the fact that she maintained a non-denominational profile in the chapel services, and resisted all pressure to appoint a college chaplain (who would have been male and Anglican). This is in accord with her stated opposition to conventional churchgoing practice.

A student described her as ' sympathetic but astringent' and she was remembered by past students as much for her interest in college activities as for her unconventional dress and indifference to what she was eating. Sitting next to her at High Table on formal occasions was no problem; she initiated the conversation, generally on topical rather than academic matters, and largely sustained it. Wise students did not attempt to discuss the evening's menu.

Career advice was not within the college's brief, but Mary Stocks's wide-ranging knowledge of the world outside college walls made her an ideal informal adviser. By the end of her régime, in 1951, a summary of career prospects for new graduates covered social work, technology, journalism, horticulture, local government, as well as the more obvious occupations for chiefly arts graduates: teaching, librarianship, bilingual secretarial work, the Civil Service.

In 1947 Westfield language students broke new ground for their year abroad – the first German speakers studied in war-torn Vienna.

Discipline was seldom mentioned in the logbook as a problem. In her memoirs Mary Stocks wrote that being a college principal in her time was child's play to what she imagined it might be twenty years later. A greater problem was the acute shortage of food in the years following the war. Student malnutrition, she noted, seemed for a year or two a real possibility. Survivors of the immediate postwar years at Westfield speak with feeling of snoek and disguised whalemeat, dried egg mixtures, endless margarine and synthetic jam, and grey unnamed substances posing as meat.

During the last five years of Mary Stocks's reign (her word) the college expanded in numbers, from just over 100 on the return from Oxford to more than twice that figure by 1951, and in buildings, roughly doubling its accommodation. Her task was to win for Westfield a sizeable share of the university grants available at the time. It was a period of generous academic funding, and Westfield did not do badly. In 1950 Mary Stocks was appointed to the University Grants Committee.

The end of the war had brought some family sadness and some pleasures. John Stocks junior left the Navy and joined a major international oil firm. He married an ex-Wren, and they had a son and a daughter. In 1946 Dr Roland Brinton died, aged 88, and a few months later Constance Brinton also died, one of the last survivors of Sir Alexander Rendel's remarkable family. For Mary the loss of both parents was made keener by a sense of lost family memories and links with their illustrious nineteenth century records. The two deaths, following soon after that of Eleanor Rathbone, perhaps impelled Mary towards picking up the threads of her writing career which had been in abeyance since Manchester. Two projects lay ahead which she entered into wholeheartedly, in tandem with her last years as Principal. Her much expanded writing commitments to some extent arose indirectly from her past acquaintance with public persons and public bodies; but there is no doubt she greatly enjoyed writing, and this was her chief medium of self-expression in the post-Westfield years.

The first of these historical publications in fact appeared when

Plate 1: Mary Stocks (née Brinton), aged 22, on her honeymoon in Rome, 1913. (Photo Mrs Ann Patterson.)

Plate 2: Mary Stocks aged 33, on holiday with (left to right) John, Ann, Helen, 1924. (Photo Mrs Ann Patterson.)

Plate 3: At a reception to welcome her husband John as Liverpool University's new Vice-Chancellor, 1937.

Plate 4: In her study as Principal of Westfield College, with Candida, her white cat, 1945. (Copyright Keystone Press.)

Plate 5: With Sir Frederick Marquis (later Lord Woolton) at an honorary degree ceremony (D. Litt.) at Liverpool University, 1955. (Copyright *Guardian*.)

Plate 6: Mary Stocks interviewing Nancy, Viscountess Astor, for the tenth anniversary of *Woman's Hour*, 1956. (Copyright BBC.)

Plate 7: The *Any Questions* team at Combe Martin, Devon, in 1959. From left: Gerald Nabarro, MP, Patrick Gordon-Walker, MP, farmer Jack Houghton-Brown, Mary Stocks and Freddie Grisewood as chairman. (Copyright Powell's Photographers, Ilfracombe, Devon.)

Plate 8: Baroness Stocks of Kensington and Chelsea with Lord Goodman of Westminster and Lord Evans of Hungershall, when Lord Evans was taking his seat in the House of Lords, 1967. (Copyright Universal Pictorial Press.)

she was in her prime as Principal of Westfield, and must have entailed some midnight-oil burning alongside her other preoccupations. *Fifty Years in Every Street* (published in 1945) was the fiftieth anniversary account of Manchester University Settlement, founded in 1895. Again the double meaning pleases: Every Street was the actual postal address of the Settlement, but it also carries wider implications. Writing the Settlement story gave her both pain and pleasure because of its close association with John Stocks for thirteen years; in the twenties he had turned its fortunes round from near bankruptcy to what Mary called 'a new golden age'. Aspects of the work of the Settlement which appealed to her most were its part in developing social reform and voluntary service in a deprived area of Manchester, and the nurturing of the Wilbraham Community Centre on a vast postwar housing estate.

Possibly her best-researched and most stylishly written book was *Eleanor Rathbone, a Biography*, published in 1949, three years after Eleanor's death. For this Mary had been given access by the Rathbone family to all necessary papers among the family archives in Liverpool, and in London her own Labour Party contacts built up a rounded picture of Eleanor's long Parliamentary careers. Mary needed little persuasion to take on the biography, even while running Westfield and half a dozen committees and standing as a candidate for Eleanor's former Parliamentary seat. Eleanor had been a personal friend and fellow fighter for more than twenty years. They had much in common.

In 1902 Eleanor's father had died, when she was 30, and she found herself taking on more and more of his philanthropic and public service commitments on Merseyside. One of these was the Victoria Women's Settlement, and here a new warden, Elizabeth Macadam, a social worker from Scotland, had recently been appointed. Eleanor and Elizabeth became friends and companions for the rest of their lives, Elizabeth dying very soon after Eleanor.

In the 1920s they set up home together in a small eighteenth-century house in Westminster, and here Elizabeth's passion for household management made it a busy centre of hospitality. Both women had their own careers, but they interacted at every point. Elizabeth's social work reinforced Eleanor's campaigning for women's rights, family allowances, the status of women in India, Jewish refugees. They both enjoyed foreign travel, driving open cars and swimming. Mary tells a story which seems to pinpoint their relationship:

> For those who accompanied Eleanor [on her travels, there was] the problem of accounting for some of the things she had chosen to accumulate. Ever fresh in the mind of one of her friends is Elizabeth's revolt at the appearance of Eleanor emerging at the zero moment of a departure from Dorset with a large stone, a coil of derelict rope and an unseemly paper bag containing loose cigarettes . . . Why, o why had she elected to add these final items to an already variegated baggage train? Her answer was simple: the stone was a nice shape. The rope might come in useful at some future date for bathing. The cigarettes had to be put somewhere.[7]

In 1934 Eleanor and Elizabeth went on an official visit to Palestine to see for themselves the nature of the Arab–Jewish problem. They went with open minds, but Eleanor returned with strong Zionist sympathies which found their outlet in her wartime work with the Parliamentary Committee on Refugees.

Bombed out of their much-loved Romney Street home, they found another just as vulnerable to air raids and carried on as if nothing had happened. At the end of the war they moved to Highgate, not far from Westfield College in Hampstead, and here Eleanor died with tragic suddenness after a routine visit to her dentist.

The biography is workmanlike and unemotional. One detects Mary Stocks's profound admiration for the woman she is writing about, but this never obtrudes. She mentions herself once or twice, in the third person. No sources are listed, but there are appendices in the form of letters from Eleanor Rathbone to 'Some Indian Friends', expressing her concern at the condition of women in India, and from Jawaharlal Nehru (then in prison) in reply to her. The biography was never reprinted, but it remains the standard work on one of Britain's first and ablest women Members of Parliament.

The preface begins: 'It was a terrifying privilege to be entrusted with the writing of Eleanor Rathbone's life'. It goes on to outline Mary Stocks's apprehensions about meeting Eleanor and Elizabeth Macadam in a possible afterlife. First, that Eleanor would rebuke her for omitting the names of so many of her friends and colleagues.

Next, that Elizabeth would recall she had specifically asked not to be mentioned. Mary Stocks had an answer ready for them both. Her excuse to Eleanor for her omissions was the postwar paper shortage; to Elizabeth she would say, 'Dear Elizabeth, you are part and parcel of Eleanor's life and cannot be disentangles from it'. She hoped they would forgive her; she was 'grateful beyond measure' for the friendship of them both.

Such a biography, written in the later years of the century, would scarcely cause an eyebrow to be raised. But in the 1940s the close relationship of two well-known women was a sensitive matter, needing to be delicately handled. Mary Stocks struck a careful balance between intrusion into their private lives and suppression of facts. Miss Rathbone emerges as a strict, perhaps puritanical figure, one who would today be labelled a workaholic, dedicated till the day she died to certain causes, fond of swimming, driving (she had her first car in 1925), country holidays. People referring to her would invariably use such words as ardour, fanaticism, persistence, doggedness. Against this had to be set the fact that 'her ardour was apt to create a mood of sales resistance', and Ministers who incurred her wrath in the House had to suffer much.

Much of the book is concerned with Eleanor Rathbone's almost lifelong fight over family allowances, recognised at last by the passing of the wartime Government's Family Allowance Bill in June 1945. Mary Stocks had of course been deeply involved in this campaign. She traces it from Eleanor Rathbone's early upbringing in a strongly philanthropic Liverpool family, through her years as a city councillor and her sixteen years as an Independent Member of Parliament.

A social historian writing in the 1970s commented that the payment of family allowances to women had seemed 'impossibly utopian despite Eleanor Rathbone's energetic campaign in the thirties' – utopian, that is, until the war changed women's circumstances and public opinion. Mary Stocks's books charts, from within, the crossing of that particular hurdle towards equality.

Later in the book she summarises Eleanor's other major contributions to lessening the sum of human misery:

> Her imagination, working as it had worked for the Huyton refugees, for wandering Jews, for African girls, for Indian child wives, for overdriven working mothers, for neglected widows

under the old Liverpool Poor Law, spared her nothing of the postwar scene . . . Sometimes it seemed as if she were unbearably oppressed by the magnitude of that sea of suffering in relation to the puny efforts of such human endeavour as could be mobilised for its redress.[8]

New problems arose to preoccupy Eleanor Rathbone: rising population, the atomic bomb, world famine. Mary Stocks attributes to her a perhaps apocryphal answer to a question about the futility of bringing children into the world with the prospect of early annihilation:

Even if the children born have to face early extinction – even granting that probability, which in fact I don't – they will have lived. Life is good. They will at any rate have had a little of it.[9]

This embraces a philosophy which Mary Stocks shared very positively with her biographical subject, who had been also a powerful role model for her in her political objectives. To criticise is to carp, but the book might have been strengthened by a closer look at Eleanor Rathbone's relationships with her Parliamentary colleagues. What did it feel like to be a woman debating, battling in an almost-wholly male House of Commons?

Mary Stocks was in the habit of saying that Eleanor Rathbone had been the third strongest influence in her life, after Edith Rendel and John Stocks. The two women had met during the First World War, when Stocks was on the committee and Rathbone president of the National Union of Women's Suffrage Societies. There was an instant rapport, and they worked together for this less militant women's rights group tirelessly until the vote was achieved in 1917. Thereafter their paths crossed often.

In 1922, two years before the Stocks family's migration to Manchester, Eleanor, then a Liverpool city councillor, stood for Parliament as an Independent for the Liverpool seat of East Toxteth, but lost to a Conservative after something of a smear campaign. Thereafter she lived partly in London, devoting herself to the cause of family allowances, the position of women in India, and various social issues important to her through her civic work in Liverpool.

Eleanor stood for Parliament again in 1929 as Independent candidate for the Combined Universities (Liverpool, Manchester,

Birmingham, Leeds, Sheffield, Durham, Bristol and Reading) and
was elected by a comfortable majority. Although canvassing was
not permitted for the university seats, it is hardly likely that Mary
Stocks, now well established in Manchester, did not contribute to
Eleanor's campaign. From 1929 till 1946 Eleanor held her seat
continuously.

Just after the 1929 election both Eleanor and Mary went to Berlin
as delegates at a conference of the International Women's Suffrage
Alliance. Mary recalled this summer visit to pre-Fascist Germany
with immense pleasure:

> The German people were liberal, feminist, pacific and lavishly
> hospitable . . . one could talk freely to one's German friends,
> watch experimental drama under enlightened Jewish direction
> . . . from time to time catch sight of Einstein in the street or at
> the opera.[10]

For the next few years Eleanor's passionate involvement in
Indian women's rights took her away from Mary Stocks's observation, but as the Second World War loomed Eleanor's concerns
focused more and more on the plight of refugees – in particular
Jewish refugees – and Mary's various committee posts brought
her more closely into contact with Eleanor Rathbone, now one of
Westminster's best known MPs.

During the war, while Mary Stocks was pursuing her new role as
college principal in Oxford, Eleanor and Elizabeth Macadam were
bombed or burned out of more than one London building, but
carried on with their work regardless, merely moving on. In 1945
Eleanor, now 72, stood for Parliament yet again and was elected
with a huge majority. The Family Allowance Act, virtually her main
life's work, became law in August 1945. She turned her attention
even more vigorously to the anomalies of rent rebates, the plight
of homeless people in postwar Europe, the Palestine question. Her
energy was no less, her concerns just as pressing. She died at the
height of her political powers.

Within a few months of her death Eleanor's family and friends
asked Mary Stocks to undertake her biography, and her political
allies had asked Mary to stand as a Parliamentary candidate in her
place. She did both with some trepidation, but willingly. For a while
it really did seem that Eleanor's mantle had fallen on her.

As it happened Mary Stocks's radio career really took off about eight months before the Rathbone biography was published, and the twin activities, broadcasting and writing, fuelled each other. The first of her many appearances on 'Woman's Hour' was on 18 August 1948. She gave an eight-minute talk, 'I Knew Eleanor Rathbone', in the series *I Knew Her*. *Woman's Hour* was approaching its peak popularity, with a daily audience of five million, mainly but by no means exclusively housewives.

In 1949 Mary's radio reputation was secure enough for her to be appointed a member of the Beveridge Committee to review the operations of the BBC before its charter (granted in 1927) came up for renewal in 1952. One of the issues under scrutiny was the possible introduction of commercial broadcasting. All but one of Lord Beveridge's committee eventually declared in favour of the public service monopoly. The dissenter was Selwyn Lloyd, a Conservative MP, and it was somewhat ironic that he and Mary were chosen to investigate how matters stood in the USA, in terms of public versus private broadcasting. Together these two, diametrically opposed politically, travelled to Canada, Washington and New York. What she saw on the tour merely reinforced Mary Stocks's disapproval of sponsored television. She was dismayed when Attlee's Labour Government delayed implementing the recommendations of the Beveridge Report. They left the way open (as she saw it) for the Conservatives, when they came to power, to bring in the 1953 Television Act which was midwife to commercial television in Britain. Mary Stocks is on record as saying that a free vote in the House of Commons might have held up the Act, but she acknowledged there was a very powerful lobby pressing for independent television. She also said the Conservative Government might have reacted differently if someone other than Beveridge, persona non grata with the Tories, had chaired the pro-monopoly committee.

Meanwhile college continued to present challenges which she relished. The first few weeks of 1948 saw an influx of noteworthy visitors, among them Mary's cousin Pernel Strachey (lately Principal of Newnham), Professor Gilbert Murray, who spoke to a crowded hall on 'What's wrong with the Sophists?' and a missionary speaker, who came to promote recruitment to the mission field. The Principal's comment on this was 'Prospect not encouraging'.

At this time staff meetings were much concerned with food and gas economies. The logbook described the postwar food situation as increasingly meagre. Most staple foods were still rationed and the daily allowance for students' bedsit teas was limited to two slices of bread (for toast), a scrape of margarine and some synthetic jam. Nonetheless a picnic lunch was provided on 20 November so that students could line the streets of central London for Princess Elizabeth's wedding. Some even took up pavement positions overnight, a chilly exercise in November.

The Lent term was enlivened by college participation in a Light Programme radio quiz against students from Haverford College, Pennsylvania. Little did the Westfield students suspect that their Principal would achieve fame one day doing something rather similar.

Still milking her wide circle of acquaintance, Mary Stocks set up a lecture on the state of the working classes during the Industrial Revolution. She invited along the industrial editor of the *Manchester Guardian* and a former colonial governor. The following term visitors included Richard Crossman (later to become Minister of Housing and Local Government in Harold Wilson's Cabinet) and Maude Royden-Shaw, an early fighter for the ordination of women priests. At the time at least two Westfield students were considering becoming Baptist ministers; the Baptists already had a number of women in post.

A Colonial Office representative came to dinner to discuss what Westfield could do for West African students, and here was a cause Mary Stocks could wholeheartedly espouse. She had already made several broadcasts in the BBC West African Service on women's educational topics; Westfield had currently two West African students in residence, from Nigeria and Ghana, and others were applying. The problem was that their particular educational backgrounds did not (with some exceptions) equip them to sit for honours single subject degrees, yet posts in the Colonial Education Service required them to have these degrees rather than general ones. Mary Stocks wrote to the Director of Scholars at the Colonial Office: 'We are always prepared by hook or by crook to find vacancies for Colonial women students whose standard of work makes it possible to sit for an honours degree'. She pointed out that at least one West African student was 'not up to standard, but we are doing our best to carry her along'.[11]

The correspondence dragged on for a year. Mary Stocks, writing to Dr E.C. Martin, a member of college staff seconded to Ghana, felt more should be done to prepare students intending to come to England, and to guide their choice of subject. The English degree course was particularly unsuitable because of its heavy emphasis on Anglo-Saxon, yet most colonial students tended to choose English: 'Could we not produce a Pass degree course for them?' Finally she wrote to Arthur Creech Jones, Secretary of State for the Colonies. 'West African students start with a linguistic handicap and a lack of European background which makes it difficult for them to get the best out of an honours degree course. Could not the regulations be modified for West African students?' The college was also prepared to interview Caribbean students, and to put them through test papers. History was recommended as the most relevant subject.

A reply came from Lord Listowel, Under Secretary at the Colonial Office. He suggested that an honours degree might be mandatory for the general Colonial Education Service, but probably not for teaching in the students' own territories. He knew of some authorities who would accept a pass degree as a teaching qualification, but 'West African students are very ambitious'. His final advice was to treat each case on its merits, and indeed Westfield did increase its intake of students from the former colonial territories.

Another attempt to broaden Westfield's intake was much less successful. After an approach from Cadbury's, the chocolate manufacturing firm, Westfield set up a scholarship for a mature student to be chosen from among Cadbury employees – 'Provided she reaches the required college entrance standard'. In the first year no applicant was found, and in the second year the chosen woman opted for social science which Westfield did not offer. After this the scheme seems to have lapsed.

A staff meeting during 1948 considered the fate of several students whose interim results had been so poor they might be asked to leave. This sad business happened every year, but 1948 was remarkable for that crisp forthrightness of the Principal's logbook comment: 'N.B.G. – consider alternative career'.

The summer vacation that year was an exceptionally busy one for Mary Stocks, who remained in residence throughout. In July a posse of Anglican overseas bishops and their wives came into residence for the Lambeth Conference (Westfield was not the conference venue, but was offering hospitality). In the middle of this major invasion Mary had two impressive dinner guests; an old friend from her early Oxford time – Tyrone Guthrie, now director of the National Theatre at the Old Vic – and the Oni of Ife, a Nigerian chief and father of that same Teju Aderemi who was so popular in the student ranks (described by the Principal as 'doing well – a very vital and intelligent young woman'). Mary Stocks recorded in her autobiography, as well as in the logbook, an incident of the Oni's visit. '[He arrived] in full African splendour accompanied by "grand vizier" and daughter. Received by M.D.S. and the Bishop of Liberia, whose wife prostrated herself on the front steps'.[12] After this singular mark of respect the Oni had sherry with college staff and no fewer than three bishops. History does not record how their womenfolk greeted him.

Visitors continued to pour in regardless of the bishops in residence: 30 American postgraduates on a course, the Archbishop of Canterbury and Mrs Fisher (dining with the bishops), and finally a crowd of old students for their annual weekend. There was a tea party, a children's party, Holy Communion, meals and talks, one on the ordination of women (a recurring topic in the Westfield archives, though still half a century away). Mary Stocks was much struck by the fact that the bishops discussed what the Church could do for displaced persons in Europe, and appeared to come to the negative conclusion that nothing could be done.

At last came August and the end of the summer invaders. The Principal's logbook for the academic year 1947–1948 concludes laconically: 'August 3: Librarians out. August 4: Bishops out. The rest is silence'.

Tyrone Guthrie came back in November to start off the new season of lectures with one on contemporary theatre. This was an outstanding success, with the hall overflowing. Westfield was beginning to score some notable successes in university drama festivals, helped by a talented current generation of actors and considerable encouragement from the Principal. There was in fact a plethora of end-of-term plays, dances, parties – one of which provoked the comment: 'Some goings-on in Philpotts Hall, and in the street, which will have the be inquired into'.

During 1949 the logbook becomes largely concerned with routine administrative matters. There are fewer acerbic remarks about student activities, perhaps because Mary Stocks had now completed a decade as college Principal and had, as the students might have said, 'seen it all before'. Visitors included Professor Ian Richmond lecturing on Roman Britain, Dame Myra Curtis of Girton College, Edith Summerskill (Minister of Health in Attlee's Government) and a batch of Cubs and Brownies from the hostel and social settlement at Hoxton, in London's bomb-shattered East End, where Westfield students ran the two packs.

Voluntary social service was another strong college tradition which Mary Stocks very much approved and sought to expand. Despite the growth of the welfare state under socialist government, and the building of infra-structures to support its new provisions, the social services were still underdeveloped and had by no means superseded the network of voluntary agencies dating back in many cases to the turn of the century. The London Blitz, evacuation and relief for the homeless had in fact generated a whole new webb of support groups offering meals-on-wheels, day centres for the elderly, children's adventure playgrounds, and the like.

A request had come from the North Kensington Council of Social Service (in the area of the Stocks family home) for students to help with teas, gardening and odd jobs at an understaffed old people's home. She deflected some students from the now well-resourced Hoxton Settlement to meet the Kensington need, for a trial period. This was not easy. A young people's hostel in the bombed wastes of the East End had more appeal for students, understandably, than an old people's home in comfortable west Kensington.

Another call for help came for Guide leaders in Hampstead, and yet another for youth club volunteers at a university women's settlement in Blackfriars, not far from St Paul's Cathedral. This organisation also ran a nursery, a playgroup, and a country holiday fund. It was bound to remind Mary Stocks of her own earliest social involvement, in Clerkenwell and St Pancras, and moreover it was a former workplace of Eleanor Rathbone's friend Elizabeth Macadam. All the causes were deserving, the need for helpers great. All Mary Stocks could do was make her students fully aware of the various problems and leave the choices to them.

The autumn term of 1949 brought 76 new students, among them four from the United States, and a little later the college's first German exchange student, from Bonn. To underline the multi-cultural theme, the inaugural lecture was on colonial education, followed by a talk on West Africa. A Stocksian innovation was an

International High Table, with guests of many nationalities. The celebrities were G.D.H. Cole and Veronica Wedgwood, historians, the Dean of St Paul's and the head of Cheltenham Ladies' College, one of Westfield's feeder institutions.

Harold Nicolson, retired diplomat and husband of Vita Sackville-West, spoke on the Principle of the Monarchy, and the novelist L.A.G. Strong talked to the English Club. Strong was another kinsman of Mary Stocks, and discussed with students at High Table the relatively new phenomenon of the newspaper 'agony aunt', being one himself.

Highlights of the summer term 1950 were a banquet with madrigals for the 1949 graduates, proposals for geography and Spanish departments, and a memorable midsummer ball. At least one student recalls it as a dazzling affair ('Where did we get all those high fashion creations when clothes were still on coupons?') but the Principal's logbook is less enthusiastic: 'A disreputable crowd of guests and (drunk or sober) they made a pig-sty of the typists' office'. So ended her penultimate year as Principal, with Westfield now firmly in the mainstream of London University and the mid-twentieth century.

The autumn term of 1950 began with 223 resident students and eight non-resident. At the time this seemed a fairly huge number. How surprised they would have been to see their successors 45 years later, men and women, over a thousand, multi-cultured and reading a range of subjects undreamed of in the 1950s.

The new year began rather unpropitiously with a partial ban on the use of gas fires in students' rooms, because of a gas strike. Mary Stocks felt most concerned about the seven American exchange students, wholly unused to the privations (rationing was still in force for many commodities) that home-grown students simply took for granted. She wrote at intervals to the Principal of Barnard College apologising for Westfield's lack of a warm welcome, and reassuring him as to the welfare of his alumnae. Their contemporaries recall them as much less delicate plants than Mary Stocks seemed to think. Her latest letter to Barnard College went like this:

Dear President Taylor,
Your two students arrived safely at the beginning of term and they seem to be happy. Unfortunately they ran straight into a London gas strike which caused some of our streets to be

reminiscent of wartime blackout, and so reduced the pressure of gas by which we cook that we were obliged to cut off gas fires and gas rings in students' rooms. As a result our American students, who under normal conditions suffer from the notorious incompetence of the English in the matter of home heating, were subject to even greater hardship . . . They seem to be making friends all round and have already started exploring London.[13]

October was marked by the christening of Mary's first grand-daughter, Kate Patterson, in Westfield College Chapel, and November by a prestigious public lecture on Taste given by the art historian Kenneth Clark (later Lord Clark) and chaired by James Gunn, RA, the eminent portrait painter. Art was not one of Mary Stocks's private passions, but she maintained her respected habit of asking the first question and scoring a bull's eye with it.

The Christmas end-of term festivities included a revue by the first years – 'Dickina Whittington and her Cat'. Was feminism already casting its shadow before?

In January the College Council appointed Kathleen Chesney as the next Principal of Westfield. In many ways this was a surprising choice: a reversion to the old procedure of choosing a single female with an almost exclusively academic curriculum vitae. It was as if Mary Stocks's innovative and by all accounts happy régime had never happened. There were some who felt she had not placed enough emphasis on academic standards, but others argued this was outweighed by the high public profile she gave Westfield under her command.

In April came a major social innovation; an academic board meeting decided to allow each student two late passes each term. This was, in Westfield terms, nothing short of revolutionary. Mary Stocks had been urging the realism of it for some time.

Soon after this she was obliged to attend the annual university degree-giving at the Albert Hall, for new graduates somewhat overwhelming, for old Principals a routine event. Mary wrote: 'Presentation, more tedious than ever, in Albert Hall, followed by Abbey service'. One of the recipients valued more highly than her certificate a postcard handwritten by Mary Stocks before the results were made public:

Dear Miss H. – Hearty congratulations on your very good second. The news of it came late last night and unofficially on the telephone, so my congratulations must be unofficial too. They are nonetheless sincere. You have got what Civil Service examiners call 'a good honours degree' – a useful possession that may come in handy at various points in your subsequent career.[14]

If she wrote by hand, personally and at this length, to all the 1950 firsts (there were two) and upper seconds (twelve) it must have taken her quite a while.

In May 1951 Westfield revived its prewar tradition of rather grand Commemoration garden parties. The guest list for this one included the Earl of Athlone and Princess Alice (he was the Chancellor of London University) as well as the French Ambassador, the Mayor of Hampstead and the local MP (Henry Brooke). Also invited were Dame Myra Curtis, and Arthur Creech Jones (the Colonial Secretary with whose department Mary Stocks had had such prolonged correspondence over the academic criteria for Commonwealth students).

Mary Stocks viewed the whole business with some trepidation. She found herself signing painfully formal letters which began Your Grace, or Your Worship, or Your Excellency. She had to borrow a hat for the occasion from Dr Beatrice White. It is not described, but since Mary Stocks labelled it 'exceedingly suitable' we can assume it was exceedingly plain. She had her letters checked by the Vice Chancellor ('is this the sort of thing? I am not accustomed to making arrangements for Chancellors, let alone Chancellors married to princesses').

In the Principal's logbook Mary was succinct as ever: 'Garden party. Weather dubious but in the end dry. Complicated arrangements for reception of Princess Alice and Chancellor. Madrigals in garden and V.I.P. tea'.

As the end of her last term approached her logbook entries became a trifle frivolous. Take this for 20 June:

Great discomfort prevails in college owing to presence of unde-tected thief. Main field of activity students' laundry [not so strange as it might seem, for smart clothes were still hard to come by on a limited allocation of clothing coupons] . . . Theft of Principal's binoculars – general search – binoculars found in housemaid's cupboard. Clearly planted there.

Three days later she reported: 'Summer dance – followed by usual inquest. Males at large . . . dubious goings-on.' After this came the end-of-year play, a Masque performed in Hall: 'very spirited performance including presentation of lovely Persian rug to Principal'.

More farewell presentations followed: a divan bed from the staff, and a portrait given by Westfield College Association. The last laconic entry in the logbook in Mary Stocks's hand was for 9 July: 'Remainder of W.C.A. members departed after breakfast'. Thereafter the logbook entries were written by Kathleen Chesney.

In 12 years Mary Stocks had guided Westfield from the rather private role of a women's college isolated in Hampstead to a mainstream institution of London University. Its range of subjects, staff and students had all broadened and competition among school leavers for entry had increased. In one respect she left it poorer than she found it – in the closing of a whole science department. This was a political move by the university, a battle she fought vigorously but lost.

Now she returned to her family roots in Kensington to write, broadcast and carry on with her committees. She did not regard it as retirement, and many would say she was now entering the busiest period of her life.

Chapter 5

The BBC Years:
1951–1966

At 60, fit, active and with a huge reservoir of experience to draw on, Mary Stocks was more than ready for new challenges. The first challenge was to find somewhere to live after twelve years in the security of Kidderpore House (or Old House), the Principal's lodging at Westfield. To her great pleasure she found a flat in the converted lodge of an historic Kensington house, not far from her previous homes. Aubrey House had a notable history in the community life and social development of Kensington. The owner, Miss Rachel Alexander, was the survivor of three sisters who had lived there for nearly a century. Mary Stocks became a tenant of the last of the Alexanders.

Her older daughter Ann, already in her thirties a senior civil servant, was settled in Campden Hill Square near by with her husband, also a civil servant, and three teenage children: Mark, Kate and Simon. John Stocks, demobilised from the Navy at the war's end, was working for the Shell Oil Company and living in the Middle East with his wife Jane (an ex-Wren), son Jonathan and daughter Sarah.

Helen, now 31, had a caring post with the Caldecott Community established by Mary's aunt Edith Rendel and continued by Leila Rendel (Edith's daughter) as a residential school for maladjusted children. The Community had moved from Kent to the war-time home in Dorset, then back to Kent. Ann, John and Helen maintained a close relationship with their mother, and her five grandchildren gave her increasing pleasure as they grew up.

The next challenge was to find something to do in line with her beliefs and experience. Mary Stocks wasted no time. She liked to tell people she was 'the statutory woman' on a number of government committees (quangos, they would now be called –

in the 1950s they were regarded with less suspicion than today). The truth was that experience and personality fitted her supremely well for this role, and it proved complementary to her increasing popularity as a broadcaster.

From 1950 till 1958 she was a member of the University Grants Committee, a joyful status at a time when, as she said, 'the golden rain of largesse had begun to fall upon . . . the universities'. She revelled in this: visiting universities to see how the money was being spent; discovering the strengths and weaknesses of the new redbrick institutions which mushroomed in the 1950s; reporting on student halls of residence. As always Mary Stocks developed independent and controversial opinions, based on her own observations. She came to the conclusion that academic mobility was not necessarily an unmitigated blessing. It might even be no bad thing for a prospective teacher to start work near his or her own place of study. But a small doubt crept in here. Was her idea 'an aged person's nightmare of a footloose generation so universally mobile that nobody has time to strike roots?'[1]

She questioned the received wisdom that academic posts should be awarded on the basis of published work rather than an interest in guiding students. She dared to wonder if too many candidates were being admitted to universities whose ambitions were social rather than academic – though at the end of that particular debate she was forced to acknowledge there should be no barriers except ability to reach the required standard.

Her next quango was the London Executive Council of the National Health Service. Probably no single appointment could have given Roland Brinton's daughter greater satisfaction. She publicly regretted that none of her children or grandchildren had chosen her father's profession. She traced her concern for the NHS back to 1909, when a minority report of the Poor Law Commission had called for a 'unified health service' unrestricted by the patient's ability to pay. Her contact with family doctors, dentists and opticians led her to conclude that hospitals were understaffed, under-equipped and provided inadequate housing for those who worked in them.

She compared the intensive use of hospital buildings to the intermittent use of university buildings and facilities. She criticised the excessive size of a general practitioner's allowed patient list (3,500) and praised the concept of group practices. Most perceptively she questioned the relationship between private and state medicine. In all these doubts she was considerably ahead of public opinion.

In 1949 she had been invited by Lord Astor (Nancy's husband) to serve on the Trust of the *Observer* newspaper. He and his son David, the editor, had set up the Trust in 1945, relinquishing their own family shares, as an experiment in newspaper control. Lord Astor wrote to Mary Stocks: 'We believe you are leftish but not intolerant and would fit into the team'.[2] He added that his wife did not approve of the paper's independent (in her view anti-Conservative) stance, and Mary Stocks wrote: 'It was with some trepidation that I confessed to Lady Astor that I had accepted this invitation'.

She served on the *Observer* Trust until 1961, for one year as its chairman, and through it on the Commonwealth Press Union. During her year as chairman the Suez crisis blew up, and Mary Stocks was happy to support David Astor's strong editorial criticism of Sir Anthony Eden's Government.

> It is true that temporarily we lost circulation. But I choose to think that we gained repute because the Editor, in addition to showing notable courage, was, as subsequent events showed, absolutely right. So I regard November 1956 as the *Observer*'s finest hour.

There are echoes here of the Mary Stocks who broadcast her trenchant comments on current affairs in 1930.

Looking back in 1993, David Astor said:

> She was a stopgap chairman who gave me tremendous support. Her predecessor, Dingle Foot, was interested in colonial causes. He wrote a signed article for the *Observer* which annoyed the other Trustees. Lord Portal of Hungerford resigned, and Arthur Mann who was a former editor of the *Yorkshire Post*. They left because they felt we should support Eden. The whole newspaper staff was on my side, but only Mary on the Trust.[3]

He admired Mary's strength of character: 'She was properly outspoken – a good quality. She was an intellectual, but character and moral qualities were more important. The staff all liked her and her disrespect for formalities. She handled my mother well too; they were quite sisterly'.

Further input into the arts world came through a seat on the governing body of the Central School of Speech and Drama, initially based at the Albert Hall and very much on Mary Stocks's home territory. She loved the contacts it brought her with distinguished theatre people: Lewis Casson, Sybil Thorndike, Peggy Ashcroft. She rejoiced when John Davis of the Rank Organisation, currently chairman of the School, bought the old Embassy Theatre at Swiss Cottage as a new home for the Central School. What she could not then know was that this move would lead to a close co-operation between the Central School and drama undergraduates at her own old college. Swiss Cottage and Westfield were within walking distance of each other.

Not such a far cry, then, from the *Observer* newspaper and a college of speech and drama to a niche in broadcasting history. Unexpectedly, the threads of Mary Stocks's life began to come together with her début as a panellist in a new programme pioneered from the West of England studios in Bristol. It involved a team of three or four knowledgeable and entertaining speakers meeting once a month in halls scattered over the West of England. It was their task to give impromptu answers to questions on current affairs put to them by a local audience. The programme was recorded, and it was called *Any Questions*.

Mary Stocks became its best-known and possibly best-loved panellist. She appeared on it more times than any other broadcaster. It made her famous, and (so she believed) it brought her a peerage. The first *Any Questions* session (a dummy run) was held at the Guildhall in Dartmouth, Devon, on 29 June 1951 – a month before Mary Stocks retired as Principal of Westfield. The coincidence is odd, and it cannot be wholly ruled out that West Region was waiting for her to be fully available.

Her first broadcast appearance on the programme – indeed the first by any woman panel member – was from the Corn Exchange, Blandford, Dorset, on 30 November 1951. The whole team had a West Country flavour, and Mary must have been delighted to make her début so near the family holiday home at Bridport. She was introduced as Vice-President of the Workers' Educational Association, and her fellow panellists were A.G. Street, farmer and author, Dingle Foot of Plymouth, Vice-President of the Liberal Party, and the opera singer, Parry Jones. The question master was Freddie Grisewood and it was a rôle he maintained with panache for fifteen years. Mary Stocks was an undoubted and immediate success, the live audience loving her dry humour and terse speaking style. The pattern was set for her to join in three or four programmes a year indefinitely, on a rota basis with A.G. Street, and the countryman Ralph Wightman. They were all seasoned broadcasters with distinctive voices and positive opinions.

In the early stages there was no consistent attempt to set up a tripartite political balance (this came later), and the main thrust of the questions was by no means as politically orientated as they eventually became. Some panellists were chosen for their identification with one of the three main parties, but Mary Stocks and her fellow-regulars were perceived as independents. She had given up her membership of the Labour Party when she took over at Westfield.

On that first programme, a month before Christmas, one of the questions was inevitably about food shortages. The panel was asked to comment on the Government's decision not to increase food rations for Christmas. Part of Mary Stocks's reply drew much applause: 'What worries me a little is that Christmas tends to become a sort of commercial Saturnalia of buying, instead of being what it once was, a religious festival'.[4] After this there was a question about the desirability of trial periods of living together before marriage, to which she answered that such a practice was not realistic. Marriage was a matter of adapting to a lifelong partnership which could not be tested in a month.

As a former Beveridge Committee investigator, she was in her element when a questioner asked if commercial television on American lines was likely to be adopted in Britain. Vigorously defending modern and classical music against the competing claims of football and boxing, she pointed out that sponsored broadcasting would mean programme selection by the advertising agents. This view was not shared by her fellow panellists. Indeed it is doubtful if many people in 1951 (some fifteen years before the advent of commercial television in Britain) could have anticipated the pressures to book prime-time slots.

Freddie Grisewood and Mary Stocks felt an immediate rapport, and years later they were to appear together on programmes recalling their respective childhoods and the way their worlds had changed. They had much in common. Frederick Harman

Grisewood, the son of a well-off Victorian rector on the borders of Gloucestershire and Oxfordshire (who may well have known Mary's father-in-law, Canon John Stocks, during his time at Oxford) was born three years earlier than Mary Brinton and, like her, lived to be 84. He went to public school at Oxford, then studied music before serving in the Oxford and Bucks Light Infantry through the First World War.

For ten years he acted as agent for his birthplace, the great estate of Daylesford which included his father's rectory. Like Mary, he had had distinguished forebears: his grandfather had owned Daylesford and developed the fine gardens for which Daylesford became famous. In 1929 – a year before Mary Stocks began to make her name as a broadcaster and birth control campaigner – Freddie Grisewood joined the BBC as an announcer, and worked for radio for more than thirty years. In 1959 he published *My Story of the B.B.C.*, collected an OBE and more or less retired; but (also like Mary) he never gave up broadcasting.

One other interest they shared. Freddie played hockey for Oxford University, as did John Stocks, and for Oxfordshire (as well as tennis and cricket for Worcestershire).

Mary Stocks wrote of him: 'One name glows with especial warmth; that of Freddie Grisewood, who for nearly 20 years acted as chairman of *Any Questions*. Few performers in the broadcasting world have been so greatly loved by so many people'.[5] Their relationship was that of close colleagues and contemporaries.

A few months later Mary Stocks made her second appearance on *Any Questions*, from Bournemouth, with the Conservative ex-minister Robert Boothby, the future Labour leader Hugh Gaitskell and (again) A.G. Street. On this occasion she roundly condemned public hypnosis, which had lately been in the news. It raised the question of personal freedom, she argued, and how far people needed to be protected from their own folly. Looking back on some of the early 'Any Questions' sessions during a Boxing Day broadcast in 1966, Freddie Grisewood and Mary Stocks relished reminiscing over the first fifteen years. Had they but known, it was a programme that would still be going strong 45 years later.

Meanwhile, through her radio commitments, Mary was getting acquainted with parts of the south west she had not visited before. In the early 1950s *Any Questions* had ranged over the West of England, sometimes finding some unlikely temporary homes. In

1952, for example, it came from a Bournemouth theatre, a Weston-super-Mare junior school and the Queens Hall, Barnstaple. In 1953 it flowed on steadily from Lynton, Sherborne, the Regal Cinema at Cheddar and an infant school at Gosport. In between these sessions Mary Stocks appeared with Isaac Foot in what was billed as a 'Younger Generation Question Time', from a Plymouth youth club. She also chaired a studio discussion from Bristol on 'What's Wrong with Snobbery?'

One of her great skills was somehow to make all her engagements fit, whether stopping overnight in a West Country hotel and driving to London at dawn for a committee meeting, or dashing from the annual Dorset family holiday to Bristol for a recording. It was rare for Mary to cancel anything, but on one occasion she had to withdraw from a BBC lunch appointment in order to collect a granddaughter from school. Neatly handwritten postcards were her favourite device for forward planning. If they had been saved, they would run into thousands.

In 1953 Mary Stocks gave the third Eleanor Rathbone Memorial lecture at Liverpool University. Her time there had been, she said 'the six most exhilarating months of my life'. Eleanor Rathbone she had 'admired as a very great woman and loved as a friend'. Only one other contemporary could be ranked as a truly great woman: Beatrice Webb. The subject of her lecture was one that harked back to the activities of an earlier generation of her own family, to her own strongly held belief that social privilege carries with it social obligation: 'The Philanthropist in a Changing World'.

She regarded the education of middle-class women during the late Victorian period as far more humane than that of men, who had to suffer the exile of boarding school and the 'almost exclusive companionship of a peculiarly barbarous masculine age group, and a pattern of existence conditioned by its immature needs'. This was a favourite topic with Mary Stocks, who abhorred the concept of boarding school, perhaps because she had an antipathy to school in general, or because her brother Ralph had suffered at its hands.

She summed up the female condition at the turn of the century in very Stocksian terms:

> I don't want to paint too rosy a picture of female upper and middle class life at the turn of the century . . . There were many small frustrations and taboos. Trailing skirts, tight neckbands,

precarious hats, hatpins, hairpins, etc., bathing dresses which reached from neck to knee. Girls can't do this – girls can do that! But things were infinitely better than they had been a generation earlier, in the age of which Antony Trollope writes . . . The medical profession was open. The nursing profession was respectable. The teaching profession had become a profession . . . Women could move about as freely as their horrible clothes would let them. They could scale the tops of buses, ride bicycles, hail hansom cabs. And they were free enough to know that they were not free enough.[6]

And so to another of her pet themes. Innumerable middle-class Victorian women, not yet cumbered with careers or domestic chores, devoted themselves to doing good. 'The crack regiment, the brigade of guards in this philanthropic army was the glorious company of maiden aunts'. They devoted their lives to the Church, hospitals and workhouses, boys' and girls' clubs, school boards, reconditioned slums, charities – and all this without pay or (in most cases) training.

She discussed the semantic distinction between a philanthropist and a social reformer and a socialist. Eventually the concept of voluntary social work had become largely absorbed in the structure of a professional welfare state. Where the great-aunts had given up their leisure to pursue unpaid good works, the great-nieces qualified as full-time housing managers or probation officers. Women, Mary Stocks told her Liverpool audience, had lived through a social revolution, but the class divide was still there and not all had equal access to education.

Finally she offered her own definition of charity in the mid-twentieth century:

> Here I think is the greatest benefit that the Welfare State has brought to our latter-day philanthropists . . . to my mind it is a word that relates to the quality of a personal relationship – the response of an individual human being to the misfortunes or defects of another individual human being . . . So please let us call it that unashamedly, restoring to the word 'charity' its ancient gracefulness in a world which offers it a new meaning.

The Rathbone Lecture reached a wider audience when Liverpool University published it as a pamphlet. Mary Stocks's next publication, in 1953, continued the theme of equal opportunity across the class barrier. In the 50th anniversary history of the Workers' Educational Association (she was invited to write it as the Association's vice-president) she could give freer rein to her radicalism. The WEA had been part and parcel of her life from the day she graduated. John Stocks had introduced her to it and she had laboured lovingly as tutor, lecturer, organiser and publicist.

The jacket blurb of *The W.E.A., the First Fifty Years*, says:

> The W.E.A. was founded in 1903 and to mark its 50th anniversary the Association commissioned its deputy president to describe its development through this momentous half century . . . her book is a contribution to a neglected aspect of the social history of the early 20th century.

It was first issued in a ten-shilling edition, a fair price for a slimmish book at that time.

It is an undramatic record of great achievements. Until 1903, the author pointed out, the great mass of British people had no education other than eight years at a free elementary school. Then an enlightened couple, Albert and Frances Mansbridge, set up an 'Association to Promote the Higher Education of Working Men' with an initial capital of 2s. 6d. ('In due course its name contracted and its membership grew.') Within a year the organisation had acquired a typewriter, a committee and its first classes – in Reading.

The WEA was boosted by the growth of the BBC, the need for adult education and the expansion of the Forces in the Second World War, and financial support in the form of donations to an endowment fund from the great and the good. Mary Stocks's review of its status in the 1950s was an optimistic one, but she sounded a warning note:

> The B.B.C. caters for a public naturally disinclined to engage in any effort of mental concentration . . . A population of satisfied half-listeners is not likely to provide a good field for the kind of adult education which demands continuous attention and active response.

Her book concludes by repeating some advice given by R.H. Tawney, her old family friend and early mentor. He had cautioned the WEA against the trap of providing education for those who could most easily be induced to undertake it, as opposed to those most needing it.

The book led to many public speaking engagements. Another major one came in September 1954, when she addressed the British Association on the type of education needed by mid-twentieth century women. 'Girls should learn at school', she told her scholarly audience, talents not learned in home-making or child-rearing. They would then 'bring to domestic problems the trained intelligence, systematic thought and mental concentration acquired during their education.' It seems possible that not all of her hearers wholeheartedly agreed; many in 1953 would have argued that an academic education would be a waste of money if it led only to marriage and domesticity.

In 1954 Mary Stocks made headlines when she was chosen as the first woman chair of an international radio programme, *Asking the World*, a question-and-answer programme linking several countries. She chaired the programme from London with her old friend Sir Ifor Evans of University College as a colleague, debating with journalists based in New York, Paris and Hamburg. The series continued for a few months but could not survive poor listening figures and technical hitches.

The press were now increasingly interviewing her and quoting her. She was described nowadays as 'writer and broadcaster', no longer as 'college ex-principal'. Early in 1959 there was a furore over her apparent revelation on *Any Questions* that she kept warm on a winter drive to the West Country with a paraffin heater in the back of her car. This greatly excited the Chief Officer of Glamorgan Fire Brigade. He told the press his men had recently been called out thirteen times to fires started by paraffin heaters. To have one in a car was 'the last thing one should do. I was absolutely horrified – a lot of silly people will copy her'.[7] In a subsequent programme Mary Stocks claimed she had merely apologised to passengers who had to share the back of her car with a heater. It was not alight. Her car had other means of heating. The matter of the heater in the car rumbled on for some time, the facts never entirely established.

A little later that year she was reported, under the headline 'Streets Act Critic', as attacking the new Street Offences Act which banned prostitutes from public streets. 'It has merely had the effects of sweeping the dust under the carpet and out of sight,' she is reported to have said. 'By driving the prostitutes from the streets the Act has increased the number of middlemen'. Prostitutes were no longer regarded as 'fallen women', but the Act had not made it any more difficult for their clients.

By her 70th year (in 1961) Mary Stocks had become firmly fixed in the public's perception as a character with outspoken views on every topic under the sun and a witty way of expressing them. More seriously, she had an established reputation as a writer, not only of books, but of solid intelligent articles on the social concerns of the day.

Frank Gillard was a distinguished BBC figure for thirty years, first as a war correspondent, then Head of Programmes in Bristol and the West, finally retiring as Director of BBC Regions. His main contact with Mary Stocks was in the 1950s and 60s, when *Any Questions* came under the Bristol umbrella. In 1993, aged 85 and a CBE, he still vividly recalled her: 'indomitable in argument, but entirely without rancour. I can't remember that she was ever caught out in *Any Questions*, with nothing to contribute . . . never outwardly shocked, and never patronising to towards people intellectually inferior to herself'.

Frank Gillard recalled an occasion when the BBC moved him at very short notice from Bristol to London, and while he was flat-hunting Mary Stocks offered him the use of her flat while she was in the Middle East. He also remembered her as having 'a mischievous sense of humour' and 'rather a headmistressy voice . . . with very little interest in the trivial gossip which broadcasters habitually exchange'. And he confirmed the general picture of Mary Stocks as without fashion sense: 'Quite uninterested in her personal appearance. No time at all for fashion or fripperies'.[8]

Frank Gillard played some part in bringing about the publication of Mary's religious talks:

> When I asked if she had thought of publishing them in print, she said her publishers feared there would be no market for such material. So I had a word with the Books Editor of B.B.C. Publications. They became paperback best-sellers and brought in quite a nice sum in royalties to their author. I am sure she gave all the money away.[9]

During the 1960s Mary Stocks sandwiched her broadcasting in with membership of the University Grants Committee, a challenge for which she was uniquely fitted, and of the London Executive Council of the National Health Service, a voluntary body of supreme interest to Dr Roland Brinton's daughter. Indeed she was probably more emotionally attached to these two quangos than to any others she served on.

All radio programmes were grist to Mary's mill. In her autobiography she admitted:

> I think I must have performed on every possible type of talks programme. I lifted up hearts, interviewed bishops, educated the young, reviewed books, selected discs for a desert island, gambolled with Renee Houston on Petticoat Line, and from Bush House expounded British ways of life to listeners . . . in the Far East.[10]

She valued also the correspondence her broadcasts generated, some from old friends, most from total strangers. Every one was replied to, for letter-writing was a special Stocks skill. She recognised the existence of 'a large circle of listeners, many of them lonely, or elderly, or both, who find in the voices of regular sound broadcasters a circle of familiar personal friends whose personalities seem to become part of their lives'.

She was not immune from the attentions of abusive or even obscene letter-writers, and found it significant that so many of these were anonymous:

> Many indicate the prevalence of what might be called 'half-listening'. The listener hears a word which for him or her has an emotional association. This sets up a train of thought which leads to the belief that the broadcaster has in fact said what the listener is accustomed to hear said in connection with that particular word, whether the broadcaster has said it or not.[11]

She saw herself as 'popular quiz artist' (her words) and Freddie Grisewood as an incomparable chairman. She liked her fellow-panellists and responded with enthusiasm to the West Country venues and audiences. So it was not surprising that she deplored the plan for *Any Questions* to become a national rather than a regionally based programme. 'I nostalgically regret . . . other changes. Its old

West Country flavour gave it a pleasing West Country personality. But perhaps its excursions all over the British Isles give it a more varied audience response'.

Another aspect of *Any Questions* that pleased her was the fact that it was to all intents and purposes a live programme, recorded in one session, on location, with a real as opposed to a studio audience. This not only gave it piquancy but enabled members of the panel to slip in an occasional indiscretion.

In 1956, at the time of the Suez crisis, they worked in some anti-government comments which were immediately censored ('Cut. Red light. Next question, please') because of the BBC's 14-day rule. This rule banned any discussion of a topic likely to be debated in Parliament in the next fourteen days. Shortly after this the censoring rule was withdrawn, and Mary Stocks always believed this was a coup for the *Any Questions* team.

In this period she averaged five or six appearances a year on the panel, and audience research suggested she was its best-known and appreciated member. She continued her occasional talks for *Woman's Hour*. One that gave her special pleasure was a talk in *Home for the Day* about her old friend and fellow-feminist, Dame Millicent Garrett-Fawcett. The occasion was the centenary of Mrs Fawcett's birth, when surviving suffragists held a wreath-laying ceremony at Westminster Abbey. Mary Stocks once again made the point that Mrs Fawcett, through diplomacy, political expertise and negotiating powers, had done more than anyone to bring about votes for women.

Three months after this she gave her first 'Letter from Britain' for the European Service, arising from a visit to Cyprus to see her daughter and son-in-law, Ann and Arthur Patterson. As a senior civil servant and Cambridge mathematician Arthur had been invited to set up a national insurance scheme on the island (as he did later for Malta, Jamaica and Kuwait).

For Mary Stocks the visit was not only a holiday but a chance to study Cypriot politics in the early stages of the Enosis movement for union with Greece, bitterly opposed by the Turkish minority and leading to much bloodshed. Later she managed to meet President Makarios and came away convinced that at the heart of the island's problems lay a failure in communication and a lack of imagination by the earlier British colonial administration.

The BBC hesitated to allow her free rein in broadcasting on this sensitive issue, and memoranda went to and fro before permission was given. This time she expressed her opinions a shade less forcefully than usual.

Soon after this *Woman's Hour* put out a discussion between Mary Stocks and the newspaper columnist Ann Temple, under the title '20th Century Woman'. Their views in many ways anticipated the feminism of the 1960s, just beginning to attract attention as a social force with Germaine Greer as its guru. Ann and Mary saw twentieth-century woman as a New Age thinker and activist. Her role was no longer that of a second-class citizen, but an equal contributor to society.

However, the *Any Questions* panel continued to consist almost exclusively of men, with an occasional nod towards female politicians – and Mary Stocks as a bi-monthly statutory woman. The roll-call may have been chauvinist, but it makes impressive reading. During 1955 Mary Stocks's colleagues included Labour leader Hugh Gaitskell, Tory Lord Chancellor-to-be Viscount Hailsham, economist Graham Hutton, notable Tory backbenchers Julian Amery and future Prime Minister Edward Heath, *Punch* editor Malcolm Muggeridge, historian A.J.P. Taylor, writer Peter Fleming and *Daily Mirror* editor Percy Cudlipp. For Labour appeared Harold Wilson, Michael Foot, Denis Healey, Patrick Gordon Walker and Richard Crossman; and for the Conservatives Gerald Nabarro and Sir Robert Boothby.

Two series emerged at this time. One was *Weekend Away* which involved three contributors spending a weekend together in a comfortable West Country hotel and discussing the immediate locality. Mary Stocks found herself uttering instant opinions on places she had never seen before, such as Porlock and St Mawes. The second new programme was *Christian Forum* – the name is self-explanatory – which she launched from Portsmouth with the veteran Canadian war correspondent, Stanley Maxted.

A notable *Any Questions* at Mullion in September 1956 threw together the future Liberal leader Jeremy Thorpe, Bob Boothby, Mary Stocks and the aged but quick-witted Labour campaigner Emmanuel Shinwell.

Less than a month later came a high point in Mary Stocks's broadcasting career. *Woman's Hour* asked her, as part of the tenth anniversary celebrations, to interview her old friend and political opponent, Nancy Astor. The idea had been mooted in a letter from

Lorna Pegram of *Woman's Hour*. She wrote to Mary Stocks on 7 August:

> The story of Nancy Lady Astor's entry into Parliament in the face of great opposition is a fascinating one that would make very good broadcasting in *Woman's Hour*, and the person who knows all the facts is yourself. Could we meet to discuss the idea?[12]

Eventually it was agreed that the interview should be recorded at Lady Astor's home. Thirty minutes would be edited down to ten, and Mary's fee would be eight guineas.

In her autobiography Mary Stocks recalls her impressions of Nancy Astor at the time of her election as the first woman MP to take her seat at Westminster.

> We had envisaged our first woman M.P. as at best a tried suffragist, at least a woman distinguished in local government or social service. But here was an American millionairess, known only to us by reputation, since we did not move in those circles, as a society hostess. . . . We feared the worst. Only Mrs H.A.L. Fisher, wife of the historian, who it seemed did move in those circles, offered a word of comfort. 'Wait and see', she said. 'She's all right. You'll be surprised'. We did; and we were.[13]

At first Mary and her colleagues in the National Union of Women's Suffrage Societies were deeply opposed to this situation, but gradually, as Nancy began to make her mark, they accepted her. Later Mary was to say: 'It was soon obvious that Nancy Astor was the fiercest feminist of all'.

Nancy's son David remembered the hostility Nancy initially had to face in the Commons:

> They did all they could to make her feel unwanted, even setting up a special debate on venereal disease in the hope that she wouldn't be able to sit through it, to prove a woman wasn't fitted to be an M.P. But this made her even more determined. She said the only intelligent thing to do was to call together women who were politically active (and of course they were all Labour supporters) and told them: 'All I can offer is to be a vehicle for you. If you can make use of me I'm at your service'.[14]

This, he explained, was how she met Mary Stocks and the two women who became her parliamentary aides, Hilda Matheson (later a BBC talks director) and Ray Strachey, member of the Bloomsbury Group and a cousin of Mary Stocks.

> She couldn't have managed to fight the case for women without these friends. Nearly all her friends in the House were Labour. The Tories refused to speak to her – they just froze her out.

David Astor regarded his mother's greatest achievement as simply surviving, showing that a woman was fully as capable as a male MP. Nancy remained an MP until 1945, when she was persuaded not to seek re-election. During those 25 years Cliveden, her Buckinghamshire home, became famous – initially as a First World War hospital financed by the Canadian Red Cross, later as a weekend gathering place for leading public figures – the so-called Cliveden set. David Astor confirmed Mary Stocks's view that the Cliveden set was a myth. (The Stockses were frequent visitors from nearby Oxford and later from Manchester.)

> The Cliveden Set was invented by Claud Cockburn as a way of working up feeling against the Chamberlain government. It went down so well that even if he'd denied it people would still have used the expression. There was no Set or conspiracy; these people were personal and political friends of my parents.[15]

Another interest that Mary and Nancy shared was reading the Bible, though from differing standpoints (Nancy was a devoted Christian Scientist). David defended his mother against charges of racism and anti-Semitism; he pointed out she had been brought up among Blacks in Virginia and was happy to invite Black visitors to her home. She also had Jewish friends and intervened personally with Ribbentrop to help some escape from Vienna.

In spite of a 12-year age gap and hugely differing views on many topics, Mary Stocks and Nancy Astor had remained lifelong friends. To interview her nearly forty years after their first meeting was an invitation she could not resist, and she made a good job of it. David Astor renewed his contact with Mary Stocks when he and his brother invited her to serve on the Trust of the *Observer*, his family's newspaper. For a year she was a stopgap chairman.

> We were very keen to have Mrs Stocks on the Trust because she was a friend of my mother. She had a healthy disrespect for formalities and a very quick mind, like my mother in being

concerned with all kinds of causes. She handled my mother very well; they were quite sisterly. Mrs Stocks gave me tremendous support as Chairman of the Trustees.[16]

However, Mary had not sought the post of chairman, and was happy to hand over after a year to her former London University fellow-principal, Sir Ifor Evans of University College.

Mary Stocks's autobiography reflects some aspects of the 1956 Stocks–Astor interview. In spite of Nancy's fine record, Mary had never wholly lost her reservations about an aristocrat's suitability to represent commoners in Parliament. This was an American heiress, an English peeress, a society hostess with four homes. However, 'she stepped into the pages of history when she became the first woman to take her seat in the British House of Commons'. So she wrote long after in the *Observer* newspaper.

Mary Stocks had always been conscious of the pressures operating on Nancy Astor. She had constantly to be at the beck and call of women's organisations, she was pursued ceaselessly by the press, the names of her guests were discussed in the gossip columns. To counteract the social butterfly image she mentions in her memoirs that Nancy counted George Bernard Shaw as a personal friend (three of his characters were modelled on her) and she was proud to have her name on Hitler's black-list of those he would round up if the Germans invaded.

Most interestingly, Mary agrees with David Astor when she vigorously discounts the myth of a so-called Cliveden set, a semi-secret political power group rumoured to meet at the Astors' country place. 'Those who came and went at Cliveden were far too heterogeneous a crowd to constitute anything resembling a "set"', she insisted.[17] But she did not tell her readers that she was one of the comers and goers, and therefore possibly biassed. However, David Astor's confirmation does lend credence to the view that the Cliveden Set was dreamed up by a few columnists.

In her autobiography (and no doubt in the 1956 interview, frustratingly no longer on record) Mary described her old friend's impatience at her enforced retirement from Parliament in 1945, her delight at being made a Freeman of Plymouth on her 80th birthday, her deep commitment to Christian Science. At feminist events such as the unveiling of a statue to Christabel Pankhurst Nancy would 'delight her hearers with the old mixture of deep feeling and impish irreverence. Who would have supposed that fate could have provided so colourful a chapter for the austere chronicle of feminist advance?'[18]

In a sense Mary Stocks was providing a commentary on her own life as well as that of Nancy Astor, and the BBC interview must have raised some poignant memories of her own abortive attempts to enter Parliament.

Towards the end of 1956 the Rev. Elsie Chamberlain, of the BBC's Religious Service, wrote inviting Mary Stocks to do a series of modernised Bible readings in the daily breakfast time slot, *Lift Up Your Hearts*. This opened the door to some twenty years of very personal reflections on her favourite Bible passages. She developed, in effect, a plain person's guide to the Old Testament.

The original invitation was to read and comment on selected Bible passages. In the event this turned into a very personal choice of modernised Biblical stories; after all Mary Stocks had thirty years earlier published a nativity play in contemporary idiom. She and Elsie Chamberlain, who later became a close friend, were to have lunched at Marshall and Snelgrove in Oxford Street. But Mary Stocks had to fetch her six-year old granddaughter from school, so the arrangements were made largely by post.

The series of six talks was broadcast on successive days of a single week, from 4 February till 11 February 1957, with these titles:

1. Eleazer and the Pork
2. Nature – or idol worship
3. Founders' Day
4. Persian oil
5. Displaced persons
6. The unread best-seller

Title number six was Mary Stocks's own view of the Bible, in later years often stressed, and eventually to become the title of a book. Elsie Chamberlain wrote to her in advance: 'Don't polish the script, will you? Keep it conversational.' To which Mary replied typically: 'It is nothing if not unpolished'.

The series led to a flood of listeners' letters. Mary summed them up in a note to Elsie Chamberlain on 13 February:

I have had a 'fair mail' which has left me breathless, innumerable requests for chapters and verses and publications, tracts from

British Israelites, Jehovah's witnesses, Protestants who regard the Apocrypha as Popish, invitations to address meetings, one exhortation to live on hazelnuts and currants, an invitation to become president of an anti-vivisection society . . . Not to mention friendly letters from everyone I ever knew, including Gilbert Murray. Does this always happen to those who engage in this programme?[19]

In her reply Elsie Chamberlain quoted an audience research panellist who had taken the trouble to write in: 'At long last you've put someone on this programme who talks sense. I notice she bases her talk on common-sense Jewish Old Testament books'.

Any Questions continued peripatetic around the West Country; among Mary Stocks's team-mates from time to time were Labour personalities Tony Benn, Tony Crosland and James Callaghan, the historian Alan Bullock, and Ernest Marples (the Conservative minister who launched the first British motorway). In August 1957 the programme went out from the Earls Court Radio Show. At about this time she became involved in a new series – an Ulster-based version of *Any Questions* from Belfast and Armagh.

1957 closed with an unscripted *Woman's Hour* discussion, 'Peace on Earth?' involving the writer Marghanita Laski, the academic Kathleen Lonsdale and Mary Stocks, with Robert MacKenzie as chairman. He was a popular Canadian presenter who later became famous for election night commentaries using a bizarre machine called a swingometer.

During 1958 there were two new topical radio ventures: a seven-minute assessment of the National Health Service for *London Calling Asia*, and an eight-minute discussion on racism and immigration – already becoming a considerable issue only a year after the first wave of Afro-Caribbean arrivals. This was for *At Home and Abroad*.

And in October of that year Frank Gillard, director of BBC West in Bristol, wrote to the head of Home Service:

When is Mary Stocks going to do *Lift Up Your Hearts* again? . . . She has a broadcasting style which is all her own, and through it she certainly made her mark last time.

The hint was taken with remarkable speed for the BBC, so that by April Mary was submitting a new set of scripts to Elsie

Chamberlain, having in the meantime appeared six times on *Any Questions*.

Throughout the 1950s Mary Stocks was a regular *Any Questions* performer, gaining a considerable reputation for outspokenness, wit and humanitarian views. She told a Bristol factory audience in February 1958 that hard work before examinations was no excuse for university students in 'rags' and demonstrations to behave in a more silly or destructive manner than wage earners; a popular answer.

Asked about the necessity for unemployment in a free economic system, Mary Stocks as the only economist on the team delved into her Manchester experience to quote Margaret Bondfield, Labour's first woman Cabinet minister:

> I remember Maggie Bondfield lecturing to some Lancashire mill girls during the Great Depression. She gave them a real proper scolding, as she could . . . She said 'You think it's your natural right to have a factory at the end of your street. Now when I left school I had to leave home [to find work] and everyone in my village assumed they had to leave home.[20]

The last questioner that night wanted to know the qualifications needed to become one of the *Any Questions* team. Mary Stocks's reply encapsulated the story of her life.

> I am what was described in the House of Lords as 'statutory woman' – the kind of woman they always put on a committee when somebody says you must have a woman on this committee. I started on persistent offenders many years ago. I did unemployment insurance, broadcasting, foreign information services, training of midwives, training of teachers, women in the services, recruitment of dentists, and university grants – I could think of a few more. As a result of this I've achieved a rather superficial knowledge of many things, so that I can talk fairly superficially on almost any question – except Scottish finance.[21]

Soon after this, in January 1959, came the opportunity to give a more extended talk than hitherto and at the same time to recall her husband's career. It was broadcast on the North of England Home Service to mark the centenary of Samuel Alexander, OM, who had been John Stocks's predecessor as Professor of Philosophy at

Manchester University. She mentioned that Alexander had become a personal friend of them both, and that he had completed a book left unfinished by her husband when he died in 1937.

Samuel Alexander looked like a philosopher, she said, bearded and patriarchal: he was her idea of the Great Jehovah. He maintained a bachelor establishment 'with the biggest aspidistra in the world', and was proud of his bust sculpted by Jacob Epstein. When Alexander presented the historian Eileen Power at a ceremony for an honorary doctorate, he delighted the audience with his paternalism: 'My Lord Chancellor, I present to you a lady who by a strange dispensation of natural history combines the glamour of the butterfly with the industry of the bee'.

This Stocks talk was followed on the Home Service, two weeks later, by 'Portrait of a Friend'. The friend was Archbishop William Temple. Here again some pleasing anecdotes surfaced: 'In philosophical debate once at Rugby a teacher said "Ah, Temple, are you not a little out of your depth?" "Yes, sir, but I can swim."'[22]

By the time John Stocks became Professor of Philosophy at Manchester William Temple was Bishop of Manchester (he had tried unsuccessfully to persuade Stocks to take Holy Orders, like so many members of John's family). Mary Stocks recalled that Temple and his wife Frances would cycle over to have tea with them ' in non-episcopal clothes'. Later she had attended his institution as Archbishop of York.

During the war years, as Archbishop of Canterbury, he was literally working himself to death, endlessly travelling, never refusing a request, presiding over meetings. Nonetheless, he had somehow found time to officiate at the wedding of Mary's elder daughter Ann, who was married in the side aisle of the bombed church (St James, Piccadilly) where he had once been rector. Mary Stocks ended her portrait with an anecdote rather typical of her broadcasting style:

> A year later I wrote asking him to christen the first baby. [Ann] said 'Isn't it a bit arrogant to ask the Archbishop of Canterbury to christen my son?' I explained I was doing nothing of the sort. I was asking William Temple to christen John Stocks's grandson. And of course he did.[23]

One outcome of this talk was a renewal of her old friendship with Frances Temple, the archbishop's widow, who wrote to say she had heard the broadcast and regarded it as one of the best accounts she had heard or read.

In April 1959 Mary Stocks repeated her success in *Lift Up Your Hearts* with a second seven-day run of short Biblical commentaries. Her scripts were submitted to the Reverend Elsie Chamberlain with this note:

> I hope they will pass muster. What I really hope is that they will reach the ears of persons waiting for the weather report, and make them think the Bible is more interesting than they supposed. . . . They made me feel I was back at Westfield College again, selecting passages of Scripture for morning chapel.[24]

The wheel had come full circle.

This particular series of *Lift Up Your Hearts* led to an invitation to give a talk on comparative religion. Mary Stocks's entertaining reply is worth quoting almost in full:

> Dear Mrs Walton – If you were to come and see me you would have to come an awful long way because I am off to Cyprus tomorrow morning at 7 a.m., for more than a month. But honestly I think you are well out of it, because I don't think I'm the right person. I can tell Old Testament stories on the air but I am neither a scholar nor a philosopher, and you would need a bit of both for this job.[25]

A year later a third series of *Lift Up Your Hearts* led Elsie Chamberlain to write in friendly vein:

> It makes a high spot for a number of listeners (a bottomest pit for the one who had to switch off lest her children should hear you refer to anything in God's Holy Word as dross) . . . May I say thank you for a very nice breakfast in your peaceful haven. I hope the kittens are thriving. If someone asks for suggestions about a vicar, do remember my husband. Again thank you for all the good things you share with us.[26]

Any Questions was now rotating with a new international current affairs series going out monthly on Sunday nights, *Asking the World*. Mary Stocks chaired this, at 40 guineas a time, and on the first panel were Sir Ifor Evans (her old acquaintance from London University) together with French and German experts.

She took part in a discussion with Walter James on policy in the new universities of the 1960s, and prepared a 13-minute talk for the Asian Service on Mary McArthur, the pioneer woman trade unionist. This prompted a request for a book to be lent by the BBC library; she doubted whether Kensington Public Library would have it. During 1961 some internal BBC correspondence between London and Bristol debated whether Mrs Stocks was becoming over-exposed on the air. Frank Gillard's reply was an emphatic 'No' – he remained a staunch Mary Stocks advocate, later prodding London to find more, not less, for her to do.

Asking the World was withdrawn in June after six programmes, apparently because some members of the BBC hierarchy did not like it. In compensation, even more *Any Questions* sessions were fitted into Mary Stocks's extremely active retirement, which now included fairly frequent visits abroad with her daughter Helen. They became familiar with Cyprus and various areas of the Middle East.

An *Any Questions* high point was the broadcast from Bristol University in February 1961 with the author Robert Henriques, Lord Boothby and John Freeman of the *New Statesman* (former Labour minister, and later Ambassador to Delhi).

Neil Crichton-Miller, a Home Service talks producer, in November 1961 invited Mary Stocks to join with Cyril Ray (best known as a wine connoisseur) in cross-examining Dr Donald Soper of the Methodist Church on his advocacy of the concept and practice of total abstinence. Miller wrote: 'I am confident that Dr Soper, Cyril Ray and yourself all have the common touch needed for a programme on this subject, and that you also have the ability to debate the subject on a high level'.

Mary Stocks's reaction to this was to welcome the idea of a debate with Donald Soper. They were old friends from *Any Questions* sessions, and she felt he combined strong opinions and tolerance. Interestingly, this was a combination that others perceived in her. The Stocks–Soper paths had crossed and re-crossed already and were to do so many times more. Donald Soper, born in 1903, had devoted his life to the Methodist Church and to left-wing campaigning. He too had studied at the London School of Economics, gaining his doctorate there, though considerably after Mary's LSE era. He had published half a dozen books on theological topics, presided over several London Methodist missions and, from his twenties onwards, preached every Sunday in Hyde Park and every Wednesday on Tower Hill.

There were other enthusiasms he shared with Mary Stocks, but most significantly he was to be created a Labour Life Peer a few months before Mary achieved the same status. They were to sit together on the Labour benches of the House of Lords for nearly ten years.

The debate on total abstinence was broadcast in February 1962 and audience research showed it was well liked, in spite of the fact (or perhaps because of the fact) that John Arlott, the poet and cricket commentator, took the place of Cyril Ray. He too was a wine expert. No transcript has survived, but it can be assumed that Mary took the line of moderation, steering a middle course between Donald Soper's passionate support for teetotalism and John Arlott's devotion to wine.

Interviewed thirty years later, Lord Soper (as he now was) recalled Mary Stocks as a doughty opponent on various radio programmes. 'We were friendly antagonists – a happy fellowship of controversy'. He went on: 'She had a capacity to speak with authority on a variety of topics. One hesitated to disagree with her. She was very quick-witted and would often win the argument'. *Any Questions* was a star programme under Freddie Grisewood, he suggested.

Questioned about Mary Stocks's personality, Lord Soper said: 'She was indifferent to many attributes of femininity. I would have to say she had no particular pride in her appearance; it was military rather than decorative'.

Of her religious beliefs, he said: 'She did not groan under a sense of sin, but she was certainly on the Lord's side. She was profoundly concerned with many moral issues, and it would be wrong to call her irreligious'.

Of her activities as a Peer, Lord Soper commented: 'She did not find it wholly congenial, so she was not the success she could have been'. He sympathised with her decision to vote against the Labour Party over the settlement of Rhodesia and the arrangements for Uganda Asian immigrants, but questioned her opposition to some forms of nationalisation ('She equated it with Socialism. It was nothing of the sort. It was a poor alternative to a true Socialist community'.)

Surprisingly for a Methodist minister, he was sympathetic also to

Mary Stocks's campaign for free contraception within the National Health Service ('I agreed with her views. The bishops sometimes caused me shock'). As to her rejection of the Labour whip in 1974 (to be discussed later), he understood her reasons but saw it as a great loss to the party. 'Socialism is a movement, and you have to move with it'.[27]

More diversification – for she rarely refused an offer – came, with a light-hearted piece for *Woman's Hour* on weather forecasts, an overseas talk on voting, and the first of a series of prestige interviews – *Frankly Speaking* – which evolved mainly as chats with bishops. The first was Lord Fisher of Lambeth, lately Archbishop of Canterbury, and the second (six months later) Mervyn Stockwood, the social campaigning Bishop of Southwark. Scripts of these controversial interviews have not survived.

This was followed by a personal talk, in a series suggested by a listener, in which well known radio voices discussed their childhood: '*In the Time of My Youth*'. Mary Stocks feared her youth might not have been sensational enough for listeners' expectations. However, she wrote to the producer: 'Nothing simpler. I will let you have a script, though my upbringing (a singularly happy one) was conditioned by (a) a sense of security and (b) by domestic service – neither available for the middle classes now.' This theme of middle-class privilege was one to which she returned again and again, in her talks and her writing. It was as if she felt the need to apologise for her comfortable background and upbringing.

In July 1962 she was involved in what must have seemed to this child of the Victorian era a remarkable technological experiment: a transatlantic conversation by means of the new Telstar communication satellite on Goonhilly Down in Cornwall. This was to have been recorded at midnight. Ironically the link-up failed and a second attempt had to be made next day. Mary Stocks's view of this futuristic space-age radio innovation is not recorded. A pity, for the comment of a septuagenarian participant, however, youthful in outlook, could not fail to be intriguing.

Later that year, to mark the centenary of the District Nursing Association, she published *A History of District Nursing* – drawing much on her Manchester experience in pioneering birth control clinics. And in this connection one of her most controversial public statements ever came on an *Any Questions* panel at Ringwood,

Hampshire in the early 1960s.

The panel was asked to give advice to Diana Dors, the somewhat notorious blonde and buxom film star, on bringing up her newborn son. Unwisely Mary Stocks said firmly: 'My advice is that she should get it adopted'. She was strenuously opposed by the Abbot of Downside and a *Daily Mirror* columnist. Diana Dors and her husband, Dickie Dawson, said the suggestion was ridiculous and the baby, Mark, would have as many photos taken as they liked. (It later transpired that £3,000 paid in advance for photos of the baby would be paid into a trust fund for his benefit.) Mary Stocks refused to withdraw her remarks, or even to admit they had been flippant. In a subsequent newspaper interview she said: 'The home life of a child whose parents live in a blaze of publicity must be very undesirable. The adoption should take place at once, the sooner the better'.

Later in 1962 she plunged into another controversy with an article in the *Sunday Times* which argued against euthanasia. Using Florence Nightingale as a model (she had actually died at the age of 91, but her faculties of sight, hearing, memory and movement had long gone) Mary Stocks suggested that what could be called suspended animation might be only temporary. Equally, the exact moment of death may be impossible to determine except by medical tests. Does this, she asked, make man any more than a conditioned automaton? A synthetic man might one day be created from transplanted tissues.

Mary Stocks had not, as far as we know, sat at the bedside of a person who would now be classified as brain-dead, for whom a legal decision might be made to end life support. Yet there seems to be a degree of personal experience in her judgment:

> Nobody who has watched the process of disintegration in a human being can ever be one hundred per cent certain what goes on in the consciousness of the inarticulate unresponding human frame. So if we accept any interpretation of death other than the physical symptoms which enable a doctor to sign a death certificate, we are indeed landed in a quagmire of uncertainty.[28]

Her conclusion is somewhat open-ended, and she calls as witness her favourite poet, Robert Browning:

This man's flesh He hath admirably made,
Blown like a bubble, kneaded like a paste,
To coop up and keep down on earth a space
That puff of vapour from man's mouth, his soul.

In 1964, she was called on to write and broadcast tributes to
Lady Astor, who died in May that year. This was something Mary
Stocks was supremely well qualified to do, and her appreciations
of her old friend threw a new light on their relationship. Nancy
Astor and Mary Stocks were as unlike, one might think, as any two
women could be: Mary an academic, a feminist, a radical; Nancy
an American Southern belle married to an aristocrat – yet over
45 years their friendship had deepened and endured into a kind
of mutual devotion, most powerful on Mary's side.

In 1963 there finally appeared a biography which had been
germinating for many years: Mary's life of her old friend Ernest
Simon, later Lord Simon of Wythenshawe. As she said, she wrote
Ernest Simon of Manchester in return for the happiness of a long
friendship with both Ernest and his wife Sheena.

They had met almost as soon as John and Mary Stocks arrived
in Manchester, where Ernest served on the city council and his wife
on Manchester Education Committee. Ernest Simon headed the
Simon Engineering Group, and was also closely connected with the
university and the Scotts of the *Manchester Guardian*, so the Simon
and Stocks paths crossed and re-crossed. Ernest Simon and John
Stocks were almost equal in age, and their educational paths had
crossed even earlier, at Rugby. Mary was convinced it was Sheena
Simon's influence which caused her to be appointed to several
important government committees during her time in Manchester,
and possibly it was also the Simons who recommended her for the
magistracy. The two families remained lifelong friends, holidaying
together in the Lake District and abroad.

As a Liberal MP for Withington, Ernest Simon co-operated on
housing issues with the Independent Eleanor Rathbone, and in the
wartime Coalition Government he was appointed deputy chairman
of the Building Trades Council in the Ministry of Works (after a
spell with the Ministry of Aircraft Production). A point of interest
for Mary was that the Minister of Works during the war was Lord
Reith, first Director-General of the BBC, and later a House of
Lords contemporary. Ernest Simon and Mary Stocks were not

contemporaries in the House of Lords, for he died six years before she was created a Peer. If they had been, she would certainly have supported his campaigns for improved higher education, public sector housing and similar concerns.

Ernest Simon of Manchester was Mary Stocks's most scholarly publication, but critics might find it not adequately impartial. It is a eulogy of a man she deeply admired, rather than an objective overview. She summed up his personality as that of one who always wanted to do good, expected others to be similarly motivated, and could not understand it if they were not:

> Under the skin of an eminent social reformer and successful business tycoon one discovered at the core of Ernest Simon a kind of innocence which was positively childlike and, to those who knew him, infinitely endearing.[29]

Here is a paradox, and at other points in his life (for example at Cambridge, where he went up with a scholarship in engineering but admitted to largely wasting his time and money on polo, race-going and cards) a dichotomy can be detected in his character. Mary Stocks hints at this discrepancy, but does not analyse it. A biographer should be able to stand back and assess his subject. Mary Stocks was probably too close to, and involved with, the Simon family to do that.

Nonetheless a clear portrait emerges of a late Victorian Lancashire philanthropist, one of a generation who inherited family wealth in coal or cotton or railways, who turned their high intelligence and superior education to good account in public service. There were several of these in Mary's own family, and she could easily recognise solid social achievement when she saw it. Moreover, she could write with fluency and lack of inhibition. The result is a good book, but not a great book.

In 1965 Mary Stocks was accorded the rare accolade, for a broadcaster, of a slot in the popular *Desert Island Discs* programme devised during the war and presented for some 40 years by Roy Plomley. It is clear from the transcript that Roy Plomley regarded her as one of his most admired castaways. He asked her directly: 'Could you endure indefinite solitude?' She told him loneliness did not alarm her at the age of 74, provided the island was warm and fertile; and she would be happy to escape the feeling that whatever she was doing she ought to be doing something else. Music had been a pleasant by-product in her life, though her only instrument had been the mouth organ. Attempts to teach her the piano had failed.

School life had not greatly interested her, she confessed, but social work did and that led her into studying for an economics degree. The first record she chose was 'Soldiers of the Queen', which she remembered listening to on a phonograph during the Boer War – when she was naturally on the side of the minority and therefore pro-Boer. Then came an opera excerpt from Rossini, followed by the Liebestod from Wagner's *Tristan and Isolde.* This she had heard at the Opera House in Berlin in 1931, and Wagnerian music she associated with her own wedding.

She admitted it might have been a blessing not to get into Parliament in 1945 since this would have meant resigning as Principal of Westfield, though she 'jolly nearly got in' against a right-wing Independent. Her next record was of Myra Hess playing Schumann's *Carnival Suite.*

After a few questions about her broadcasting career, Roy Plomley asked which pronouncement of hers on *Any Questions* had raised the biggest rumpus. And Mary Stocks told the story of her gaffe over Colin Cowdrey's feet – he had been rejected for military service because of a foot problem but soon afterwards was chosen to play cricket for England. Freddie Grisewood picked on her first, said Mary, because he knew she would be ignorant of the Colin Cowdrey affair. So what did she think about Colin Cowdrey's feet? To which she said: what was his feat?

Her fifth record was of Gracie Fields singing 'The Little Pudding Basin that Belonged to Auntie Flo' – a reminder of early days in Manchester, and perhaps a gesture towards the anti-snobs. After that a Paul Robeson song she associated with her husband's brief time as Vice-Chancellor of Liverpool.

Her practical streak came to the fore when she suggested she might use her spectacles on the desert island to kindle a fire and fry fish, and as an optimist she chose 'Transatlantic Lullaby' – an American song recalling the worst days of the London blitz when this song raised morale. Her last choice of record was the final chorus from Bach's *St Matthew Passion,* and that would be her first choice if she could take only one record.

The book she would take (all castaways automatically have the

Bible and Shakespeare) would be the collected novels of Jane Austen in big print, and her luxury a transistor radio. And the programme ended on an original note: Mary Stocks regretting that she could not invite Roy Plomley to join her because if he did, the island would no longer be a desert one. She was far from sure that she would want to be rescued in view of the threat to the world from nuclear war and overpopulation.

The script of a radio programme without the participants' voices is like a person with no taste buds eating rich fruit cake. Yet in reading through the script of Mary Stocks's session on *Desert Island Discs* one seems to hear snatches of her sharp incisive speech, the very slight lack of roll in her r's, the dry humour. This was vintage radio.

Later in 1965 she was busy stirring up controversy again. Several tabloid newspapers covered a meeting of a women's organisation in Sussex at which she reportedly proposed that castration might be the best way of dealing with compulsive psychopathic sex offenders. This, she argued, would be a merciful operation rather than a form of retribution. Such a scheme was operated in Denmark, provided the offender and his wife agreed. However she did not advocate it as a matter for women to campaign for. In 1965 such views were sensational – Mary Stocks made headlines.

Later that year an opponent called Pat Baker (the name is ambivalent; it is not clear whether the journalist was a man or a woman) interviewed Mary Stocks for the *Advertisers' Review*[31] on her publicly perceived critical attitude towards advertising. This, Baker alleged, was frequently in evidence in asides on the *Any Questions* programme. Mary Stocks was asked if she regarded advertising as an economic waste. 'Not altogether. Some advertising I know is necessary. But there is too much advertising altogether – it absorbs money which could be used to better purpose'. Which particular advertising did she have in mind? 'Well, take for instance tobacco and beer . . . the extensive advertising of these puts pressure on young people by glamorising smoking of cigarettes and the drinking of beer'. The advertising of medicines had improved greatly since her youth and 'Dr Williams' Pink Pills'.

Her comment on television advertising was that detergents had ruined the image of advertising on television. Pressed to name a detergent, she reluctantly admitted she used Surf, probably because it was so heavily promoted. What about women's magazines and advertising? 'They certainly educate women readers, show them how to better themselves physically and how to improve their homes'. The final question: which newspapers did she read? 'The *New Statesman*, *Listener*, *Observer* and *Evening Standard*. Before *Any Questions* I bone up on things by reading the *Daily Express* and the *Daily Mirror*'.

The first four publications she mentioned accurately reflect her world view. The *New Statesman* as the intellectual reader's left-wing guide, the *Listener* as the main written organ of the BBC, the *Observer* because she had served for years on its Trust, the *Evening Standard* because of her increasing militancy over what she called the rape of London.

The year 1965 was indeed an *annus mirabilis* in Mary Stocks's broadcasting career. She was well into her eighth decade, at a time of life when most women of her generation had long faded quietly from the public eye. Not so Mary Stocks. The BBC file for 1965 under her name is a bulging folder punctuated with telegrammese postcards sent from Aubrey Lodge. (As she grew older her postcards became more succinct and wittier.)

One unexpected treat was to interview John Badley, founder of the unorthodox Bedales co-educational school in Hampshire, then 97 but still active. Bedales started in 1893 and, closely associated with the Arts and Crafts movement, had educated many famous names. Because of John Badley's great age it was necessary to send a recording car to his Hampshire home, but there proved to be nothing aged about his mind. He himself had been at Rugby in the 1870s, he told Mary, and found its educational base very narrow: hours devoted to classics but hardly any attention paid to mathematics, science or French.

At Cambridge his best friend was Garrett Anderson, whose sister John Badley married. (Strange how often the Garrett Anderson family, Elizabeth, Millicent and others, had come into the life of Mary Stocks.) From the Anderson family Badley absorbed the idea that co-education was a good thing. So with other educational reformers he founded Bedales at a time when co-education in Britain was almost unknown. (In its centenary year, 1993, Bedales flourishes.) It was to be an independent place of learning with emphasis on the creative arts. The school prospered. Bernard Shaw sent a ward there, Oscar Wilde and Sir Oliver Lodge sent their sons. Although it was non-denominational, the Bible was regarded as important. But was it too upper-class in composition, Mary asked? The old man defended this by arguing that high fees were inevitable for an avant-garde place of learning. When she asked about the future of the school he implied that economic viability might depend on overseas students. (Since the time of the interview Bedales has had two royal pupils.)

Meanwhile Mary Stocks was diversifying even more in her radio output. One of her most popular talks, often re-broadcast, was on the theme 'What would you do if you were in charge of a Cabinet of Women?' Her proposed reforms included nationalising the distribution of water and of sewage disposal, two of her favourite topics on air. This was followed by a Home Service talk on Cyprus, the island divided uneasily between Greek and Turkish communities. This talk was prompted by visits there to stay with her daughter Ann and son-in-law Arthur (the Civil Service expert on national insurance). This 15-minute talk, 'Cyprus, the Troubled Island', caused a good deal of controversy.

Mary had first been to the island in 1953 when the Greek demand for Enosis (union with Greece) was emerging. When she returned in 1955 the Enosis movement had become violent, the British Institute Library had been burned down by Greeks, and a British policeman shot. By 1958 the troubles had escalated into full-scale war. By 1959, under the benevolent governorship of Sir Hugh Foot (brother of Dingle and Michael, her fellow *Any Questions* panellists), NATO forces had moved in to keep the peace. But the integration of Greek and Turkish communities, which Mary had hoped for, did not come. She made no secret of her criticism of the British Government for its handling of the Cyprus problem, and advocated limited independence before the idea was fashionable. Her view was that the problem had been compounded by Britain's failure to provide good education during the colonial years, and by what she called 'an unimaginative colonial administration'. BBC memoranda circulated at a high level before she was allowed to give the talk, and there are indications that it was much modified from her original script.

Soon after this she was planning a review of a book on Victorian lady travellers, a talk about Mrs Beeton in *Home This Afternoon* ('Take 24 Eggs') and a 'Salute to Old Age' for *Woman's Hour*. It is strangely ironic that the non-domesticated Mary Stocks, aged 72 and known to say that her favourite food was tinned spaghetti, should pay tribute to Britain's most famous cook on the centenary of her death, aged 28, in 1865.

Next she was asked to compile a collection of texts and sayings for a successor programme to *Lift Up Your Hearts*, to be called *Ten to Eight* (this was the time when it went on air). She was keen to refer in rather unorthodox terms to Robert Browning, in particular *Bishop Blougram's Apology* and *Ben Izarshish*. The broadcast, in June, provoked some decidedly hostile reactions. Mary wrote to the then Head of Religious Broadcasting 'See what you have let me in for'.

Some lighter fixtures in 1965 were a talk on 'Saturday's Child' (her birthday was a Saturday), another entitled 'Flattery will get you Nowhere', and a choice-of-holiday books programme with the South African anti-apartheid novelist Ruth First (later killed by terrorists) and the foreign correspondent James Cameron. On two Saturdays in August she filled the *Outlook* slot for the religious broadcasting service, and worked on a theatre review piece for Monica Sims of *Woman's Hour*.

The theatre review, a new genre for her, caused her some difficulty. Postcards revealed that she 'could not make head or tail of the play *Inadmissible Evidence*, she found *The Killing of Sister George* 'disgusting and offensive'. Nonetheless she reviewed them. Then came a half-hour reassessment of Mrs Gaskell's biography of Charlotte Brontë, favoured Stocks reading, and a portrait of her old friend Mrs Sidney Webb for a series called *Twentieth Century Thinkers*. Another theatre round-up covered *Spring and Port Wine*, *Say Who You Are*, and Shaw's *Too True to be Good*.[32]

Throughout the 1960s she was in demand for book and theatre reviews, Sunday evening Good Cause appeals, and what might loosely be called chat-shows. The year 1965 ended and 1966 began on an extended high note. On Christmas Day, Mary Stocks gave the early morning *Thought for the Day*, and in the New Year Honours it was announced that Harold Wilson had created her a Life Peer. So Dr Brinton's daughter finally and indisputably joined the ranks of the Establishment which she had so often rebelled against. She chose to explain it away as being a reward for her longevity as a broadcaster, but friends of the new Baroness felt that nearly all her life's activities has played their part in her ennoblement.

Chapter 6

The House of Lords Years: 1966–1975

The taking of her seat in the Upper Chamber was undoubtedly a double-plus high point in Mary Stocks's career – which had not been short of high points. She bought the obligatory black tricorne hat which rather suited her personality, and her daughters advised on suitable clothes to be worn under the somewhat oppressive scarlet and ermine robes. The event had been postponed because of a car accident, but it finally took place on 16 February 1966, almost exactly twenty years after she had last failed to be elected to the House of commons. The new Baroness might have been forgiven for feeling a quiet sense of triumph that her debating skills could now be exercised in a fitting forum.

Her chosen sponsors were Barons Archibald and Piercy. Lord Archibald of Woodside in the City of Glasgow, now 68, had been created a Life Peer in 1949 after an impressive career in education and documentary films, most notably for the Central Office of Information during the war. He had been a Glasgow city councillor and magistrate in the 1920s, and more recently Assistant Chief Whip for Labour in the Lords. There is no record to show that Mary Stocks knew him personally, so it seems probable that it was in his capacity as a Whip that he supported her. Harold Piercy, five years older than Mary, had remained a friend since their student days. He was created 1st Baron Piercy of Burford in 1945 (the year when Labour came to power in postwar Britain) after holding many prominent business posts, among them a directorship of the Bank of England and chairmanship of the Wellcome Trust. What would especially have pleased Mary was his status as a governor of Birmingham University and their old Alma Mater, the London School of Economics.

So the three socialists, the film-maker, the banker and the

broadcaster, walked together behind the Gentleman Usher through corridors of power that Mary Brinton the Kensington doctor's daughter had never dreamed of entering; and she joined the ranks of the highest in the land.

The ceremony is recorded for ever in the *Journals of the House of Lords*:

> Mary Danvers Stocks, being by Letters patent bearing the date of the 17th day of January in the 14th year of the reign of her present Majesty, created Baroness Stocks of the Royal Borough of Kensington and Chelsea, for life, was (in her robes) introduced between the Lord Piercy and the Lord Archibald (also in their robes) the Gentleman Usher of the Black Rod and Rouge Dragon Pursuivant preceding: her Ladyship, on her knee, presented her Patent to the Lord Chancellor at the Woolsack.[1]

The Patent was then read aloud:

> Elizabeth the Second by the Grace of God . . . do by these presents advance, create and prefer our trusty and well-beloved Mary Danvers Stocks, widow of our trusty and well-beloved John Leofric Stocks, Esquire, Companion of our Distinguished Service Order, to the state, degree, style, dignity and honour of Baroness Stocks of our Royal Borough of Kensington and Chelsea . . . Witness ourself at Westminster . . . Coldstream.

After this the Writ of Summons was read:

> We . . . command you . . . you be personally present at our aforesaid Parliament with Us, and with the Prelates, Nobles and Peers of our said Kingdom, to treat and give your counsel upon the affairs aforesaid.

The Journal continues:

> Then her Ladyship, at the Table, took and subscribed the Oath, pursuant to the Statute, and was placed on the Barons' Bench next below the Lord King-Hall.

It is not clear what the plain-living and plain-speaking Mary Stocks thought of all this antiquated and ceremonious English, the fancy dress and the mediaeval ceremony. One suspects she was thrilled by it.

There were other familiar faces. She nervously approached Lord

Reith, the BBC's formidable first Director General, to explain who she was. He overwhelmed her by saying he would have been happy to sponsor her entry into the Lords. Her old London University fellow principal, Ifor Evans, was now Lord Evans of Hungershall. And of course Donald Soper was a recent recruit to the Methodist peerage ranks as Lord Soper of Kingsway.

Another broadcasting peer of Mary's generation was the former naval commander Stephen King-Hall, a defence expert who had graduated to radio commentary and presentation, and become a favourite voice on *Children's Hour*. She found many friends of all political persuasions, and not unreasonably she came to think of the Upper Chamber as 'an eventide club'. It did not then have an influx of younger socialists created Life Peers to bring in new blood.

No one was ever sure, least of all Mary Stocks, who had recommended her for her title. She attributed it at one time to her 'superannuated gaiety on the Light Programme'. Others pointed to her lifelong commitment to the Labour Party and her various forms of social service over the years. She had given in total about thirty years to government committees. Her name was a household word, her voice one of the most instantly recognisable on radio. She said later:

> What the B.B.C. did was to force me into the public eye – or rather ear – and focus a lot of personal publicity on any other activities I might pursue. Without this advertisement I should have lapsed into a decent obscurity.[2]

It is slightly puzzling that she was offered a peerage by Harold Wilson and accepted the Labour Whip, although she had not been a party member for almost thirty years and indeed had stood as an independent Parliamentary candidate. Frank Gillard, long a senior BBC man, throws some light on it:

> When Life Peerages were introduced it occurred to me the Labour Party might like to have someone in the Lords with Fabian leanings, and that Mary would meet that need admirably. She was, moreover, a well liked public figure through *Any Questions* and other broadcasts . . . I mentioned this idea to Sir Robert Boothby, knowing that although they belonged to opposing political parties Boothby and Harold Wilson were on good terms . . . Bob Boothby later telephoned to say that

Wilson was definitely interested. Mary, of course, knew nothing of all this.

Her name was in the next Honours list. There is little doubt that her *Any Questions* work had a lot to do with the bestowal of the peerage, but no doubt all her efforts in her great cause of education (which meant so much to her) and all her diligence as a 'statutory woman' on Government and other committees were taken into account.[3]

She could have sat on the cross benches. But she chose Labour sponsors and sat with other Labour peers; indeed soon after she renewed her party membership by joining the Kensington Labour Party. At heart this was still the Mary Stocks who had marched as a suffragette, married a passionate socialist academic, and organised Labour Party meetings in Oxford and Manchester.

On that first day the House of Lords sat until 7.38 p.m., and the new Baroness listened to debates on the exemption of milk from a new Weights and Measures Order, the draft of a Woollen Textile Amendment Order, and the functions of traffic wardens in Scotland.

The procedure was not unfamiliar to her. Her first visit to the House of Lords had been in 1918, to hear a women's suffrage debate, and there had been subsequent visits when the matters under review were especially relevant to her concerns. She did not need briefing, she was an accomplished off-the-cuff speaker, and she had friends in the Chamber.

Baroness Stocks's maiden speech was made two months later, on 28 April. She spoke in favour of a government proposal to include family doctors' deputising services (the system of transferring their night call-outs to an agency) in the National Health Service. The *Times* reported her speech at some length:

Lady Stocks said that when her father was a general practitioner in West London his practice was entirely fee-paying and he was never overworked. The leisure of a G.P. today, under the National Health Service, was nil, and his wife was his receptionist, cook, children's nurse and everything.[4]

When the Bill came before the Lords for a second reading, she argued that the dream of 1946 (when the Health Service was set up) was 'a service giving men, women and children in this country the services of a G.P. based on the old doctor–patient personal relation. The question is: Have we got it?' A legal case-load of up to 3,500 patients made for perfunctory visits at the surgery – 'an experience with which noble Lords in this House will not be familiar, but others are'.

Meanwhile, for the new Peeress, life at the BBC went on as vigorously as before. Soon after her introduction, plans were in hand for her to give an hour-long talk under the title 'A Year in my Life: 1951'. This was later changed to 'The Time of My Life'. Mary wrote to the producer, John Blunden:

> I was fairly heavily engaged during [1951] in the fight for the Beveridge Report. It was of course the year in which the Labour Party sold the pass by extending the B.B.C. Charter and handing it on a plate to the Conservatives and the pressure group [which had advocated commercial television, always fiercely opposed by Mary Stocks]. It is therefore sad that one can't get the voice of Beveridge on his Report.[5]

Her talk was to include a good deal of actuality (BBC jargon for on-the-spot recordings) and she had hoped for the voices of other pro-BBC campaigners from the 1950s – Lord Hailsham, Christopher Mayhew. 'Alas, I cannot unearth any voices concerning my activities as a statutory woman, or my elevation to the Principalship of Westfield'. Later she wrote (perhaps somewhat tongue-in-cheek) 'The thought of talking about myself for close on an hour fills me with horror'.

'The Time of my Life' finally went out in July 1966, with not one speaker but two – Mary Stocks and Freddie Grisewood – discussing their memories of 1951. Afterwards John Blunden wrote that listeners' letters had poured in. 'I am quite sure that you and he must be among the most popular broadcasters of today'.[6] Sadly, a BBC memorandum the following October admitted that the programme recording had been 'destroyed in error'.

Also that summer the new Baroness, still at 75 a campaigner for women's rights, spoke on *Woman's Hour* about women's suffrage ('rational creatures and free citizens'), carried on with an early morning religious slot, and teamed up with the folk singer Julie Felix and the novelist G.W. Target to talk about their choice of novels. Julie Felix picked John Steinbeck's *The Grapes of Wrath*, G.W. Target chose *To Kill a Mocking Bird* by Harper Lee, and Mary

Stocks opted for the nineteenth-century classic, Samuel Butler's *The Way of All Flesh*.

In October she diversified still further, joining the panel of a rather trivial radio parlour game called *The Petticoat Line*. Christopher Searle, at one time its producer, recalled that her presence gave distinction to a lightweight programme. Most of her friends thought her unwise to get involved. In total contrast she supplied for the religious department a talk on morals and philosophy, a review of some religious books, and a further series of *Outlook* (the 10-minute early morning reflection.)

1966 reached a climax on Boxing Day with a memorable West Region dialogue, again with Freddie Grisewood, linking excerpts from *Any Questions*. They also reminisced about their childhoods, and compared past and present generations. The title – after some debate – 'Two Old Squares'. Not for the first time Mary deprecated her contribution to *Any Questions* by saying the programme called for 'a superficial knowledge of a number of unrelated subjects'.

So she came to the midpoint of her 75th year still immensely active as a broadcaster, as a House of Lords speaker and a public figure. She espoused some controversial current causes; abortion, the state of the Health Service, and campaigning against what she called the rape of London. The epilogue to her autobiography makes it clear that she valued her access to the House of Lords while refusing to take it too seriously:

> The House of Lords can, by the nature of its composition, produce a debate of exceptionally high quality and sustain it in an atmosphere of mutual respect. So long as a second Chamber reflects these qualities I, for one, would like to let it alone.

On the other hand:

> It is difficult not to contemplate with a tolerance, amounting to affection, the quaint forms and ceremonies which clearly waste time, sometimes border on absurdity, and may indeed occasion inconvenience.[7]

Among the time-wasters she mentioned the slow method of voting in the division lobbies, among the splendours of the Upper House the ceremonial State Opening of Parliament.

In 1967 a more intellectual tone can be observed in her general broadcasting. She was picked to debate a controversial new book,

Vatican Observed, with the Bishop of Ripon, who had attended the historic second Vatican Council as an observer for the Church of England. One senses that she was now recognised as an authority on contemporary religion. This was confirmed with yet another series in the early morning five-minute religious slot, and the culmination of moves over the years to publish a collection of her popular talks on the Bible. This had been pressed for by listeners, by Mary Stocks herself, and by her old friend Elsie Chamberlain.

Finally the slim volume, a BBC publication, appeared in July 1967 under her own choice of title: *Unread Best-Seller: Reflections on the Old Testament*. It sold out and was reprinted twice in the same year. Some of the talks had already been printed in *Nursing Mirror* as far back as 1962, but they were now assembled in a more streamlined and logical order.

Her introduction refers with typical realism to:

> random reflections on the Old Testament by a broadcaster who is neither a scholar nor a theologian. They were given 'live' between 1957 and 1964 in a B.B.C. programme at 7.50 a.m. entitled *Lift Up Your Hearts*, which involved early rising and careful timing to make way for the weather report at 7.55. Thus they were heard, among others, by a number of inadvertent listeners, normally allergic to religious homilies but anxious to be tuned in to the weather report.

Baroness Stocks passionately defends the Bible as poetry as a source of very present help in trouble, and for its 'overwhelming consciousness of the responsibility of man to God and of God to man'. And she prefaces her reflections with a very practical exhortation:

> I know that some of my readers are happy with their old familiar Bibles and like them just the way they are. But I do hope that instead of writing to tell me so, they will think of all those – especially young people – who don't read the Bible because they don't like the look of it, and therefore don't know what they miss.

She suggests that one such missed experience may be 'disturbing onslaughts of the unseen', or unexpected spiritual insight.

Many of the talks were concerned with Old Testament folk heroes, and surprisingly often she equates what happened to them with contemporary European events. Thus the Hitler Youth have some roots in Jeroboam, the revolutionary leader who destroyed Solomon's kingdom; and the frivolous young women of Jerusalem castigated by Isaiah are compared unfavourably with 'a sunburnt young woman in shirt and shorts living the simple life on a kibbutz'. The author justified the title by observing how often Bibles are found by hotel beds, or given as prizes or presents, yet seldom read. She regretted that the great songs and poems of the Old Testament were printed until recently as prose – 'for they have the thunder, the pathos, the rhythm and the beauty of real poetry, and they should be presented as such'.

She found relevance in unlikely parts of the Bible: 'When Jerusalem was threatened by the kings of Assyria the Jews sang [a cruel song] . . . When I read it in college chapel on one of those crucial days when the Germans were battering at the walls of Stalingrad, I found it very satisfying'. At a critical period of the war, in 1940, she was at a service in Oxford Cathedral, when the lesson referred to the Battle of Megiddo where Israel held out against a mighty army; a Serviceman in the congregation called out 'Splendid'.

Travellers, she felt, might have their consciousness enlarged by an awareness of the Bible – 'the way the past lives with the present'. And she gained particular delight from comparing the overdressed daughters of Zion, with headbands, rings and nose jewels, to their counterparts in 1960s London.

Perhaps the most memorable and Stocksian line in *Unread Best Seller* is this: 'Deborah was, I think, the Winston Churchill of her people'. Mary Stocks is of course likening the Song of Deborah as a call to arms with some of Churchill's wartime speeches. But one suspects the feminist in her took special pleasure in finding a female Biblical *alter ego* for Churchill.

Many of the Old Testament and Apocryphal personalities who preoccupied Mary Stocks were women: Deborah, Jezebel, Esther. The most unexpected is Susanna, perceived as the inspiration for one of Daniel's finest exploits:

I mean his rescue of Susanna by a very simple court procedure known to all magistrates today, namely the separate examination of witnesses out of hearing of one another to prevent collusion.

Susanna, a married woman, was accused by two Babylonian elders of improper behaviour in a garden. Daniel, defending her, extracted conflicting evidence from the watchers – 'with that the case against Susanna collapsed'.

The book, and the talks which gave rise to it, were popular for two reasons. One was Baroness Stocks's practical and down-to-earth interpretation of sometimes obscure Old Testament stories. Another was her ability to relate them effectively to the twentieth century, with rare insight. Anglican and Catholic theology were balanced by some talks on great philosophers. One was Bertrand Russell. Mary Stocks introduced recordings of Russell in an analysis of his books and career.

Other 1967 activities included an appreciation of Emily Brontë for *Woman's Hour*. This followed a very Stocksian postcard when the BBC could not decide whether it should be Brontë or Walter De La Mare ('whichever suits you best. Meanwhile I stand by for further marching orders').[8] Another characteristic postcard was generated by discussion about a possible title for a new *Woman's Hour* talks series: 'Future Perfect is O.K. by me – as long as I can say that it isn't!'

The year was busy with *Any Questions* and *Petticoat Line*. In October she was special guest at a *Woman's Hour* anniversary party, and went to Bristol for an unusually left-oriented *Any Questions* with the Australian writer, Russell Braddon, and John Mortimer, the barrister-author.

Early in 1968 Mary Stocks interviewed both Freddie Grisewood and her old friend from Manchester days, Kingsley Martin, on his autobiography. Between these two broadcasts, in March, she was briefly a patient in Woolwich Memorial Hospital, but well enough in June to be back on a vintage *Any Questions* with the politicians Norman St John Stevas (later Lord St John of Fawley) and Lord Robens, and the actor Peter Ustinov.

In July *Woman's Hour* accorded her the rare honour of wishing her many happy returns on the air. She appeared on the programme six times in 1968, most notably in a discussion on euthanasia arranged by the National Secular Society. Another lively debate was entitled 'Can Marriage Survive Success?' Baroness Stocks took part with the author Shirley Conran and Marjorie Proops of the *Daily Mirror*. She was in demand for book reviews and *The Week's Good Cause*, the regular Sunday evening charity appeal. Later in the year she interviewed the Bishop of Southwark; and joined the Liberal Party leader Jeremy Thorpe and the economist Peter Jay in

Any Questions at Malmesbury. By now members of her family were
used to driving her around the West Country ('The B.B.C. always
entertained us well,' said one of her daughters who was often roped
in as chauffeur).

However, in February 1969 *Any Questions* was held in her
well-remembered Manchester – possibly the first session to be held
outside BBC West Region. So the wheel had come full circle, and
at 76 Mary Stocks was back broadcasting on topical issues where
she had given her first radio current affairs talks almost forty years
earlier.

In March 1969, still active in the House of Lords and on matters
of controversy concerning London, Mary Stocks in a letter drew
the BBC's attention to the problems faced by elderly patients when
their family doctor died suddenly. As a result she was interviewed
on *The World this Weekend* about rheumatism. Elderly yet still
powerfully articulate, she was coming to be seen as a guru on
matters medical associated with old people.

During 1969 she continued on the panel of *Any Questions*,
Petticoat Line and yet another radio parlour game, *Call my Bluff*
(in which panellists challenged each other on invented word defini-
tions; the truth proved often more bizarre than the invention). Plans
were mooted for a talks series on the most significant decade in the
lives of a number of well-known people: Malcolm Muggeridge,
René Cutforth, Mary Stocks. Baroness Stocks opened the New
Year of 1970 with a challenging look back at the first decade of
the century: 'Turn of the Decade, 1900 to 1910'.

As it was almost her broadcasting swan-song it is worth quoting in full:

The first decade of the century naturally made a lasting impression on me because it brought me out of childhood, at the age of
nine, through adolescence, to adult status as a first-year undergraduate at the age of nineteen. I will record three outstanding
impressions of those years:

First, they covered a ten years' battle with my otherwise
greatly loved mother, over the kind of clothes I had to wear.
I wanted clothes that took on and off easily and allowed free
movement. She was aware that such clothes were not then worn,
and naturally did not want her daughter to look eccentric.

Second, I did not want to associate with my own barbarous,

and I thought foolish, age group. I liked mixing with adult persons and doing the things they were doing. As a social worker after 1908 I was able to do this.

Third, I was not interested in sex and had no wish to attract young men – though on two occasions I seem to have done so. But then I was not perpetually reminded that I ought to be interested in sex, by cinemas and T.V., which did not then exist; or by unending talk – which, if it did exist, did not come my way.

How different then is the comparable decade enjoyed (or not enjoyed) by my grandchildren and their contemporaries. They can dress as they like, comfortably or not as the mood takes them. They only seem happy when associating with their own contemporaries – preferably in large groups. And our highly organised and financially profitable mass media are so busy reminding them that they have sex instincts which should be freely enjoyed, that it is difficult for them to stop thinking about the matter.[9]

So she bowed out (almost) from the airwaves with a wholly typical then-and-now broadside about clothes, sexual mores and the social behaviour of young people. But by now the views of a near-octogenarian had far less impact on listeners than those of younger social observers.

However if by 1970 the BBC attracted for her a less sympathetic audience, the House of Lords did not. This was a forum where her views were still listened to with respect and close attention, where age counted. In the previous year she had spoken in twelve debates. To her the most important was on divorce reform, but she intervened on matters as diverse as the cost of building Concorde, the ritual slaughter of animals and the Street Offences Bill.

In May 1970 she put a question on noise pollution, asking: 'What expenditure the Ministry of Technology has committed to sponsoring research and development in the field of aircraft noise?' The Government's reply was that currently over a million pounds year was being spent on research into sonic booms and the like. A year later Mary Stocks was elected a vice-president of the Anti-Concorde Noise Abatement Group, saying 'If people ask me to back something I agree with, I do so'. It could have been her family motto.

In the same month another Peer put a question about the design of the new Knightsbridge Barracks, not far from Mary Stocks's home. She contributed: 'Would my noble friend tell us whether any Ministry was consulted as regards the design of this banausic excrescence?'[10] The Minister concerned agreed he did not find it 'all that pleasant' and the unofficial keep-London-lovely group followed up with a question on the preservation of the Holland Park Orangery.

'Banausic' was a favourite pejorative term with the Baroness. She used it in interviews, in her autobiography and in speeches. So rare is it that most people need to look it up, to discover that it means materialistic, uncultivated, suitable for artisans. Did the upholder of adult education appreciate the social snobbery inherent in the term, or did she overlook this because she liked the sound of it?

The preservation of historic London became one of her chief preoccupations in her last few years. She devoted much energy and word-power to condemning what she saw as the rape of parts of the city she knew well, particularly the Kensington and St Pancras areas, as demolition and redevelopment accelerated in the 1960s and 70s. In 1970 she wrote to *The Times* urging the Government to let well alone rather than carving up the Greater London Council's Parks Department among several boroughs. She sympathised with Kensington's desire to run Holland Park, but 'the London parks as at present administered command the admiration of the civilised world'.[11]

Higher education was a field on which she spoke in the Lords with authority and not a little experience, and from time to time she wrote an article on some aspect of university education. In November 1970 she startled her fellow ex-academics by suggesting in *The Times* that the power and influence of former vice-chancellors and college principals in the Upper House was excessive in proportion to their numbers ('they combine more than average intellectual quality with capacity for convincing and articular exposition'). Lord Robbins had lately put forward a motion to consider future demands for higher education, and there were many of his fellow Peers to support him.

Baroness Stocks boldly questioned the priorities involved. There was not, she pointed out, a comparable pressure group to promote the needs of the police, the medical services or (for example) primary education. The university system in Britain was still modelled on the Oxbridge pattern, no longer relevant to the needs of most young people in the 18 to 21 age group pursuing education at public expense. Might the existing courses not adequately be covered in two-thirds of the existing time?

The demand would grow, university places would increase. But 'whether more young people should have university education' should be seen against a background of the needs of 'overdriven hospital doctors, sub-standard hospitals, overcrowded prisons, and an over-extended police force'. In short, she dared to question the sanctity of that very higher education which had won her a first-class degree, a career and a place among the senior academics of the land. Mary Stocks later took up the same theme in one of her books, pitting her mature practical world-view against the idealism with which she had argued as a young woman for free education for all those who wanted it, of whatever age. And in a sense she was acknowledging that her own careers, in another age, had not been fought for or carved out of dwindling public funds.

Another recurring hobby was reminding young women of the battle fought when she was a girl to win the vote. She told a newspaper reporter in 1969: 'The National Union of Women's Suffrage Societies did a lot of hard work in getting small but useful Acts on to the [statute] books. On the whole we have done much better with regard to legislation than to social standing, where we still have a long way to go'.[12] She wrote often to the press arguing the case for women to be ordained – in this she was a pioneer pleader.

Progress in birth control and family planning had made it far easier for women to take up careers, she said in a lecture to the Family Welfare Association, but taxation still discriminated against them. Many had careers in the social services, inheriting the tradition of maiden aunts of her youth. She told the *Sunday Times* she had backed three main causes: 'Votes for women, family allowances, and contraception. They've all gone through, but there's still a lot to be done in the social services.'

In the same interview, given in February 1969, she was invited to comment on her domestic skills.

I've never cooked, and I never will. I do a little housework. I like to read novels, but not modern novels because they are concerned with the psychological distortions of people with odd sexual lives. It used to be marital infidelity, now it's homosexuality. But I think there's something to be said for reticence.[13]

She wrote to *The Times* when a statue of Mrs Pankhurst was planned for Westminster:

I do not grudge Mrs Pankhurst her statue. She was a heroic woman who rendered great service in 1903 for the cause which the 9d. stamp commemorates . . . But why in the report on the anniversary stamps is there a reference to the militant organisation which she founded as 'the movement which brought about the extension of votes to women in 1918?' Her organisation packed up in 1914 after militancy had degenerated into sabotage, and the fight was carried on by the older constitutional society . . . it continued the agitation until the achievement of equal franchise in 1928. It is important that the young women of today should know the true story of how their vote was won, and particularly important that they should realise that it was not all done by violence.

Fifty years on Mary Stocks was still loyal to the National Union of Women's Suffrage Societies and still concerned to debunk the myth that militancy won the day for universal suffrage. It was her philosophy that more can be achieved by negotiation than by brute force.

The Medical Termination of Pregnancy Bill, brought before the Lords on 16 July 1967 (the day after her 76th birthday) was Baroness Stocks's finest hour in the Upper House. This was a Private Member's Bill inspired by David Steel, then a very young Liberal MP and the son of an Edinburgh Congregational minister. (Later he became leader of the Liberal Party and was eventually knighted.) The Bill sought for the first time to legalise abortion, up to the twelfth week of pregnancy. This was a deeply controversial issue, bitterly contested between the women's welfare organisations and the traditionalists.

Many amendments were tabled, and Mary Stocks spoke on a number of them. This was an area on which she knew her ground probably better than any other Peer who spoke. Most of her life she had been involved in campaigns to help pregnant women: setting up birth control clinics, advising on the training of midwives, promoting welfare for disadvantaged mothers. In the House she was Baroness Stocks rampant and supremely well informed. She had already nailed her colours to the mast in a letter to *The*

Times, which had carried a report to the effect that two-thirds of the 5,000 doctors questioned wanted the existing Abortion Act repealed or modified. She pointed out that this was a tiny minority of all Britain's 34,000 GP's. She went on:

> In a well-ordered educated society, demand for abortion should be confined to a minority of cases, including victims of rape, and mothers who, having started a planned pregnancy, are faced with a diagnosis of risk to their own health or the likelihood of a defective child. Abortion is in most cases, I am sure, a counsel of despair. But where despair exists we must accept that counsel, while exerting ourselves to attack its causes, among which I would class . . . the apathy of some local authorities in failing to provide an effective family planning service.[15]

During the debate itself she spoke passionately in support of the Bill, first presenting the case of a mother having a planned pregnancy, who might contract German measles during pregnancy and thus run the risk of a blind or handicapped child. Under the present law this woman could force a doctor to recommend termination only by threatening suicide, or persuading a psychiatrist to diagnose her as mentally disturbed. 'What she is doing is not sacrificing one life. She is exchanging the possibility of a good life, a normal life, for a handicapped child, because she will have another pregnancy if she wants to increase her family'.

A number of Peers were concerned that hospitals would find themselves understaffed if anti-abortionists refused to carry out the operation. Mary Stocks's view on this was that legislation was unnecessary: hospitals should be left to make their own alternative arrangements.

The debate moved on to consider the case of a young girl who had attempted an abortion on herself and been refused medical help. One Peer said:

> At the moment a great many women, for various causes, would be refused an abortion. I do not know what they will do with themselves. Objections were raised that it is difficult to construct a form. If you sit at any desk in this country forms come down on you like brown snow. It is easy to make out a simple form which . . . is secret and confidential.[16]

This form would then direct her to an authorised welfare officer who would guide her towards motherhood or adoption.

Mary Stocks dealt with this very briskly. There was already ample provision, she insisted, for mothers, married or unmarried, to have care and information. She did not say so, but she must have been wondering where the noble lords had been all these fifty years since the first birth control clinics opened.

Then came her moment of glory, the moving of her own Amendment. The Bill as it was drafted stipulated that of two doctors recommending an abortion, one should be a National Health Service consultant or approved by the Minister of Health for the task. Baroness Stocks assumed that the thinking behind this clause was to prevent collusion. A newspaper editorial had suggested that without this safeguard there would be a real risk of 'a couple of doctors running a profitable abortion racket'. Collusion, she admitted, did happen in the medical world. Insisting that one doctor should be a National Health Service consultant was not going to stop it happening.

> We must trust two doctors acting in good faith – and most doctors act in good faith – to recommend or give their consent to abortions . . . performed in a proper place under professional, hygienic and expert conditions. That is the security which the Bill gives.

Furthermore, it had been stated that there were no more than 740 NHS consultants in the whole country available to perform this service. Many women would find themselves out of range of the necessary two doctors. This would tend 'to push distressed, disconsolate women back into the clutches of the old back-street abortionists.'[17] She did not believe her Amendment would wreck the Bill, unlike several previous Amendments (which to her relief had failed). 'It is not a nice way to kill a Bill. It suggests the technique of a slow poisoner rather than the swift blow of a public executioner'.

After speaking for ten minutes, she begged their Lordships to carry the Amendment standing in her name. Two government ministers and the Archbishop of Canterbury, among others, spoke in favour of the offending clause. Baroness Stocks's Amendment was supported by Lord Kennet, Lord Amulree and the Earl of Selkirk. In her summing up she argued that many hospital beds were currently and tragically occupied by women who had attempted abortions on themselves or had them carried out by back-street abortionists.

When the Amendment was put it was convincingly passed, by 113 votes to 79. Several bishops, Lord Longford (a Catholic Peer) and Baroness Wootton of Abinger (Barbara Wootton, the economist) voted against it, but the Archbishop of Canterbury and seven Peeresses were in favour. Teller for the Labour party was Mary Stocks's old *Any Questions* colleague, Lord Soper.

Another controversy in which Mary Stocks had a special and informed interest was the advent of commercial broadcasting, whether on radio or television. In February 1970 the Broadcasting Policy for Sound Radio Bill came before the House of Lords. The Conservative Peer Lord Hill (Charles Hill, dubbed 'the Radio Doctor' and by then, as Lord Hill of Luton, chairman of the BBC governors) pleaded for agreement to commercial radio as a way of raising much-needed extra revenue. By and large, he said the BBC had done a wonderful job and could not be expected to meet public demands in the 1970s without the wherewithal to do so.

Mary Stocks hit back vigorously:

> Some two or three years ago the B.B.C. made a considerable breach with what one might call the Reith tradition by appointment of the noble Lord, Lord Hill of Luton, as chairman. To some of us, perhaps to the noble Lord, Lord Reith, and certainly to me, that appeared to be calling in a chairman from what we regarded as an opposition 'gang' . . . it involved a quite considerable re-orientation of the relationship between the Chairman, the Governors and the Director General. Very soon afterwards the B.B.C. advertises *Broadcasting in the Seventies*, a completely new look at its programme policy.[18]

She went on to accuse the BBC planners of major change in traditional broadcasting standards, this despite the natural conservatism of listeners who did not like change in the style, naming or timing of their favourite programmes.

Now it was vintage Mary Stocks in full (if not always logical) cry:

If they [the planners] know a lot about the ethos and composition of the radio listening public, so, too my Lords, do I, because for about 20 years I have been an addicted radio listener and a very frequent radio broadcaster. I think that in the course of those years I have been on every form of talks programme from *Lift Up Your Hearts* to *Petticoat Line*. In the course of that experience one learns a great deal about the listeners . . . The radio listening public is exceedingly conservative (I use that word with a small 'c'.) Any change in the title and times of programmes causes distress. When *Lift Up Your Hearts* was supplanted by *Ten to Eight*, that is a programme title which seems to me to suggest peppermint creams rather than religion . . . Instead of feeling that they were being preached at by somebody who had risen in the dark hours of a cold morning to clock in at Broadcasting House at 7.30, [listeners] felt they might be being preached to by somebody who was possibly fast asleep at the time of the broadcast, or sitting in bed drinking early morning tea and reading the *Daily Express*, and as such had no right to speak to them in that way.[19]

She went on to challenge the assumption that people will constantly look in the *Radio Times* to choose programmes; and her comments may have attracted charges of sexism, prejudice and over-reaction:

Radio listeners are not all housewives who like sweet music. They are not all young men who like 'Pop'. Many housewives are exceedingly intelligent. They rely on sound radio to lighten the burden of cooking, ironing and cleaning. I have two daughters, both quite intelligent, and that is the way they listen. That is the way that they hear things they do not expect to hear, and perhaps they would not have otherwise switched on to hear them. That certainly was the case with *Lift Up Your Hearts*. A number of people . . . found themselves involuntarily listening to *Lift Up Your Hearts* for fear of missing the weather programme. If the sequence had been different it would not have happened, because nobody can 'lift up their hearts' after an English weather report.

Her final plea was for 'mixed' programmes rather than an all-day-the-same service. She urged the framers of *Broadcasting in the Seventies* to think again.

After a lively debate the published report was accepted, thus opening the way to advertising on independent radio and television. But Mary Stocks never accepted its validity, and more than once laid herself open to the charge of being hopelessly out of date in terms of the medium and the message. To which her answer was, as always, 'There is altogether too much advertising. People today are exploited for money in their pockets, whereas what formerly oppressed them were high poverty and low wages.'

Baroness Stocks was now nearing her 80th birthday, with five grandchildren and eight great-grandchildren living close at hand, so that family activities occupied much of her time. A great grief, not mentioned publicly, was the terminal illness of her son John. But she derived much pleasure from the academic achievements of her grandchildren, variously becoming qualified as a teacher (Mark), a polytechnic lecturer (Simon), an overseas teacher (Kate), a hospital nurse (Sarah) and a chartered surveyor (Jonathan). All the family lived in the Kent or London area except Mark, teaching in Cambridge. His small daughter Rebecca, born in 1969, was the apple of her great-grandmother's eye.

In October 1970 her first volume of autobiography was published, dedicated 'To my great-granddaughter Rebecca; who, if she ever reads it, will think it all rather odd'. *My Commonplace Book* attracted a lot of press attention, and reporters queued to interview the author.

Winifrede Jackson of the *Sunday Telegraph* found 'nothing frail about her voice, clear and incisive to the point where one wondered whether a question might be too stupid for her consideration'.[20] With some foresight Baroness Stocks listed Joan Vickers, Margaret Thatcher and Barbara Castle as women politicians of stature. She expressed concern that so few women were appointed as heads of co-educational schools. The permissive society did not worry her unduly, but she believed it disadvantaged women more than it did men.

Celia Brayfield of the *Daily Mail* approached the interview with some trepidation, conscious that here was a woman who had spent most of her 79 years fighting on behalf of women.

As an architect of many of the freedoms which I and other women unthinkingly enjoy every day, Mary Stocks has seen many of her innovations turn out unexpectedly. For instance, she considered that sexual freedom brought a new set of problems . . . With the best will in the world there is doubt, but you don't want to be thought square by your young man.[21]

There was an age gap of 54 years between reporter and interviewee, yet a rapport was quickly established and Celia Brayfield paid a handsome acknowledgment to the woman who might have been her grandmother:

> If she and her contemporaries hadn't worked so hard I might never have been able to meet this fascinating woman at all, let alone be paid for it. I'd have been a prisoner in someone else's home, meant only to breed, feed and knit socks.

The most detailed and perceptive interview appeared in *The Times* under the byline of Kirsten Cubitt: 'Surely the isn't-she-wonderful syndrome should have overtaken her years ago. Yet here she is at 79, highly vocal, incurably purposeful and waspish as ever.'[22]

Summarising the book, this reviewer called it the record of a lifetime's fight to bring about change. Baroness Stocks had lived to see the dissolution of the old class-based world into a new world disturbed and in many ways disturbing to an old woman, but far kinder than the one she had grown up in. The reviewer regretted that she had so little to say about her experiences as 'an archetypal reluctant débutante'.

She portrayed Mary Stocks sitting in a deep armchair, stroking the ears of her white cat (mentioned by every interviewer) and uttering scathing criticisms of higher education institutions and courses, especially the mushroom growth of sociology – not intellectually disciplined (in her view) and attracting too many students who were merely interested in current affairs. Wasn't this a touch uncharitable coming from one who took part in the suffragettes' Mud March of 1907? But Mary Stocks exemplified the virtues of 'hard grind and stamp-licking' in her own suffragist career. Now, she told her interviewer, if you disliked a government's action you sat down outside the embassy and threw stones.

Kirsten Cubitt noted that the cover of *My Commonplace Book* showed an Edwardian beauty, but one who had waged war on female clothing from an early age. Photographs had led her to expect an old woman with a face criss-crossed with lines like

W.H. Auden. Instead she discovered someone 'quite extraordinarily young', with good complexion and shining brown hair – 'dressed to make no show, in grey trousers, a grey-green blouse and a well-cut stone-coloured windcheater. The only eccentricity, perhaps, was her sensible schoolgirl sandals'.[23]

Was she afraid of death? 'No, no. But I am afraid of the process of dying. I don't want to be incontinent and senile and calling for a large share of nursing attention. It's undignified. I would like to sign a declaration that if I'm in that state I would like to be finished'. She admitted to the much younger reporter that she was uncomfortably arthritic and dreaded the prospect of false teeth.

She fully intended to continue her regular attendance at the House of Lords and to fight for those remaining unresolved issues. Had she had regrets? She would have liked to have written a play that went further than the Oxford Playhouse. She was concerned about youthful affluence and the power of the mass media. Perhaps she should extricate herself from too many committees . . .

The photograph accompanying the article shows a slim short-haired woman dressed in rather masculine clothes, radiating energy and lips parted as if engaged in earnest dialogue. It was the last public picture taken of Mary Stocks, and it brilliantly captured her personality.

In July 1971 she celebrated her 80th birthday with little ado, and plunged soon after into a fight to save the threatened casualty wards of her own local St Mary Abbots Hospital, and also the about-to-be-demolished Gaumont Cinema in Notting Hill Gate, which in its time had been a notable theatre.

Speaking as chairman of the Kensington Society and a member of the Friends of St Mary Abbots Hospital (where she had more than once been a patient), she condemned the closure of small hospital wards all over the country in favour of larger units at regional hospitals. While the big centres might be 'super-efficient', she argued that they did not meet local wishes. In the case of St Mary Abbots she wrote to *The Times* pointing out that heart patients or old people who had fallen down needed the reassurance of a hospital close at hand.

The Gaumont Cinema claimed her attention because as the Coronet it had provided a stage for Sarah Berhardt and Ellen Terry, who had opened there in 1907 in Bernard Shaw's *Captain Brassbound's Conversion*. It became a cinema in 1923. Now the

Rank Organisation wanted to develop the site for shops, flats and offices. The Kensington Society opposed this, and it was lobbying Kensington and Chelsea Borough Council with Baroness Stocks as its chief spokesperson.

In 1973 she published a second volume of memoirs, *Still More Commonplace*. This, she said, had not been planned, but she felt an urge to put into print those parts of her earlier manuscript which had been edited out by the publishers. These included recapitulations of some of her more controversial views – on Cyprus, Lord Reith, William Beveridge, the future of the universities. She paid more tribute to Nancy Astor, Marie Stopes and William Beveridge. She dwelt lovingly on her recollections of Dorset as a holiday base. But for the most part the second volume held little that was new, and relatively few copies were printed or sold.

In 1974, aged 83, Mary Stocks was still making news and headlines. In April she led a protest against the renewal of a late-night music and dancing licence to an avant-garde Kensington High Street fashion store, Biba, extremely popular with young people. It was proposed to allow music up to midnight, even on their roof garden. This was reported under the headline 'Battling Baroness Fights for Quiet'.

In a speech to the Greater London Council entertainments licensing board Mary Stocks said much of Central London was turning into a wilderness of offices, hotels catering for tourists and 'quaint' areas. She feared this latter process was happening to the old High Street, Kensington (always so called), 'a private place where the residents shop and have shopped for generations'. Unlike many adjacent areas Kensington was still largely residential.

What was being threatened, she argued, was 'the function of London as a place where people can still live and work and bring up their children'.[24] Which was exactly what Dr and Mrs Roland Brinton had done, a mile or so from the High Street, in the later years of the last century. Perhaps family sentiment and nostalgia over-coloured Baroness Stocks's thinking, but she could still put a case with fire and spirit.

Another resident, Brigadier James Thorburn, told the GLC committee in an inflammatory speech that the influx of boutiques was turning Kensington High Street into a place of notoriety comparable with Kings Road, Chelsea (where some would say the permissive society first took root).

Quite possibly these two elderly pleaders, seen as anti-youth or out of touch with reality, did their cause no good. When she was cross-questioned by a GLC lawyer, Mary Stocks had to admit she did not live near enough to be disturbed by late-night activity at the store. In her heyday she would surely have anticipated that point and produced evidence that others were disturbed. For whatever reason, the committee agreed to renew the music and dancing licence on weekdays till midnight.

In July she made even more sensational headlines: 'Now Lady Stocks Quits' – 'On the Stocks' – 'Blow for Labour'. She had written to the Labour Party General Secretary resigning from the Party, which she had first joined as a student at the London School of Economics (although her membership had by no means been continuous).

Various reasons were given for her surprise decision. In an interview she told the *Daily Mail*

> I have resigned because I have lost all confidence in Mr Wilson as Prime Minister. I am frankly terrified by the policies he is following. I began to lose confidence when he let down Mrs Barbara Castle, when she wanted a prices and incomes policy. From then on I became more disillusioned. Harold Wilson, I honestly believe, only thinks of the interests of the Trade Unions. Mr Wedgwood Benn is a menace. His policy of wholesale nationalisation is crazy.[25]

Pressed to say if she would join another party, she unhesitatingly denied this. She would sit on the cross-benches of the House of Lords. She could suggest no other potential prime minister. Perhaps a coalition between the Liberals and Edward Heath might work. Nothing would ever induce her to join the Conservatives, however. 'They simply give in to every sordid interest in the country. For me commercial radio was the last straw'.

The *Daily Telegraph* was alone in pointing out that she had been a council candidate for Labour in Manchester in 1932, an Independent Progressive candidate for London University in the 1945 general election, and an Independent for Combined English Universities in the 1946 by-election following Eleanor Rathbone's death. She had always taken the line that the business of a politician was not to find out what people thought, but to take the initiative and stand or fall by the result. Her role model in this respect was W.E. Gladstone.

Other papers speculated that her disillusionment with Labour stemmed partly from Harold Wilson's decision to give his former secretary, Marcia Williams, a life peerage. To this she commented that she saw it as a tactless move, but her resignation had been planned before the announcement. Another political commentator suspected Mary Stocks's main reason for leaving the party was dislike of what she saw as government by the trade unions. It seems at least possible she was disenchanted with Harold Wilson's leadership because of a straightforward clash of personalities.

It was her swan-song. There were to be no more major speeches in the House of Lords, no more letters to the press, no more broadcasts. Mary Stocks did not so much retire as wind down. As she said: 'We've come a long way since I started in politics. And now my life is coming to an end, I can look back and say I have won my fight'.[26]

Increasingly she spent her days at Aubrey Lodge, occasionally being driven down to the House of Lords or sightseeing around London with one of the family, often her grandson Mark. Aubrey Lodge suited her perfectly both in terms of its whereabouts and in its character. Today it is an austere four-storey house in yellowish brick, standing high on Campden Hill at the very top of Kensington, adjoining the redbrick mansion of Aubrey House, which stands in its own grounds shaded by giant horse chestnuts and plane trees. Through an iron gate one glimpses a lawn, shrubs, a black cat. Baroness Stocks had the garden flat, and sat on this same lawn with her white cat.

Close by are the cool shady semi-public gardens and grand terraces of Campden Hill Square. South of this the whole neighbourhood has something of the feel of a Victorian village, with cobbles, camellias in tubs, rustic ironwork, small flowery villas and the highly Italianate St George's Church. One might be forgiven for thinking of it as Mary Stocks's patch, every street nameplate bearing her title: the Royal Borough of Kensington and Chelsea.

Her daughters recall that as she grew older they had to persuade her more to go out sometimes 'and have a proper meal'. She still preferred something out of a tin, and her constant companion was always a white cat. This dynasty of cats dated back to when the historian H.A.L. Fisher bred white kittens at Oriel College in

Oxford and gave Mary one as a present. Thereafter all her cats came from the same source. Throughout most of her years at Westfield the resident companion was Candida, who lived to be 13, and descendants of Candida ruled at Aubrey Lodge.

Baroness Stocks died exactly as she would have wished, without fuss or ado. She had not been ill (except for a hip operation); her eyesight, hearing and mental powers were as keen as ever. But grief perhaps contributed to her sudden death, for her only son John died of cancer in June 1975. He had become ill in Malaya, returned to England and continued to work for Shell in London, but as a very sick man. He died aged 57, only a little older than his father (also John Stocks) had been when he died in 1937. Mary Stocks insisted on attending her son's funeral in south London. Three weeks later she died after having Sunday lunch at home with Helen, on 6 July, 19 days before her 84th birthday.

Her life had come full circle, for she died in her own home, barely a five-minute taxi drive from the house where she was born, almost on the eve of her birthday, and again at a time when women's rights were high on the social agenda.

Epilogue
The Mary Stocks
Legend and Legacy

Some remember her as a great eccentric, an academic who dressed like a farmer. Others would say her golden years were given to broadcasting, to making radio listener-friendly and a happy vehicle for her opinions, invariably down to earth, sometimes outrageous, most often wise. 'Wasn't she the *Any Questions* woman?' they would ask. Hard-pressed working women who came to her evening classes or her birth control clinics would praise her for making their lives easier. Students, suffragettes and socialist colleagues would speak of her tough determination in fighting their causes. People who saw her plays, heard her *Lift Up Your Hearts* broadcasts or listened to the battling Baroness in the House of Lords found her ideas inspirational.

Mary Stocks was all these. For seventy years she argued relentlessly for what she believed in, injecting a good deal of satire into her message.

Hundreds gathered for her memorial sevice at St Martin in the Fields. Lord Soper gave the address, the Bishop of London pronounced the blessing, and among those represented were the Speaker of the House of Commons, the Mayor of Kensington, London University, the Royal College of Midwives and the Commonwealth Press Union.

What Mary Stocks did best was to speak for women's needs and rights and to be, herself, a statutory woman on so many public bodies that would have been womanless a generation earlier.

Notes

Chapter 1   The London Years

1. Mary Stocks, *My Commonplace Book* (Peter Davies, London, 1970), p. 237.
2. Workers' Educational Association hymn.
3. *New Zealand Herald*, 14 Sept. 1925.
4. Article by Kia Kaha, *NZ Herald*, 13 Sept. 1932.
5. *The Times*, 19 Jan. 1867.
6. *Kidderminster Shuttle*, 23 July 1932.
7. Stocks, *My Commonplace Book*, p. 2.
8. *Evening Standard*, 3 Nov. 1973.
9. Ibid.
10. Stocks, *My Commonplace Book*, p. 62.
11. Ibid., p. 27.
12. *Daily Graphic*, 16 Apr. 1904.
13. Stocks, *My Commonplace Book*, p. 9.
14. Frances Gray, *Gladly Wolde He Lerne* (1938) p. 89.
15. *The Times*, 10 Feb. 1907.
16. *Manchester Guardian*, 10 Feb. 1907.
17. Stocks, *My Commonplace Book*, p. 73–4.
18. Ibid., p. 56.
19. Ibid., p. 74.

Chapter 2   The Oxford Years

1. From J. Sherwoood and N. Pevsner, *Buildings of Oxfordshire* (1937).
2. Stocks, *My Commonplace Book*, p. 100.
3. *Daily Telegraph*, 26 Feb. 1937.
4. Stocks, *My Commonplace Book*, p. 143.

5. Mary Stocks, *The Industrial State* (Collins, London, 1920), p. 15.
6. Ibid., p. 308.
7. Ibid., p. 175.
8. Helen Stocks, conversation with author.
9. Ann Patterson (née Stocks), interview by author.
10. From *Oxford and District*, Ward Lock, 1937.
11. Ibid.

Chapter 3   The Manchester and Liverpool Years

1. Helen Stocks, conversation with author.
2. BBC North of England Service talk, 6 Jan. 1959.
3. Mary Stocks, *Everyman of Everystreet* (Sidgwick & Jackson, London, 1929), p. ix.
4. *Manchester Guardian*, 1931.
5. From *Everyman of Everystreet*, pp. 32–3.
6. Mary Stocks, *King Herod* (1931) p. 7, p. 18.
7. *Manchester Guardian*, Sep. 1934.
8. *Daily Express*, 1934.
9. *Washington Post*, 22 Apr. 1937.
10. *Daily Mail*, Jan. 1932.
11. Mary Stocks, *Still More Commonplace* (Michael Joseph, London, 1973), p. 19.
12. Ibid., p. 22.
13. Ibid., p. 27.
14. Ibid., p. 28.
15. Charis Frankenburg, *Not Old, Madam, Vintage* (Galaxy, London, 1975) p. 134.
16. Ibid., p. 136.
17. Extracts from *Manchester Evening News*, Mar. 1932.
18. Ibid., Jul. 1931.
19. Mary Stocks, 'Impressions of a Russian Village', *Journal of the W.E.A.*, 1933.
20. Ann Petterson, conversation with author.
21. Letter in *Manchester Guardian*, 29 Mar. 1933.
22. BBC North Region Current Events talk, 15 Oct. 1930.
23. Helen Stocks, conversation with author.
24. Ibid.

25. *Daily Telegraph*, Spring 1935.

Chapter 4   The Westfield Years

1. Stocks, *My Commonplace Book*, p. 190–191.
2. *Evening News*, 1942.
3. *Reading Standard*, 19 Feb. 1942.
4. *Daily Express*, 1942.
5. *Manchester Guardian*, Apr. 1944.
6. Ann Patterson, conversation with author.
7. Mary Stocks, *Eleanor Rathbone* (Gollancz, London, 1949).
8. Ibid.
9. Ibid.
10. Stocks, *My Commonplace Book*, p. 133.
11. Letter to Colonial Office, 17 Jan. 1947 (in Westfield College archives).
12. Letter to Colonial Office, 20 Feb. 1948.
13. Letter to Barnard College, USA, Autumn 1949.
14. Postcard in author's possession.

Chapter 5   The BBC Years

1. Stocks, *My Commonplace Book*, p. 207.
2. Ibid., pp. 215–17.
3. Hon. David Astor, interviewed by author.
4. *Any Questions* script, BBC Archives.
5. Stocks, *My Commonplace Book*, p. 219.
6. Mary Stocks, *The Philanthropist in a Changing World*, Eleanor Rathbone Memorial Lecture, (Liverpool University press, 1953).
7. *Daily Mail*, 13 Jan. 1959.
8. Frank Gillard OBE, letter to author.
9. Ibid.
10. Stocks, *My Commonplace Book*, p. 218.
11. Ibid., p. 219.
12. Letter dated 14 April 1964, BBC Archives.
13. Stocks, *My Commonplace Book*, p. 143.
14. Hon. David Astor, interviewed by author.

15. Ibid.
16. Ibid.
17. *Observer*, 3 May 1964.
18. Ibid.
19. Letters to and from Rev. Elsie Chamberlain, BBC Archives, Caversham.
20. *Any Questions* scripts, BBC Archives.
21. Ibid.
22. BBC Archives, script.
23. Ibid.
24. Ibid.
25. Ibid.
26. Ibid.
27. Conversation with author.
28. Various statements to author.
29. BBC Archives, postcard.
30. *Sunday Times*, 1962.
31. Advertisers' Review, 22 February 1963.
32. Letters, BBC Archives.

Chapter 6   The House of Lords Years

1. Hansard, 16 Feb. 1966.
2. Frank Gillard letter to author.
3. Ibid.
4. *The Times*, 29 Apr. 1966.
5. Letter dated 24 May 1966, BBC Archives.
6. Ibid.
7. Stocks, *My Commonplace Book*, p. 234.
8. Postcard in BBC Archives.
9. BBC Home Service talk, Jan. 1970.
10. *The Times*, 11 May 1970.
11. *The Times*, 7 Jan. 1970.
12. *The Times*, 27 Mar. 1968.
13. *The Guardian*, 8 Nov. 1968.
14. *The Times*, 28 May 1968.
15. Hansard, 26 Jul. 1967, p. 1034.
16. Ibid., p. 1098.

17. Hansard 1967, p. 1398.
18. Hansard, 25 Feb. 1970.
19. Ibid.
20. *Sunday Telegraph*, 11 Oct. 1970.
21. *Daily Mail*, 13 Oct. 1970.
22. *The Times*, 12 Oct. 1970.
23. Ibid.
24. Speech to GLC committee, Jan. 1970.
25. *Daily Mail*, 17 Jul. 1974.
26. Stocks, *Still More Commonplace*, p. 153.

Bibliography

Books

Frankenburg, Charis, *Not Old, Madam, Vintage* (Galaxy, London, 1975).

Greenwood, Walter, *Love on the Dole* (Manchester, 1933).

Grisewood, G.H., *My Story of the BBC* (London, 1959).

Hill, Octavia, *Homes of the London Poor* (London, 1899).

Hubback, Eva and Simon, Ernest, *Education in Citizenship* (Manchester, c. 1930).

Langhorne, Elizabeth, *Nancy Astor and Her Friends* (Praeger, New York, 1974).

Muggeridge, Malcolm, *The Thirties* (Collins, London, 1940).

Pethick-Kawrence, Emmeline, *My Part in a Changing World* (Gollancz, London, 1938).

Rose, June, *Marie Stopes and the Sexual Revolution* (Faber & Faber, London, 1992).

Russell, Dora, *Extracts in The Dora Russell Reader* (Routledge & Kegan Paul, London, 1983).

Sherwood, Jennifer, and Pevsner, Nikolaus, *Buildings of Oxfordshire* (Penguin, London, 1974).

Sondheimer, Janet, *Castle Adamant in Hampstead* (Westfield College, London, 1983).

Spark, Muriel, *Curriculum Vitae* (Constable, London, 1982).

Stocks, Mary, *The Industrial State* (Collins, London, 1920).

—— *Everyman of Everystreet* (Sidgwick & Jackson, London, 1929).

—— *King Herod* (Sidgwick & Jackson, 1931).

—— *Hail, Nero!* (Sidgwick & Jackson, 1931).

—— *Fifty Years in Every Street* (Manchester University Press, 1945).

—— *Eleanor Rathbone, a Biography* (Gollancz, London, 1949).

—— *The W.E.A., the First Fifty Years* (Allen & Unwin, London,

195

1953).

—— *The Philanthropist in a Changing World* (Liverpool University Press, 1953).

—— *A Hundred Years of District Nursing* (Allen & Unwin, 1960).

—— *Ernest Simon of Manchester* (Manchester University Press, 1963).

—— *Unread Best Seller* (BBC Publications, London, 1967).

—— *My Commonplace Book* (Peter Davies, London, 1970).

—— *Still More Commonplace* (Michael Joseph, London, 1973).

Stopes, Marie, *Married Love* (1918).

—— *Wise Parenthood* (1918).

—— *Birth Control Today* (1934).

Journals and Monographs

Hermes, 1950, 1951 (student magazine of Westfield College, London University).

Paulina (journal of St Paul's Girls' School, Hammersmith).

Eleanor Rathbone Memorial Lecture, Liverpool, 1960.

The Newsbasket, 1922 (staff journal of W.H. Smith Ltd).

Hansard 1966–1972 (records of the debates of the House of Lords).

Manuscripts

BBC Written Archives, Caversham, files relating to Mary Stocks, various periods between 1930 and 1966.

Correspondence in the Nancy Astor Archives, Reading University.

Principal's Logbook of Westfield COllege, 1939–1951.

Correspondence in the Archives of Queen Mary and Westfield College, London University.

Recordings

BBC Radio 4 programme, 1993: 'Feminist or Fogey? Portrait of Mary Stocks'.

Index

Abortion Bill, 169, 177-80
Aderemi, Tejumade, 115, 125
Advertisers' Review, 160-61
Alexander, Prof. Samuel,
    52-3, 151
Alexander, Rachel, 131
Alice, Princess, 129
Anderson, Dr Elizabeth Garrett,
    98, 161
Anstey, Vera, 26
Anti-Concorde Group, 174
Any Questions, 134, 136-7,
    140-44, 149-50, 155-56, 160,
    166-7, 169, 172-3
Arch, Joseph, 35
Archibald, Lord, 164
Arlott, John, 154
Ashcroft, Peggy, 134
Astor, David, 133, 145-47
Astor, Nancy (Viscountess Astor),
    38, 40, 81-4, 133, 144-48,
    157, 185
Athlone, Earl of, 129
Attlee, Clement (Prime Minister),
    122
Aubrey House and Lodge,
    131, 187-8

Badley, John, 161-2
Balfour, Arthur (Prime Minister),
    8
Ball, Sidney, 30
Barker's Store, 11
Barnard College, USA, 126-8
Barnett, Charis (also see
    Frankenburg), 20

Barrie, J.M., 10
BBC: Asia Service, 149; *Asking the
    World*, 140,152; *Calling West
    Africa*, 99; *Children's Hour*,
    166; European Service, 143;
    Good Cause Appeals, 163;
    Home This Afternoon, 162; *Lift
    Up Your Hearts*, 148-9. 152,
    163, 181; Light Programme,
    123, 166; North Region, 76-8;
    West Region, 136-7, 141, 169;
    Woman's Hour, 98, 143, 144-5
Bedales School, 161-2
Beeton, Mrs, 162
Benn, Tony Wedgwood, MP, 186
Besant, Annie, 35
Bevan, Aneurin, MP, 114
Beveridge, William, 27, 122, 185
Bible, The, 148, 152
Black Forest, 33
Bloomsbury Group, 25
Blunden, John, 168
Bondfield, Margaret, MP, 46,
    97, 150
Boothby, Robert, MP, 136, 144,
    153, 166
Brayfield, Celia, 182-3
Bridges, Robert, 35, 48, 62
Bridport, Dorset, 15-16, 30,
    45-6, 104
Brinton, Constance (Mary's
    mother), 2, 5, 11-12, 71,
    106-7, 116
Brinton, Edith (Tiddy, Mary's
    aunt), 8, 12
Brinton, Jack (Mary's cousin), 12

Brinton, Dr James (Mary's grandfather), 5
Brinton, Joanna (also see Baillieu) (Mary's sister), 10, 39, 90
Brinton, Marion (Mary's aunt), 8
Brinton, Mary (also see Stocks), birth, 8; childhood and sightseeing, 11-13; whooping cough, 12; childhood clothes, 12-13; domestic non-skills, 13; schooldays, ; art exams, 18; public exams, 20, 25; first political march, 21-23; social work, 24; entry to LSE, 25; student union secretary, 26; political activism, 29
Brinton, Maud (Mary's aunt), 16
Brinton, Ralph (Mary's brother), 10, 16, 37, 137
Brinton, Dr Roland (Mary's father), 5-6, 8-9, 11, 15, 32, 37, 39, 186-7, 116
Brittain, Vera, 41
Browning, Robert, 156-7, 163
Bullock, Alan, 149

Cadbury's, 124
Caldecote, Lord, 101, 111
Call my Bluff, 173
Callaghan, James, MP (later Prime Minister), 149
Calling West Africa, 99
Cameron, James, 163
Candida, 188
Carroll, Lewis, 10, 44, 46
Casson, Lewis, 35, 134
Cazalet, Thelma, MP, 102
Central School of Speech and Drama, 134
Chamberlain, Revd Elsie, 148-50, 152
Chartist Movement, 58
Chesney, Kathleen, 128, 130
Chichele, Archbishop, 34
Churchill, Winston (later Prime Minister), 12
Clark, Kenneth, 128
Cliveden (Astor home), 81, 146-7

Cole, G.D.H., 127
Colet, Dame Christian, 16, 20
Colet House, Stepney, 20
Colet, John, 16
Commission on Conditions in Women's Forces, 102-3
Committee on Habitual Offenders, 62
Committee on Unemployment Insurance, 76
Committee into Training of Midwives, 114-5
Concorde, 174
Conran, Shirley, 172
Creech Jones, Arthur, MP, 124, 129
Crichton-Miller, Neil, 153
Cripps, Sir Stafford, MP, 81
Crossman, Richard, MP, 123, 144
Cubitt, Kirsten, 183-4
Curtis, Dame Myra, 126, 129
Cyprus, 143, 162, 185

Daily Mail, 61, 182, 186
Daily Mirror, 156
Daily Telegraph, 104, 182
Danvers, Emily (Viscountess Hambleden) (Mary's great aunt), 7
Danvers, Mary (Mrs James Brinton) (Mary's grandmother), 5
Desert Island Discs, 158-60
Dors, Diana, 156
Downside, Abbot of, 156
Dr Scholefield of Manchester, 58
Du Maurier, Gerald, 8

Eden, Anthony (Prime Minister), 133
Elliott, Mrs Walter, 102
Engels, Friedrich, 54, 58
Epstein, Jacob, 51
Equal Pay for Equal Work, 45
Evans, Ifor, 147, 152, 166
Evening News, 102
Evening Standard, 161
Everyman of Everystreet, 54-57

Index

Fawcett, Millicent Garrett, 26-9, 39, 143, 161
Felix, Julie, 168
Fields, Gracie, 50, 85, 159
Fifty Years in Every Street, 117
First, Ruth, 163
Fisher, Geoffrey (Archbishop of Canterbury), 155
Fisher, H.A.L., 187-8
Fletcher, Kitty (sister-in-law of Mary), 52
Foot, Dingle, 133-4
Foot, Hugh, 162
Foot, Isaac, 137
Foot, Michael, MP, 144
Frankenburg, Charis, 67-70
Frankly Speaking, 155
Frere, Margery, 24
Freud, Sigmund, 10

Gaitskell, Hugh, MP, 136, 144
Gaumont Cinema, Kensington, 184-5
Gedge, Evelyn, 99, 110
Germany in the thirties, 74-78
Gielgud, John, 48
Gill, Winifred, 56
Gillard, Frank, 141, 149, 153, 166-7
Gimson, Dr Olive, 109
Gladstone, William (Prime Minister), 187
Glamorgan Fire Brigade, 140
Gloag, John, 78
Graham-Little, Sir Ernest, 108
Grahame, Kenneth, 11
Gray, Frances, 17-19
Great Exhibition of 1851, 10
Greenwood, Arthur, MP, 77
Greenwood, Walter, 50-51, 53
Grisewood, Freddie, 134-6, 159, 169, 172
Gugenheim, Theo, 26
Gunn, James, 128
Guthrie, Tyrone, 47, 125

Hail, Nero!, 58-61, 88, 101-2
Hailsham, Lord, 144

Hamilton-Smith, Emma, 3
Hammond, Barbara, 40, 81
Hammond, J.L., 40, 81
Heath, Edward (Prime Minister), 144, 186
Herbert, A.P., 81, 109
Hermes (Westfield College journal), 105
Hill, Lord, 180
Hill, Octavia, 24-5, 38, 98
History of District Nursing, 155
Hobson, Eliza (Mary's grandmother), 2
Hobson, Polly (Mary's great-aunt), 13-14
Hobson, Capt. William (Mary's great-grandfather), 2-4, 85-6, 88
Holland Park, 175
Holst, Gustav, 20
Holtby, Winifred, 41
Home for the Day, 143
Home This Afternoon, 162
Hubback, Eva, 64, 72, 81-2
Huxley, Julian, 79
Hymn of the Workers, 1-2, 90-91

Industrial State, The, 42-5
International Women's Suffrage, 75
In The Time of My Youth, 155
Irving, Dolly, 8

Jackson, Winifrede, 182
Jay, Peter, 172
Jones, Dame Katherine, 105
Jones, Parry, 134

Kensington High School, 16
Kensington Labour Party, 167
Kensington Society, 184
Kenyon, Kathleen, 20
Keynes, J.M., 25, 80
Kidderminster Shuttle, 5
King-Hall, Lord, 165-6
King Herod, 57-8
Kipling, Rudyard, 44, 46
Knightsbridge Barracks, 175
Knowles, Lilian, 26, 32

Labour Party, 27, 41, 45, 52, 62, 80-81, 135, 154, 164, 166-7, 186-7
Langhorne, Nancy (see Astor)
Laud, Archbishop, 34
League of Nations, 82
Liddell, Alice, 46
Lift Up Your Hearts, 148-9, 152, 163, 170-71
Listener, The, 161
Listowel, Lord, 124
Liverpool Cathedral, 90-91
Liverpool University, 62, 84, 87-90, 137-8
Lloyd, Selwyn, MP, 122
Lloyd George, David (Prime Minister), 27, 42
London Council of Social Service, 92
London School of Economics, 25-30, 35-6, 80, 88, 164, 186
Lowry, L.S., 50-52

Macadam, Elizabeth, 117-121, 126
MacDonald, Ramsay (Prime Minister), 28
Makarios, President, 143
Mallam, Emily (Mrs J.E. Stocks, Mary's mother-in-law), 31
Manchester Guardian, 51-4, 58-60, 72, 75-6, 84-5, 105-6, 123
Manchester Repertory Theatre, 80, 85
Manchester University, 49-52, 79
Manchester University Settlement, 54, 76, 84
Mansbridge, Albert and Frances, 139
Maoris, 3-4,, 85-6
Markham, Violet, 102-3, 105, 107-8
Markiewicz, Constance, 40
Martin, Kingsley, 51, 53-4, 172
Matheson, Hilda, 82, 145
Maxted, Stanley, 144
Meaning of Family Endowment, The, 45

Mill, John Stuart, 28
Montessori, Maria, 35
Morgan, William de, 80
Morris, William (Lord Nuffield), 33
Mortimer, John, 172
Mud March, 21-23
Muggeridge, Kitty, 53, 72
Muggeridge, Malcolm, 51, 53, 72-3
Murray, Prof. Gilbert, 36, 81, 97, 105
My Commonplace Book, 182-4

Nabarro, Gerald, MP, 144
Nash, Walter, 88
National Council of Women, 85
National Health Service, 132, 142, 167-8, 179-80
National Trust, 24
National Union of Women's Suffrage Societies, 22-3, 28-9, 40, 176-7
New Statesman, 153, 161
Nicolson, Harold, 127
Nightingale, Florence, 156
Nursing Mirror, 170

Observer, The, 133, 146-7, 161
Odlum, Doris, 35
Oni of Ife, 125
Our Towns (report), 105

Pankhurst, Emmeline, 28-9, 177
Patterson, Ann and Arthur, 103, 107, 151, 153, 162
Person or Persons Unknown, 61-2
Pestalozzi School, 16
Peterborough Cathedral, 31
Petticoat Line, 169, 173
Piercy, William (later Lord Piercy), 26, 164
Plomley, Roy, 158-60
Popham, Miss A.E., 111
Portland Bill, 65-6
Potter, Beatrix, 10, 46
Power, Eileen, 26, 52, 95, 97
Power, Rhoda, 92-3

Priestley, J.B., 62, 109
Proctor, Christabel, 18
Proctor, Joan, 18
Proops, Marjorie, 172

Queen Victoria, 3, 10-11
Queens Gate Terrace, 6, 9, 11,
    185, 188

R101 airship, 77
Rathbone, Eleanor, MP, 9, 38, 70,
    109, 113, 117-122
Ray, Cyril, 153-4
Reith, Lord, 166, 180, 185
Relf, Granny, 15
Rendel, Sir Alexander (Mary's
    grandfather), 2, 5-6, 14-15, 38
Rendel, Constance (see also
    Brinton, Mary's mother), 2, 8,
    11-12, 23
Rendel, Edith (Mary's aunt), 6-7,
    101, 131
Rendel, Elsie, 7
Rendel, James (Mary's uncle), 7,
    91
Rendel, James Meadows (Mary's
    great-grandfather), 2, 88
Rendel, Leila (Mary's cousin), 7,
    131
Rendel, Stuart (Later Lord
    Rendel), 2
Rickettswood, Surrey, 14-15
Rieu, E.V., 111
Robbins, Lord, 175
Roe, Humphrey Verdon (husband
    of Marie Stopes), 63-4
Roe, Harry Stopes (son of Marie
    Stopes), 65-6
Royal Commission on Lotteries
    and Betting, 76
Royden-Shaw, Maude, 41
Rugby School, 31, 41, 145
Russell, Bertrand, 25, 41, 172

Sackville-West, Vita, 127
St John's College, Oxford, 32-33,
    39, 41, 47-8
St Martin in the Fields, 1, 66, 189

St Mary Abbots, Kensington,
    32, 184
St Michael's Street, Oxford, 33-34
St Paul's School for Girls,
    16-21, 24, 67
St Peter-le-Bailey Church, 96,
    97, 108
St Peter's Hall, Oxford, 96-97,
    101, 105, 111
Salford Mothers' Clinic for Birth
    Control, 67-70, 72
Sayers, Dorothy, 40, 58, 100
Scott, C.,P., 51, 53
Searle, Christopher, 169
Sharp, Dame Evelyn, 20
Shaw, G.B., 147, 161, 184
Shinwell, Emmanuel, MP, 144
Simon, Sir E.D., 113
Simon, Ernest (later Lord Simon),
    53, 73, 157-8
Simon, Sheena (later Lady
    Simon), 53, 85, 157-8
Smith, Percy Delf, 114
Smith, W.H., 7, 8
Soper, Donald (later Lord Soper),
    153-5, 166, 180, 189
Soroptimists, 88
Starkie, Dr Enid, 41
Steel, David, MP, 177
Stevenson, Robert Louis, 10-11
Still More Commonplace, 185
Stocks, Ann (Mary's daughter,
    also see Patterson), 36, 39, 46,
    52, 71-5, 80, 88-90, 103, 107,
    128, 131, 143, 182
Stocks, Frieda (Mary's sister-in-
    law), 89
Stocks, Helen (Mary's daughter),
    39, 46, 51-2, 71-3, 79, 89-90,
    107, 131, 164, 181, 188
Stocks, John (Mary's son), 37-9,
    52, 71-3, 107, 116, 182, 188
Stocks, Canon John Edward
    (Mary's father-in-law), 31
Stocks, John Leofric (Mary's
    husband), 30, 31-3, 36-7,
    39, 45-9, 50-54, 71-2, 74,
    78-81, 84-91

Stocks, Mary, wedding, 32; honeymoon, 32-3; first year in Oxford, 33-35; birth of older daughter, 36; birth of son, 37; lecturing, 37; and First World War, 37-8; and child allowance campaign, 38; return to Oxford, 39; and suffragism, 40; birth of second daughter, 39; first book, 42-5; pamphlets, 45; family life in Oxford, 45-7; Oxford Playhouse and OUDS, 47-8; discovering Manchester, 50-52; Manchester friends, 53; WEA in Lancashire, 53; collecting art, 50; writing plays, 54-62; and Marie Stopes, 63-70; founding of birth control clinic, 67-70; appointed to Lotteries Commission, 72; in Russia, 72-74; in Germany, 75; first broadcasts, 76-8; theatre activities, 79; and Nancy Astor, 81-4; farewell to Manchester, 84-6; Liverpool Vice-Chancellor's wife, 87-9; death and civic funeral of husband, 89-91; BBC scripts, 92-3; Gen. Sec. London Council of Social Service, 92; becomes Principal of Westfield College, 94-6; various reactions to Second World War, 96-100, 101-2, 105-7; eccentric dresser, 101, 179; acts in staff revue, 101, 104; appears at Oxford Magistrates' Court, 101; stands for Parliament, 108; gives inaugural lecture on London, 110-111; social contact with students, 111-2; closure of botany dept, 114; career advice, 115; biography of Eleanor Rathbone, 117-122; Beveridge Committee, 122; students and social work, 126; overseas students, 123-4; college garden party, 128-9; resigns as Principal, 128; University Grants Committee, 132; *Observer* Trustee, 133; Central School of Speech and Drama, 134; first *Any Questions* broadcast, 134; chairs studio discussion, 137; lectures at Liverpool, 137; postcards, 137, 152; history of WEA, 139-40; chairs *Ask the World*, 140; campaigns for free contraception, 155; views on euthanasia, 156; biography of Ernest Simon, 157-8; on *Desert Island Discs*, 158-60; advocates castrating sex offenders, 160; views on advertising, 160-1; views on Cyprus, 162; theatre reviews, 162; becomes a Life Peer, 163; enters House of Lords, 164-7; maiden speech, on NHS, 167-8; views on abortion, 169, 177-80; views on Lords, 169; book critiques, 168-9; looks back 60 years, 173-4; speeches on divorce reform, noise pollution, street offences, 174-5; views on preserving London, 175; speech on higher education, 175-6; speeches and views on future of radio, 180-2; publishes autobiography, 182-4; defends hospitals, 184; second part of autobiography, 185; defence of Kensington, 185; leaves Labour Party, 186-7; death of son John, 188; death of Mary Stocks, 188; memorial service, 1-2, 189
Stockwood, Mervyn (Bishop of Southwark), 155
Stopes, Marie, 62-70, 72, 76, 185
Strachey, Lady, 7, 22, 29
Strachey, Pernel, 7, 122
Strachey, Philippa, 7, 22, 29
Strachey, Ray, 7, 27, 81
Strachey, Sir Richard, 7
Strauss, H.G., 113

Street, A.G., 134
Street Offences Act, 140-1
Strong, L.A.G., 127
Summerskill, Edith, MP (later
  Baroness Summerskill),
  102, 126
Sunday Telegraph, 182
Sunday Times, 105, 156

Target, G.W., 168
Tawney, R.H., 31, 39, 71, 85,
  90, 139
Temple, Ann, 144
Temple, Frances, 71, 106-7,
  151-2
Temple, William (Archbishop of
  Canterbury), 31, 39, 71, 90-91,
  93, 95, 106-7, 151
Thorndike, Sybil, 35
Thorpe, Jeremy, MP, 144, 172
Thought for the Day, 163
'Time of My Life' (radio talk), 168
Times, The, 167, 175, 184
Tolstoy, Serge, 74

University Grants Committee,
  116, 132, 141
Unnamed Society, 58
Unread Best Seller, 170-72
Ustinov, Peter, 172

Vaughan, Dame Janet, 40

Waitangi, Treaty of, 2-4, 85-6
Webb, Beatrice, 25-28, 38, 41, 73,
  137, 163
Webb, Sidney, 25-28, 41, 73
Welles, Orson, 60
Wells, H.G., 66
Wedgwood, Veronica, 111, 127
West Africa, students from,
  99, 123-4
West African BBC Service,
  99, 123
West Bay, Dorset, 15-16, 46, 64-5
Westfield College, 17, 93-96,
  97-116, 122-130
Westfield College Logbook, 97,

98, 101, 102-4, 106-8, 111,
  114, 124-5, 127-130
White, Dr Beatrice, 104, 129
White Sir Thomas, 34
Wightman, Ralph, 135
Wilbraham Road, Manchester, 52,
  79
Wilson, Harold, MP (Prime
  Minister), 144, 163, 166, 186-7
Wirral Girls' High School, 86-7
Woman's Hour, 143-4, 155, 162,
  168, 172
Woman's Leader (Journal), 64
Women's Social and Political
  Union, 21, 28
Woolton, Lord, 90
Workers' Educational Association,
  35, 53, 71, 85, 88-90, 139-40
Wormald, Sidney, 113

Yasnaya Polyana, 73-4